NEW SEXUAL AGENDAS

New Sexual Agendas

Edited by

Lynne Segal

NEW YORK UNIVERSITY PRESS
Washington Square, New York

First published in the U.S.A. in 1997 by
NEW YORK UNIVERSITY PRESS
Washington Square
New York, N.Y. 10003

This book is printed on paper suitable for recycling and
made from fully managed and sustained forest sources.

Library of Congress Cataloging-in-Publication Data
New sexual agendas / edited by Lynne Segal.
    p.   cm.
Includes bibliographical references and index.
ISBN 0–8147–8076–8 (cloth).— ISBN 0–8147–8075–X (pbk.)
1. Sex.   2. Sex (Psychology)   3. Sexuality in popular culture.
4. AIDS (Disease)—Prevention—Moral and ethical aspects.
I. Segal, Lynne.
HQ23.N48   1997
306.7—dc20   96–46014
                                                            CIP

Printed in Great Britain

Contents

III SEXUAL SUBJECTIVITIES, SOCIAL CONFLICTS

Notes on Contributors

Lucy Bland is a senior lecturer in Women's Studies at the University of North London. She is author of *Banishing the Beast: English Feminism and Sexual Morality, 1885–1914* (1995), and is currently starting work on a book on 'Sexuality, Race and Nation in Interwar Britain'.

Bob Connell is Professor of Education at the University of Sydney, and the author of many books and articles on a wide range of themes. His most recent books are *Gender and Power* (1987) and *Masculinities* (1995). A past president of the Sociological Association of Australia and New Zealand, he is a member of a range of policy advisory committees, and a contributor to research journals in sociology, education, political science, gender studies and related fields.

Martin Durham is a senior lecturer in Politics at the University of Wolverhampton. He is author of *Sex and Politics: Family and Morality in the Thatcher Years* and editor of the special issue of *Parliamentary Affairs* (April 1994) on Abortion, Morality, Law and Politics.

Simon Forrest is based at Canterbury Christchurch College. He has long experience of working with young people in research and in projects related to health and sexuality.

Stephen Frosh is a senior lecturer in Psychology at Birkbeck College, University of London, and a Consultant Clinical Psychologist in the Child and Family Department at the Tavistock Clinic. He has published extensively on psychoanalytical thought and its relevance to understanding contemporary issues of gender, culture and identity. His most recent books are *Identity Crisis: Modernity, Psychoanalysis and the Self* (1991) and *Sexual Difference: Masculinity and Psychoanalysis* (1994).

Lesley Hall is senior assistant archivist in the Contemporary Medical Archives Centre, Wellcome Institute for the History of

Medicine, London. She has published *Hidden Anxieties: Male Sexuality 1900–1950* (1991), and (with Roy Porter) *The Facts of Life: The Creation of Sexual Knowledge in Britain 1650–1950* (1995), as well as numerous articles and reviews in a wide variety of journals. She is currently researching the biography of the feminist sex-radical Stella Browne (1880–1955)

Graham Hart is assistant director of the MRC Medical Sociology Unit, University of Glasgow, and head of the Unit's Programme on Sexual and Reproductive Health. For the past ten years he has been involved in research on risk behaviour for HIV infection. He is editor of *AIDS Care* (Carfax) and co-editor (with Peter Aggleton and Peter Davies) of the *Social Aspects of AIDS* series.

Jill Lewis is associate professor of Literature and Feminist Studies at Hampshire College, Amherst, Mass. She has worked on a variety of AIDS Health Education and Youth Initiative projects in both the UK and the USA, and helped found 'Care to Act', an experimental project in Brighton, for HIV/AIDS and sexual health education for young people. Currently based in Oslo, she worked with the Norwegian AIDS Association as organizer for their conferences on *Women and HIV/AIDS* (1995) and *HIV/AIDS and Human Rights* (1996).

Mary McIntosh teaches Sociology at the University of Essex. She has been a gay and feminist activist for many years and wrote one of the seminal articles of contemporary gay and lesbian theory, 'The Homosexual Role' (1968). She edited *Sex Exposed: Feminism and the Pornography Debate* with Lynne Segal (1992).

Mandy Merck teaches Media Studies at the University of Sussex. She was series editor of *Out on Tuesday* for Channel 4 television from 1988 to 1991, and her many publication include *Perversions: Deviant Readings* (1993).

Frank Mort is reader in Cultural History at the University of Portsmouth. He is the author of *Dangerous Sexualities* (1986) and *Cultures of Consumption: Masculinities and Social Space in Late Twentieth-Century Britain* (1996). He is currently writing a history of commercial culture in Britain, 1945–64.

Shirley Prendergast is a senior research fellow in the Sociology Division at Anglia Polytechnic University. She has researched and written about different aspects of young people's lives in school for many years.

Lynne Segal is Professor of Gender Studies at Middlesex University. She has written extensively on feminism, sexuality and gender. Her books include: *Is the Future Female?: Troubled Thoughts on Contemporary Feminism* (1987); *Slow Motion: Changing Masculinities, Changing Men* (1990); *Sex Exposed: Feminism and the Pornography Debate* (ed. with Mary McIntosh) (1992); and *Straight Sex: The Politics of Pleasure* (1994).

Andrew Samuels is Professor of Analytical Psychology at the University of Essex. He is a training Analyst of the Society of Analytical Psychology and a Scientific Associate of the American Academy of Psychoanalysis. He has published widely, including *Jung and the Post-Jungians* (1985); *The Plural Psyche* (1989); *Psychopathology: Contemporary Jungian Perspectives* (1989); *The Political Psyche* (1993); and *The Secret Life of Politics* (1997). In addition to clinical work, writing and lecturing, he works as a political consultant.

Alan Sinfield is Professor of English and convenor of the MA programme, Sexual Dissidence and Cultural Change, at the University of Sussex. Recent writings include *Faultlines: Cultural Materialism and the Politics of Dissident Reading* (1992); *The Wilde Century: Effeminacy, Oscar Wilde and the Queer Moment* (1994); and *Cultural Politics — Queer Reading* (1994).

Anna Marie Smith teaches Politics at Cornell University. She author of many articles in the area of sexuality, gender, race, post-Marxist theory and discourses of the Moral Right. Her latest book is *New Right Discourse on Race and Sexuality* (1993)

Leonore Tiefer is Associate Professor in the Department of Urology and Psychiatry, Montefiore Medical Center, New York. Working as a sexologist-psychologist in university and medical centre settings, she has published extensively on gender, sexology and feminism. Her most recent book was *Sex is Not a Natural Act* (1995).

Jane M. Ussher is a senior lecturer in social psychology at University College London. Her books include *The Psychology of the*

Female Body (1989); *Women's Madness: Misogyny or Mental Illness?* (1991); *Gender Issues in Clinical Psychology* (co-edited with Paula Nicholson) (1992); *The Psychology of Women's Health and Health Care* (co-edited with Paula Nicholson) (1992); and *Psychological Perspectives on Sexual Problems* (1993). Her next book, on sexuality, soon to appear, is called *Fantasies of Femininity: Reframing the Boundaries of Sex.*

Jeffrey Weeks is Professor of Sociology and head of the School of Education, Politics and Social Science at South Bank University, London. He is the author of numerous articles and books on the history and social organization of sexuality. His most recent book is *Invented Moralities* (1995), and he is currently working on a study of 'families of choice'.

Ine Vanwesenbeeck teaches Women's Studies at Tilburg University, Utrecht, and is a researcher at the Netherlands Institute of Mental Health. She has published widely in the area of gender, health and sexuality. Her latest book is *Prostitutes' Well-Being and Risk* (1994).

Carla Willig is a lecturer in psychology at Middlesex University. Her research and teaching interests include discourse analytic work in psychology. She is currently conducting research into the rhetoric and practice of trust in intimate relationships, particularly concerned with the links between discourse and practice, and the possibilities of change.

Preface

The domain of the sexual is unique – unique in relation to the contradictions it embraces and the disputes it generates, quite as much as the varying experiences it attempts to encompass. Supposedly the most private aspect of our lives, 'sex' has never been merely a private affair. Seen as the heart of our individuality, public pronouncements about the sexual serve to titillate and excite at the very same time as they create scapegoats and instil fear and anxiety. As many others have noticed: 'It is not sexuality which haunts society, but society which haunts the body's sexuality' (Godelier, 1981:17).

Bringing together some of the most creative scholars and researchers currently attempting to grapple with the complexities of sexuality, this book has its origins in a conference, which was held at Middlesex University in July 1995. Its goal was to promote an exchange of ideas between a wide variety of disciplinary fields and differing research, clinical and applied perspectives. Since the general awareness of the advent of HIV and AIDS well over a decade ago, conferences on the theme of sexuality and, especially, its accompanying risks have increased dramatically. Usually, however, they have remained within distinct disciplinary boundaries. The largely sexologically inspired social science research only rarely interacts with psychoanalytical and clinical perspectives, and seldom pays attention to the cultural concerns of historical and literary analysis. The novelty of the 1995 conference, and the discussions it generated, lay in its attempt to tackle some of the urgent practical and conceptual challenges in the sexual arena by crossing all the customary practical and theoretical divisions.

The current diversity of sexual debate and the theorizing which it represents itself reflects the highly conflictual, even violent, struggles which have been waged against dominant definitions and controls of sexuality – in particular the subcultural resistance and political campaigning coming from recent feminist, lesbian and gay challenges. These struggles to illuminate and overturn the power relations at play in both institutional and personal investments in normative heterosexual beliefs and practices point to the high levels of coerciveness and constraint which shape our sexual desires and experiences. The fact that many men don't *feel* individually powerful in relation to women, despite institutional arrangements and cultural discourses which continue to subordinate women, serves only to fuel the tensions between women and men which are apparent in much sexual fantasy and practice and spill over, all too often, into men's use of sexual harassment, coercion or even violence against women.

Gender and sexuality still provide two of the most basic narratives through which our identities are forged (for all the tensions and instabilities they are increasingly known to inspire). We become aware of our individual identity, first and foremost, as a gendered one, and gender differences themselves draw upon what are seen as fundamental differences between male and female sexuality. In the West, at least, we live in subjective worlds where the dynamics of gender are underpinned by an image of the heterosexual couple in which men are positioned as the active and dominant sex, women as the passive and responsive one. Yet much of the research and theorizing of the last hundred years has called into question this very notion of a definitive or stable core of either gender or sexuality, thereby problematizing the links still routinely made between them. The inescapable predicament of our times is therefore that what we still most take for granted about human nature is also what is most frequently called into question. It is this which makes sexuality such a troublesome, even destructive, affair, both in theory and in practice.

The gulf between popular and academic discourses in the sexual domain reflects this predicament. On the one hand, most people still like to think of 'sex' as something that comes naturally, with everything taken for granted as the promptings of our inner urges or instinctual forces. Building on this, sections of the popular press are busily promoting their 'hot tips' for better 'sex', even as tabloid headlines and media pundits are just as earnestly denouncing sexual 'permissiveness' and the pursuit of pleasure as the source of all social ills: a threat to public health and decency. Either way, our sex lives are placed at the centre of both personal identity and social well-being. On the other hand, in the most recent poststructuralist theorizing about the socially constructed and culturally defined nature of sexual subjectivity, 'sex' is seen as no more than a fictional unity, with personal testimonies of lived experience relegated to a space within discourse. From this perspective we have no inner sexual essence or fixed identity, whether seen as a product of innate promptings or some set of acquired responses or beliefs.

However, there are other ways of viewing sexual identity and behaviour which reduce them neither simply to biology nor to the external forces which construct and regulate them. And while both biological and social construction theories at times line up on the same side in suggesting that men and women exhibit a stable and abiding pattern of sexual behaviour (perhaps through internalizing sexual scripts), from psychoanalysis through to poststructuralist and recent queer theory, stability and consistency in sexual behaviour and desire is not what we should ever expect to find. Here sexual life and its social codes are seen as forever troubled by *conflict, fluidity* and *contradiction*. These controversies over sexuality both within and between popular and theoretical trajectories are further complicated by political disputes over sexuality as a site of personal power and social regulation. Feminist thinking has pointed to the cultural construction and institutional regulation of sexuality as a vehicle for men's power and control over women's bodies and pleasures. At times feminists have sought to reclaim and affirm women's 'autonomous sexuality' and 'difference'; at other times – and increasingly since the later 1970s – they have tied women's sexual engagement with men ineluctably to women's subordination. In the now widely influential writings and campaigning of Catharine MacKinnon, Andrea Dworkin and Sheila Jeffreys, notions of women's autonomy and selfhood have been turned against the idea of sexual pleasure – at least in heterosexual encounters (Dworkin, 1981; MacKinnon, 1987; Jeffreys, 1990). These feminists have targeted the pioneers of sexology, and their descendants, for entrenching women's oppression by encouraging them to seek pleasure in heterosexual relations: an encounter in which, they argue, women are inevitably positioned as subordinate. Dominant sexual discourses and iconography are seen to link female sexuality, and hence identity, with submission. And indeed they have – although never quite as seamlessly as voices like MacKinnon's or Jeffreys' suggest. Despite the definite connections which exist between sexuality and gender, we cannot derive one from the other: the study of sexuality does not simply reduce to the dynamics of gender (Segal, 1994).

The essays in this volume engage directly with the intersecting debates and controversies stimulated by these conflicting perspectives, while trying to map a way forward for understanding and living with the diversity of people's sexual lives today. As Lesley Hall suggests in her opening paper, the legacy of the turn of the century sexologists remains an ambivalent one. They challenged the punitive moral conservatism of their day and the medical reluctance to provide help or advice on sexual problems and anxieties, whether for disease, contraception or a multitude of personal fears and anxieties. But they also played their part in reinforcing gender polarity and the biological necessity of male domination with their depiction of the 'sex act' as male-initiated and orchestrated. Deploying more recent conceptions of sexuality in their historical reflections, Lucy Bland and Frank Mort critically elaborate both poststructuralist and psychoanalytical reflections to explore the complex relationship between the self and the social. The way in which psychoanalytical theory in particular disrupts conventional understandings of gender and sexuality – at least in some of its versions – forms the basis of Stephen Frosh's contribution; while Andrew Samuels argues that clinical insights can offer suggestions for progressive political agendas, despite the conceptual difficulties of moving from psychic to social reality.

Addressing themselves directly to the need for a sexual politics for our time, both Jeffrey Weeks and Bob Connell provide overviews of contemporary debates. Connell is in search of a conscious practice for eradicating the inequalities of sexually invested social structures. Weeks seeks to define a value system which can respect diversity and choice while recognizing shared human interests. In my own contribution I examine the obstacles facing a feminist sexual politics that would challenge the traditional meanings attaching to heterosexuality and 'the sex act' which position women as the subordinate sex. Exploring the other end of the political spectrum, Martin Durham looks at the rise of the conservative 'pro-family' crusaders in Britain and the United States over the last few decades. This illustrates the intensity of the feelings generated by the changes that have occurred in sexual and gender relations, on the one hand, and the dangers that have attended conservative calls for a 'return to basics', on the other.

Meanwhile, it would be a mistake to think that the new theoretical work on the social practices governing sexuality and the complex formation of sexual subjectivity have simply replaced the older biologistic perspectives in any straightforward way. They live on in both academic discourse and clinical interventions. Sexological reflection and research have increasingly shifted towards an emphasis on sexual diversity. Yet, as Leonore Tiefer describes from her experience as a clinician and sexologist operating in medical centres in New York, the medical model of sexuality is still dominant amongst practising sexologists, who continue to detach the sexual body from either the social or psychic dynamics which help to construct it. This is why sexologists characteristically endorse, rather than challenge, prevailing normative aspirations, as seen, for example, in the medicalization of male impotence and the acceptance of men's 'need' for proof of phallic masculinity – by whatever prosthetic means necessary.

A reliance on medically informed, individualized health education about transmission and preventive measures has provided the chief governmental response to the continuing threat of HIV infection and AIDS, when it finally got underway, at least in Britain and the United States. However, Graham Hart argues here that recent studies suggest that this is a necessary but far from sufficient response to halt the spread of AIDS. He draws mainly on community-oriented initiatives reported by researchers and gay activists in the United States, which indicate that the provision of medical knowledge alone is ineffective when compared with the success of the 'safer sex' preventive work pioneered within gay subcultures as a form of sexual politics aiming to establish new group norms and collective practices. In searching for more effective preventive action, especially for gay men who (in the West) remain the group most at risk of AIDS, it is important to bear in mind that unsafe sex (and HIV transmission) occurs most often in the context of the trust and commitment of regular relationships. This is an issue Carla Willig tackles in discussing her research on the limits of trust in intimate relationships. As other studies have also indicated, the importance of expressing 'trust' has the ironical effect that younger women were more able to protect themselves from pregnancy and disease in casual sex, but found it harder to request condom use from 'boyfriends' within relationships.

A number of other essays address the problem and effects of phallocentrism in language, sexual discourse and representation. Jane Ussher looks at pornographic representation and the idea of the 'lesbian phallus' to explore how women can resist and subvert the traditional subordinate positioning of women. Ine Vanwesenbeeck, drawing on her study of prostitutes' interactions with clients in Holland, similarly suggests that women can gain control over their lives in sexual engagements with men, although never without difficulty. However, focusing on those difficulties, Shirley Prendergast's research graphically highlights the gendered stereotyping, conflict and confrontation so prominent in the way young girls and boys in school negotiate contact with each other when moving towards heterosexuality from within the security of their single-sex groupings.

The inevitability of gender conflict accompanies the near ubiquity of forms of policing lesbian and gay sexuality. Each derives from the same source: the way in which both women and men, but particularly men as the dominant sex, rely upon heterosexual normativity to confirm gender identity and difference. Non-heterosexual engagement always threatens to undermine the parallels routinely made between the masculine/feminine divide and the supposed active/passive positionings of heterosexual sex. To the extent that men need to affirm a sense of 'masculine' dominance and difference through sex, intimacy with women can easily arouse fears of their own neediness, dependency or passivity; while the visibility of sexual rule-breakers − especially gay men and lesbians − can fuel hostile, even murderous, aggression.

Confronted with a homophobic culture, Alan Sinfield addresses the continuing tactical usefulness of affirming lesbian and gay identities as a strategy for demanding equal rights and for consolidating gay subcultures, despite his recognition of the hybridity, provisionality and constructedness of any such identity claims or sexual communities. In a similar vein, Mary McIntosh looks at the world from a lesbian and gay standpoint, in order to problematize and shed light upon the taken-for-granted nature of heterosexuality. Focusing primarily on the United States, Anna Marie Smith explores the growth of a more confrontational lesbian and gay activism in recent years as a direct consequence of the intensified homophobic rhetoric and policies of the Right in power both in the United States and in Britain, throughout the 1980s. She argues that this has now produced a new or modified form of homophobia, which aims to distinguish the 'good homosexual' (who does not threaten existing gender and sexual hierarchies) from those radical activists now refusing the liberal 'tolerance' of a homophobic society. It is a radical strand of recent gay theorizing, one equating intense sexual pleasure with self-annihilation, that Mandy Merck examines in her contribution, which questions where this leaves women's search for sexual subjectivity, whether straight or lesbian.

The volume closes with an essay by Jill Lewis on the continuing difficulties reported to her by so many people working to promote progressive sexual agendas. It is still hard to find sufficiently sensitive and open language to talk about new sexual realities: 'Safer forms of sexuality can only evolve if there is a will to reassess, dare to shift and reformulate the way we talk together, question and acknowledge the very terms in which sex functions in our culture.' There are weighty obstacles in the way of any sexual politics seeking to increase the potential confidence of all people (both individually and collectively) to pursue the differing comforts, pleasures and perils of the body, free from intimidation and threat. These include the perpetual displacement of people's fear, envy or anxiety into rage against others' pursuit of pleasure, never stronger than when they are seen as violating gender or sexual norms. The unrelenting lobbying and attacks of the corporate Right in the United States against the expansion of women's, lesbian and gay rights is just the most obvious and organized side of this mobilization of sexual fears and gender panics in the face of social change. In America, feminists have come under fire not just from the ideologues of the old male order like Jesse Helms, but from new 'post'-feminist polemicists like Camille Paglia (1992) or Rene Denfeld (1995), who have gained instant celebrity through the media attention accorded their totalizing caricatures of feminism as prudish and puritanical. Posing as outrageously radical, Paglia's reactionary dispatches serve up anti-feminist backlash as jaunty comedy: 'We cannot regulate male sexuality. The uncontrollable aspect of male sexuality is what makes sex interesting. And yes, it can lead to rape in some situations.... The powerful, uncontrollable force of male sexuality has been censored out of white middle-class homes' (1992, p. 63).

Meanwhile, the scholarly endeavours or subversive practices of other feminist and 'queer' theorists or performers are dismissed by their critics as inattentive to the daily material burdens faced by women, gays and lesbians. There has been an ever-greater gulf forming between campaigning activists and contemporary theorists of sexual signification and regulation. Yet few poststructuralists doubt that alongside discursive disruption of sexual and gender norms, we need to pay attention to specific anatomical bodies and how they are distinctively vulnerable – in ways which are as much socially as anatomically determined – along the lines of gender, age, illness or disability. Our bodily and psychic formations intertwine and are never separable from their particular positioning within a multitude of privileging or oppressive social meanings and relations.

Those seeking new sexual agendas based on the acceptance of plural sexualities will continue to deplore the asymmetries of power in the definitions and relations still dominating sexual conduct today. Those who wish to prevent any erosion of more conservative traditions will continue to oppose the expansion of sex education, information or products that might make sex safer and more pleasurable, unless sanctioned by marriage. This is now, as it always has been, a crucial battle, whichever side one is on. To take but one example: the success of the Moral Right in the United States over the last decade has dramatically reduced sexually active young women's protection from unwanted pregnancy, lowering the use of contraceptives in first heterosexual encounters to under 10 per cent, compared to their increased protection in the Netherlands (where sex education begins at the age of 8), where 95 per cent of people are reported as using contraception in their first heterosexual encounter (Baxandall, 1995). Sex education in Britain falls somewhere between these two extremes. Clearly, there is a lot at stake for those who wish to replace the old sexual agendas maintaining the heterosexual male as the uniquely empowered sexual agent by asserting new affirmations of sexual diversity, mutuality and respect. The highly charged issues surrounding sexuality are far from resolved to anyone's satisfaction. There is a lot more agenda-setting ahead.

I
HISTORICAL ROOTS, NEW SHOOTS

1 Heroes or Villains? Reconsidering British *fin de siècle* Sexology and its Impact

Lesley A. Hall

In 1895 the trials of Oscar Wilde crystallized certain sexual attitudes of the era, and had an impact which continued to resonate for decades. Shortly afterwards, two seminal works of British sexology appeared: Edward Carpenter's *Love's Coming of Age* (1896) and *Sexual Inversion* (1897), the first volume of Havelock Ellis's *Studies in the Psychology of Sex*. The writings of these two pioneers have been depicted as precursors, even begetters, of the sexual revolution, although this took a good 70 years to germinate. Views on the desirability, or otherwise, of the developments of the 1960s have therefore affected the way these writings, and these individuals, have been viewed. Their influence has been much debated, but has often been seen in either simplistic terms of the triumph of liberation from sexual repression, or the reinscription of oppressive patriarchal models of sexuality in a new, modernizing, medico-scientific discourse. In this chapter I shall suggest that there are many questions still to be posed (if not conclusively answered) about the reception of these works and their impact upon sexual attitudes and mores, and that the backlash against what was perhaps an initial, uncomplicated depiction of figures such as Carpenter and Ellis as heroic founding fathers of sexual liberation led to a demonization which was at least as misleading and unhelpful.

What was the context in which these early sexological pioneers, among whom Ellis and Carpenter were included, were writing? We all think we know what Victorian attitudes to sex were. If we no longer believe, after Foucault, that there was a total silence on the subject, when we look at what was being written in the proliferation of discourses he adumbrated, this was largely negative and repressive, and often restricted to very specific audiences. Men as a sex were targeted by voices from the highest in the medical profession to the sleaziest of quacks warning against self-abuse and the dangers of seminal losses (Hall, 1991). Women were not subject to equiva-

3

lent horror-mongering, but at the cost of almost complete silence on female sexual nature. There was a brief flurry during the 1860s in reaction to Isaac Baker Brown's controversial views that various disorders in the female were the result of self-abuse, and his equally controversial treatment by clitoridectomy. However, his professional colleagues were as offended by his aspersions on British womanhood as by his performance of a mutilating operation, and this episode remained just that (Porter and Hall, 1995).

Even writers coherently articulating the ideas generally supposed to be those of Victorian sexual respectability were few and far between. William Acton – author of *Functions and Disorders of the Reproductive Organs* and *Prostitution* – was the recognized authority on the subject from the 1850s until the end of the century, if only because there were few other serious, legitimately medical works on the subject; few apart from doctors were even licensed to speak about it (Hall, 1994).

Michael Mason has done a considerable service in his recent *The Making of Victorian Sexual Attitudes* by pointing out the existence in Victorian Britain of a conventional sexual moralism – what he calls 'classic moralism' – which was hardly ever explicitly formulated. This operated, he suggests, 'more in private precept than in essays and books', and was 'opposed to the theoretical...had a distaste for systematic and speculative inquiry into sex: it operated from the given...stock of inherited beliefs which it did not choose to enquire into' and 'not too troubled about consistency... [i]t liked to think it had its feet on the ground.' He has described a phenomenon analogous to those astronomical bodies, invisible to the naked eye, which can only be detected by observing their effect upon other bodies and which explain previously obscure anomalies (Mason, 1994).

The cast of mind Mason describes can be obliquely perceived through the observations made by Ethilda Budgett Meakin Herford (1872–1956), a woman doctor who qualified in 1898, in a letter to the Medical Women's Federation on the co-education issue during the 1920s. As a medical student and young doctor she had found that sexual questions were 'unwelcome and no information was available...in all the medical curriculum or text books'. However when 'attending [medical] congresses where women were not usually present [she] was astounded at the prominent place given to these matters as a subject of laughter and jest' (Meakin Herford, 1922).

This influential set of ideas about decency and the natural seldom emerged in any coherent form, except occasionally in reaction to those things which it had pre-defined as indecent and unnatural. There is a certain style of the journalism of moral outrage in which the voice of this 'classic moralism' can be persistently heard, or at least a voice directing its appeal towards its implicit tenets. A mid-twentieth-century figure who typified it was James Douglas of the *Express*, though by that time a certain note of defensive shrillness was becoming audible in his tirades against anything that offended against this assumed norm. He was given to making pronouncements like 'LORD DAWSON MUST GO!' when in 1921 Dawson, the King's personal physician, publicly addressed the Church Congress in favour of birth control. Douglas is most notorious for his vituperative and gratuitous attack on Radclyffe Hall's *The Well of Loneliness*, which led to its prosecution and banning after it had been on sale for some time and well reviewed in serious journals.

This 'classic moralism', as disinterred by Mason from subtext more than actual text, should not be confused with what we think of as 'typically Victorian' moral values on sexuality, influenced by evangelical religion. It was hostile to the enthusiasm and undue emotionalism of evangelicalism, while its inexplicit assumptions about the natural tended to mean the acceptance of – or at least readiness to excuse – some degree of male licence. It was basically conservative, assuming innate differences between the sexes, the necessity of the Double Moral Standard, and a male-defined heterosexual norm. Its very nature means it cannot readily be traced in specific textual formulations: it only surfaces explicitly in, for example, transactions in courts of law, or parliamentary debates. Age of consent debates from the nineteenth to the twentieth centuries provide a rich trove for hearing voiced seldom explicit, male ruling-class beliefs about sexual morality and young lower-class women.

Thus, the sexologists of the final decade of the nineteenth century were writing in a context in which there was a pervasive if unspoken assumption that sex was simply not something to be written about and analysed, except perhaps in warning of dangers. However, there had already been several decades of protest against the complacent conventional silence of society on a range of issues concerning sex and gender. These were very largely protests by, or on behalf of, women, against the various iniquities of marriage within the existing law (several of which had already been ameliorated by the 1890s) and, of course, attacking the existence of, and the ideas about sexual morality inherent in, the Contagious Diseases Acts. These protests focused on what one might call proto-feminist discontents and angers.

To ensure the better health of serving soldiers and sailors, the Contagious Diseases Acts ruled that in designated garrison and port towns women suspected of being prostitutes could be detained by the police and medically examined. If found to be suffering from venereal disease, they were incarcerated until 'cured' – though both diagnosis and therapeutic measures were open to serious criticism. By the 1880s, when the Acts were suspended and then repealed, the movement had already extended into wider areas of social morality, turning into a crusade for Social Purity, which as a movement was far from monolithic (Bland, 1995; Porter and Hall, 1995). There were important divisions of opinion both between the various bodies in the field and within them. Although some social purity policies were authoritarian, repressive and censorious, the movement as a whole struck a note of protest against the Double Moral Standard, and believed that sex was too important to be treated as 'a subject of laughter and jest'.

A similar seriousness, a refusal to dismiss the subject as trivial and amusing, appropriate to times of recreation and relaxation, characterized the early sexologists. They came from backgrounds of social protest, closely connected with feminist and radical politics Edward Carpenter, initially educated for a career in the Church, was an idealistic socialist reformer and influenced by Indian mysticism: an anti-imperialist, early 'Green', vegetarian and advocate of the simple communal life. He was himself a member of what he designated 'the Intermediate Sex' – homosexual – in a position where he was able to live a relatively 'out' lifestyle with his working-class lover. He published *Love's Coming of Age* in 1896, based on three earlier pamphlets discussing questions of sex and gender in a free society. However, early editions, significantly, omitted the chapter based on the pamphlet *Homogenic Love and its Place in a Free Society*, which was only incorporated a decade later when publishers' nerves had become a little steadier. Carpenter also published a separate extended version as *The Intermediate Sex* in 1908.

Havelock Ellis came from much the same milieu of an idealistic humanitarian utopian socialism tinged with mysticism. Unlike Carpenter, Ellis was medically qualified, although his qualification, the

Licentiate of the Society of Apothecaries, was the humblest means of entry to a medical career: he was far from the eminent member of the profession some writers have depicted. Ellis recognized the strategic benefits of medical legitimacy for investigating sex, but only practised for a short while after gaining his qualification and then devoted himself to the study of sex, combined with freelance writing. A year before his death, he was admitted to Fellowship of the Royal College of Physicians, but this was explicitly in recognition of his services to sexual science.

In 1897 Ellis published the first volume of his projected *Studies in the Psychology of Sex*, a collaborative volume on *Sexual Inversion* (i.e. homosexuality) with the writer and critic John Addington Symonds. Symonds had already written two pamphlets on the subject – *A Problem in Greek Ethics* and *A Problem in Modern Ethics*, privately printed for restricted circulation only – and in 1892 he approached Ellis, through an intermediary, to propose collaboration. However, Symonds, who had tuberculosis, died early in 1893 before the volume was completed. A German edition under both names appeared in 1896, but British publishers were reluctant to be associated with the venture, until a rather dubious character called de Villiers undertook to publish *Sexual Inversion* in Britain under his imprint, the Watford University Press. The entire first edition was, however, bought up by Symonds' executor Horatio Brown, who prevailed upon Ellis to remove Symonds' name, and all material attributed to him, and undertake considerable rewriting, in order, Brown averred, to spare the feelings of Symonds' surviving family. This substantially revised edition appeared in 1897 under Ellis's name alone.

It was not the best time to publish even the most serious and scholarly of works on the subject in Britain. Ellis's difficulties in finding a publisher were only the beginning. Watford University Press also published *The Adult*, the journal of the Legitimation League, a small society with the aim of removing the legal disabilities of illegitimacy, but also concerned with free love, the iniquity of the marriage laws, and other radical causes. The editor, George Bedborough, sold the journal out of his front room, along with other publications including *Sexual Inversion*, and was already under police surveillance because of their suspicions about anarchist associations with the League.

His sale of *Sexual Inversion* gave the police the opportunity to pounce. Detective John Sweeney bought a copy and then applied for a warrant for Bedborough's arrest, to strike a blow against 'free love and anarchism' allegedly 'flood[ing] of the country with books of the "psychology" type' – although according to Ellis's biographer Phyllis Grosskurth, far from flooding the country, this was only the third copy to be sold. The police were less interested in *Sexual Inversion* as such than in getting a lead to the dangerous nest of anarchists they believed to exist. However, the case against Bedborough was that he had 'sold and uttered a certain lewd wicked bawdy scandalous and obscene libel in the form of a book entitled *Studies in the Psychology of Sex: Sexual Inversion'*.

A Free Press Defence Committee was formed, including such major contemporary literary figures as George Bernard Shaw, Frank Harris and George Moore, and the socialist H.M. Hyndman. Bedborough eventually struck a deal with the police, claiming to have sold *Sexual Inversion* in innocence and laying all blame on the elusive de Villiers, who turned out to be very shady indeed, with a record of floating dubious enterprises. The trial thus never dealt with the issue of whether or not *Sexual Inversion* was obscene, but only with who was responsible for publishing it: its obscene nature was assumed and there was no chance to argue in its defence. Ellis was devastated by this outcome (Grosskurth, 1980).

Volume II of the *Studies* was also published in Watford – though claiming to be from the University Press, Leipzig – but subsequent volumes and further editions were published by the F.A. Davis Company in Philadelphia. All seven volumes of the *Studies in the Psychology of Sex* have never been published in Britain. Ellis and Carpenter and their works were, certainly on their first appearance, marginal and oppositional.

It is frequently alleged that Ellis was either participating in, or initiating, a medical discourse on homosexuality with *Sexual Inversion*, but this is very hard to substantiate as far as the British context is concerned. Ellis's own perception was that 'the matter was in special need of elucidation and discussion'. He commented, in the Preface to the first edition, that 'a peculiar amount of ignorance exists regarding the subject', and added that he was acquainted with experienced medical men who had 'never, to their knowledge, come across a single case'. The scientific literature as a whole was extremely sparse, while (until Ellis began publishing his own cases) 'not a single British case, unconnected with the asylum or the prison, had ever been recorded'. Yet, as he pointed out, in England, more than any other country, the law and public opinion combine to place a heavy penal burden and a severe social stigma on the manifestations of an instinct which to those persons who possess it frequently appears natural and normal.

In his chapter on 'The Study of Sexual Inversion', the authorities whose work he discussed were, with the exception of Carpenter and Symonds (neither of them medical men), either European (predominantly German, Swiss and Austrian) or American (Ellis, 1915).

In an era when the British medical curriculum omitted any study of the venereal diseases which at that time constituted a major menace to public health and were clearly definable as a medical problem, even less clearly defined issues to do with sexuality were not something that most doctors wanted to grapple with, at least not in any serious way. The medical press was prepared to present Ellis as a (serious medical) man unjustly treated at the time of his prosecution, although one cannot extrapolate from the editorial opinions of the *Lancet* or the *British Medical Journal* what the average doctor thought. There was, these journals said, 'nothing about the book itself... to pander to the prurient mind' (*Lancet*, 1898), and it dealt with certain 'unpleasant matters with which members of the medical profession should have some acquaintance' (*BMJ*, 1898). It is, however, perhaps more indicative of medical attitudes that not a single doctor was actively associated with the defence of *Sexual Inversion*.

However, once the furore of the trial had died down, and *Studies in the Psychology of Sex* were being published on the distant shores of the United States, there was some modified approval for Ellis's works from medical reviewers. In 1902 a *British Medical Journal* reviewer praised his 'serious and honest attempts to deal with his subject', though expressing regrets that such 'honesty of purpose was not turned to better account' (*BMJ*, 1902). By 1910, the *Lancet*'s reviewer could be found recommending Volume VI of the Studies, *Sex in Relation to Society*, 'to the medical world and to serious students of social problems'. Ellis had become 'a scholar in his peculiar field, and... given the dignity of scholarship to a very delicate and difficult subject' (*Lancet*, 1910).

Lacking Ellis's medical credentials, Carpenter did not receive similar approbation for *The Intermediate Sex*; the *British Medical Journal* published a long and damning review. The reviewer began his four-column attack with complaints of having 'been subjected to so many publications of this character since *Psychopathia Sexualis* and *Sexual Inversion*'. 'These articles', he fumed, 'reiterate *ad nauseam* praise and laudation for creatures and customs...generally regarded as odious.' Discussing the terms 'Urning' and 'Uranian' he rather gratuitously added, 'To avoid any confusion we may here remind ourselves that the word "urinal" comes from a different root.' He concluded that 'Urnings' ought to emigrate to

> some land where their presence might be welcome, and thus serious people in England might be spared the waste of time reading a low-priced book of no scientific or literary merit, advocating the culture of unnatural and criminal practices which, while having a pernicious tendency, remain chiefly but not wholly ridiculous. (*BMJ*, 1909)

Members of the general public, however, were reading these books, telling others about them and writing to or making pilgrimages to see their authors. Ellis wrote to Carpenter in 1918,

> The process of evangelising intermediate folk seems to go on regularly and steadily. At almost regular intervals they write or call mysteriously and unexpectedly. Either they read your book and want mine, or they read mine and of course I put them on to yours...I heard from a man of nearly 40 who has only just now found the clue to his mystery by reading your book. And so it goes on. (Ellis, 1918)

Over some four decades Carpenter received numerous letters of appreciation from grateful readers of both genders and varied sexual orientation. The following comments are typical: 'we may make a pilgrimage to see you about next Easter...My wife joins in sending hearty greetings' (Goodey, 1912); '"The Intermediate Sex" and "Iolaus" especially...have shewne [*sic*] me that I need not be ashamed of what I had always felt...to be my noblest emotion' (Sharp, 1921); 'though I am not a true Urning, your book has... opened my eyes to the true facts of this vital subject' (Bluham, 1921).

While Ellis's surviving correspondence contains rather fewer tributes from grateful readers among the general public, his name crops up in accounts by several individuals who were part of the same contemporary ferment of ideas. It is clear that he did not appear to them as a guru laying down a new gospel to be followed, but a fellow pilgrim-soul providing useful food for thought on a subject about which little was known and upon which conventional morality severely discouraged thinking. The suffragette Lady Rhondda wrote that *Studies in the Psychology of Sex* 'was the first thing of its kind I had found. Though I was far from accepting it all, it opened up a whole new world of thought.' She had been able to peruse the *Studies* in the Cavendish Bentinck Library at the International Women's Suffrage Club: her father, a mine-owner and politician, subsequently a Cabinet minister, found that when he tried to buy the volumes 'one had to produce some kind of signed certificate from a doctor or lawyer to the effect that one was a suitable person to read it' (Rhondda, 1933). Emmeline Pethick-Lawrence wrote to Ellis around 1918 that 'the issues that you live for are... closely connected with the spirit' of the suffrage struggle in which she had been for so long a leading figure (Pethick-Lawrence, ?1918).

Neither Ellis nor Carpenter nor any other member of the 'British school' of sexology created a school of thought in the way that Freud, for example, did. The British Society for the Study of Sex Psychology, inaugurated in 1914, was one outcome of their influence. However, it was a characteristic product of their style of thinking and writing in that it did not lay down any single correct line. Rather, it aimed at 'the consideration of problems and questions connected with sexual psychology from their medical, juridical, and sociological aspects'. These questions were said to be especially '(1) The Evils of Prostitution (2) Inversion (3) Sexual Ignorance (4) Disease (5) Aberrations of various kinds'. Membership and eligibility for office were 'open on precisely the same terms to women as to men', working 'together for a common understanding' upon 'matters which vitally concern both sexes'. The Society was 'for *investigation*', and the open-minded attitude which made it possible (BSSSP, 1914; Browne, 1918). It aimed to organize 'reading of papers in agreement with the general objects of the Society', and to issue occasional pamphlets. There was also the hope (never fully realized) that it might serve as a focal point for the collection of data 'on matters within the scope of the society' (BSSSP, 1913).

The areas with which those who joined were associated were extremely diverse, including politics, education, anthropology, birth control, divorce law reform, anti-censorship, eugenics, nudism and sunbathing, psychoanalysis and social purity. There were a few doctors and several clergymen among the membership. A number were additionally concerned with sex education. The BSSSP did not dismiss what adherents of social purity might be able to offer, and very early on an invitation to join the committee was extended to the eminent woman doctor and social purity stalwart, Mary Scharlieb. The committee's list of suggested reading included *An Address to the Young* by long-standing purity advocate Canon Lyttelton alongside more predictable works by Ellis, Carpenter and continental sexologists such as Iwan Bloch, Auguste Forel, Edvard Westermarck and Otto Weininger. While there is evidence of common interests between social purity advocates and sex reformers in the BSSSP, it would also be possible to demonstrate an increasing infiltration of the concepts of the sexologists into social purity writings and activities. The Association for Social and Moral Hygiene's enquiry into the State and Sexual Morality following the end of the First World War certainly considered seeking evidence from Ellis and other members of the BSSSP, such as Jessie Murray, the psychoanalyst, and Norah March, the sex educator and suffragist (Hall, 1995; Porter and Hall, 1995).

While the membership of the BSSSP was largely sympathetic to psychoanalysis, on the whole this was regarded as but one of many means by which sexual enlightenment was being brought about in the new century. A number of members were of the Left politically, however some were forthright reactionaries, such as the Reverend Montague Summers, Roman Catholic priest of occultist interests, widely suspected of satanism. There has been a persistent impression, from its contemporaries up to the present day, that the Society 'concerned itself almost exclusively with the homosexual question' – a view explicitly put forward by the famous birth control advocate and marriage manual writer, Marie Stopes, in 1931. The actual interests of members and the activities of the Society do not really bear this out. Members' own personal sexual interests/identity covered a wide spectrum, certainly including homosexual activists such as Laurence Housman and George Ives, but also married couples (the communist Pauls, the Malthusian Drysdales), the happily celibate Cicely Hamilton, women such as Harriet Shaw Weaver whose primary emotional engagements appear to have been with women, and Stella Browne who shunned both marriage and motherhood, but was in practice as well as in principle a proponent of heterosexual 'free love'. Members were aware that the enterprise upon which they were engaged could be regarded as dubious, leading to anxiety about safeguarding the Society from undesirables. Allegedly 'groundless fears concerning "spies" and similar obsessions', and the subjection of candidates for membership to 'vexatious inquisition' endured well into the 1930s (Hall, 1995).

Distinguished persons addressed the Society, including Dora Russell, Marie Stopes, Freud's leading British disciple Ernest Jones, the anthropologists Edvard Westermarck and Bronislaw Malinowski, biologists Julian Huxley and F.A.E. Crew, and foreign notables such as Robert Michels, the American psychologist Homer Lane and Dr Georg Groddeck. However, the Society by no means privileged 'experts': Bertram Lloyd informed Edward Carpenter in 1916 that Marie Stopes regarded the Society as composed of 'well meaning dilettantes and amateurs in need of proper organisation and leading' (Lloyd, 1916). Norman Haire seems to have been on a rather similar track in his 1920 complaint to Havelock Ellis that 'most of the people were enquirers on the same plane as myself', rather than authorities 'at whose feet I might sit and drink in wisdom' (Haire, 1920). The line was distinctly non-authoritarian. Many individuals whose only qualification was intelligent interest addressed the Society and do not seem to have drawn significantly smaller audiences than more famous names, and the opportunities for discussion provided were valued. On the whole attitudes were broadminded and tolerant. Bertram Lloyd wrote enthusiastically to Carpenter about 'a really extremely open and good discussion on masturbation... such as wd. [*sic*] have been utterly impossible in London not so very long ago' (Lloyd, 1917). However, upon one – possibly the same – occasion 'a virtuous lady... nearly [gave] up the ghost' when one member (almost certainly Stella Browne) 'defended female masturbation' (Housman, 1931).

The interests comprised within 'sex reform' were diverse and not always harmonious; for example, the Society included individuals who believed that homosexuality was an innate tendency and ought to be decriminalized, and others who saw it as the product of social and educational practices, which might be 'cleared up' by, for example, healthy-minded co-educational schools, as well as those who felt that while 'inverts' had a hard lot and the law should be changed, birth control (the primary interest of many members) was disgusting and reprehensible. It is thus not entirely astonishing that the Society very seldom managed to reach agreement which might have led to action on any given topic of concern.

This small and rather obscure society's impact on reforming laws, or even moderating more than a small corner of public opinion, was thus apparently minimal. By 1950 – a good half-century after the first appearance of Ellis's and Carpenter's books – homosexuality was still criminalized, sex education was only nominally part of the educational curriculum, birth control was not available within the National Health Service, and divorce continued to operate on concepts of innocence and guilt. None the less, some 30 years after the Society's wartime collapse nearly all the reforms it had desired had been implemented, with easing of laws on obscenity, greater availability of birth control and abortion, the no-fault divorce and homosexual law reform. While these may have been the result of other social changes, arguably the BSSSP (and other societies with similar attitudes and aims, such as the Federation of Progressive Societies and Individuals, and Norman Haire's own Sex Education Society) had influenced in their youth individuals who by the 1960s had risen to positions of power and influence. Gerald Gardiner, defence counsel in the obscenity trial of *Lady Chatterley's Lover* and Lord Chancellor of the reforming Labour government of the 1960s, had, as a young barrister, been an active member of the BSSSP, and indeed had provided it with legal advice about whether one of its pamphlets might fall foul of the obscenity laws (Hall, 1995).

Ellis and Carpenter's actual writings were certainly very much of their time. However, specific elements perhaps have been given undue prominence by some historians, who have spent more time on those passages where these writers were somewhat uncritical or unthinkingly accepting of contemporary assumptions, rather than those in which they were extremely, radically critical. Both writers were undoubtedly biological essentialists, but they believed and argued that society had erected upon natural differences (which were still, they contended, anyway imperfectly understood) an unnaturally exaggerated superstructure. As Carpenter put it in *Love's Coming of Age*:

> These distinctions have...been strangely accentuated and exaggerated during the historic period – till at last a point of maximum divergence and absolute misunderstanding has been reached. (Carpenter, 1930)

The fact that Ellis was engaged in an encyclopaedic compilation is often ignored: much of the *Studies* consists of more or less direct quotations from his sources, rather than his own opinions.

But what they said is, perhaps, not the question (though much of their writings are still thought-provoking and should not be dismissed). That they were saying it at all, that they were saying sexuality should be discussed, and opening up new ways of doing so, was the crucial revolution they were making. They were putting forward what may now seem a perhaps one-sided case for sex to be considered seriously as an important subject, because, at the time of writing, it was seen either as a dangerous negative force, or else trivialized. Inherent in their arguments was the belief that contemporary prudery and neglect had, to quote Carpenter, 'created worse ills and suffering... by giving sexual acts so feverish an importance' (Carpenter, 1930). If in some ways they were breaking a silence, in other ways they were trying to find different and better ways of talking of something already too much talked about.

They were hesitant, as has been indicated, about laying down new laws. To them, what mattered most was opening up an occluded topic for investigation and discussion. As Carpenter put it in the opening pages of *Love's Coming of Age*:

> Words on the subject being so few and so inadequate, everything that *is* said is liable to be misunderstood. Violent inferences are made and equivocations surmised, from the simplest remarks; qualified admissions of liberty are interpreted into recommendations of unbridled licence.... There is in fact a great deal of fetishism in the current treatment of the question. (Carpenter, 1930)

It could be argued that little has changed. There have been other, less visible, factors which have conduced to the giving of an exaggerated importance to sex. Sexual ignorance is still rife, even while (or because) the commercial deployment of sexuality – Marcuse's 'repressive desublimation' in action – has increased in an increasingly consumerized society. The media present sexual desirability in seriously circumscribed terms, very far from Carpenter's Utopian suggestion that 'there are no limits of grace or comeliness... within which love is obliged to move' (Carpenter, 1930). British society today is very far from taking sex with the seriousness, responsibility and tolerance Ellis and Carpenter advocated.

Many more people than even so much as heard the names of Ellis or Carpenter would have come into contact with and gained ideas about sexuality from – among even less recoverable sources

(Porter and Hall, 1995) – the not usually particularly sympathetic press reportage of public events such as the trials of Oscar Wilde, Marie Stopes's libel action against Dr Halliday Sutherland, the prosecution for obscenity of Radclyffe Hall's *The Well of Loneliness* and divorce cases. Even the medical profession, notwithstanding growing acclaim for Ellis during the 1930s, was very little influenced by his writings. The pioneer of Social Medicine, Professor John Ryle, asked in 1943:

> How many practitioners, how many teachers of medical students, I wonder, have read...*Psychology of Sex* or *Sex in Relation to Society*, or given serious thought to the teaching which in turn they might have given to others had they taken the trouble to inform themselves better? (Ryle, 1943)

Reading this, and reading the letters Marie Stopes received from the general public during the interwar years describing the medical profession's lack of interest in and even disgust with sexual problems (Hall, 1985), one becomes inclined to doubt the overwhelming and cataclysmic effect upon society and sexual relations sometimes attributed to sex reformers such as Ellis and Carpenter.

We may find Ellis, Carpenter and their colleagues old-fashioned, even plain wrong: however, that is no reason to demonize them or patronizingly condescend to their quaintness. We should rather recognize how much we owe to their resistance to moral conservatism and public inertia. This volume would not be in existence if a hundred years ago they had not set going, in the teeth of serious and persisting opposition, debates which still continue.

2 Thinking Sex Historically

Lucy Bland and Frank Mort

INTRODUCTION: NARRATIVES OF SEXUAL MODERNITY

In March 1912 the socialist and feminist Stella Browne wrote to the British journal *The Freewoman* about her views on sexuality:

> The sexual experience is the right of every human being not hopelessly afflicted in mind or body and should be entirely a matter of free choice and personal preference, untainted by bargain or compulsion. (Browne, 1912, p. 354)

Browne's libertarianism stood in opposition not only to a double moral standard which enforced female chastity while disregarding male resort to prostitutes, but also to a feminism that called for sexual moderation, even abstinence, for all. She saw herself as a modern sexual pioneer, campaigning for personal morality and sexual freedom (see Rowbotham, 1977). To Virginia Woolf, reflecting back ironically on approximately this same period, sex was something her Bohemian circle was likewise concerned with, but not so much as a political right as a verbal obsession:

> Sex permeated our conversation. The word bugger was never far from our lips. We discussed copulation with the same excitement and openness that we had discussed the nature of good. It is strange to think how reticent, how reserved we had been and for how long. (Woolf, 1976, pp. 173–4)

Both Browne and Woolf implicitly contrasted their contemporary world-view with Victorianism. The end of the Victorian era marked the end of sexual reservation. The new epoch represented a shift from sexual repression, reticence and silence to one of the perceived freedom and self-expression of modernity: the freedom to *speak* sex and to act upon one's sexual desires.

Since the 1960s there has been an explosion of interest in the historical dimensions of sexuality. Many of the themes announced by Browne and Woolf have emerged as core concerns in this work. The creation of the notion of progressive sexual modernity around a break with the Victorian past, the extraordinary tangled relationship between sexual knowledge and sexual identity, sex as a cultural field on which modern social relations (both between men and women and in their homosocial forms) have been dramatized. Our chapter focuses on a number of these questions. As practising historians, working on aspects of British cultural history of the nineteenth and twentieth centuries, we have confronted such concerns in our own work. But what place does history have in the proliferation of discourses about sex? Is history simply one of the many forms of competing contemporary knowledge which continue to expand at an accelerating rate? Since the late nineteenth century histories of sex have functioned in a symbolic and paradigmatic way. Sex as history has frequently served to dramatize pressing contemporary social and political questions, either implicitly or explicitly. At their most grandiose, a number of historians of sexuality have made powerful claims for the relationship between the present and narratives about the past. Such arguments have been put most strongly by Michel Foucault in his insistence that the present itself needed to be conceived historically as the product of an intersecting set of genealogies which have been unstably yoked together (Foucault, 1979). These positions are not specific to research on sexuality; they have occurred in all areas of historical work which have problematized positivist approaches to the past. Yet sexual historians do seem to have exhibited a particular personal and political investment in their material – what we might term 'a love affair' – which demonstrates the ways in which historical knowledge produced about sex has been deeply entangled with personal narratives of the past and evocations of the future. We would not see ourselves as outside that process. Rather, we would want to unpack its assumptions as part of a more self-reflexive process of writing history.

We begin with a brief review of some of the dominant tendencies among Anglo-American historians of sexuality in the twentieth century, and the challenges posed to these traditions, both by the more explicit agendas of sexual politics tabled since the 1970s and by the work of cultural theorists, especially Foucault. The core of our argument is that a series of confrontations between a Whiggish history of increasing sexual enlightenment and a more assertive set of theoretical and political concerns for a new type of history of sex has been both productive and problematic: productive in as much as it has challenged an earlier confident vision of sexual progressivism; problematic in that the new historical approaches have inevitably thrown up a fresh set of research issues which currently remain unresolved. It is these questions we wish to centre on. Many of the issues relate to what has recently been termed the 'linguistic turn' in the human sciences.[1] Such debates raise broad-based questions of language, meaning and the part played by these practices in the historical formation of identities. For the historian debates of this kind have recently become focused on the project for a new type of cultural history.

Woolf's Bloomsbury coterie was at the forefront of proposing a new modernist chronology of sexuality, in the years before and after the First World War. And Bloomsbury's thesis about the moral end of Victorianism was part of a much broader set of arguments advanced by more mainstream professionals and cultural commentators after 1900. With the aid of reformulated scientific knowledges, encouraged by the gradual dissemination of Freud's own theses on the mechanisms of repression, and abetted by the social impact of the war, Victorianism became constructed as a monolithic and restrictive force from which the twentieth century had broken free. Such a teleological narrative of social advancement was initially set in place during this early twentieth-century moment. But the chronology of sexual modernity was expanded and consolidated during the revival of interest in Victorianism which occurred in the 1960s and 1970s. Once again the repressive Victorians were a necessary foil for contemporary sexual progressivism. This binary imagery gave meaning to a wide variety of contemporary debates. Politicians and pressure groups, intent on securing the passage of reforming sexual legislation in the 1960s, frequently advanced their arguments via a modernizing logic. The remnants of 'the Victorian era' were part of the cultural debris which needed sweeping away in the interests of a more efficient and a more tolerant society (Crosland, 1956; Jenkins, 1959; National Deviancy Conference, 1980). The transformation of sexual manners and morals was cast as central to that process of reform. More academic commentators produced a different narrative of Victorian sexuality, which combined a familiar thesis about repression with a distinctive structure of desire for contemporary readers. Ronald Pearsall's flamboyant accounts of nineteenth-century sexual hypocrisy typified much of the writing on the subject at this time. In *The Worm in the Bud* he salaciously described the sexual consequences of the bourgeois ideal of purity, lingering over the pornographic texts and the sexual confessionals of middle-class men in ways which re-eroticized these encounters (Pearsall, 1969). Although Steven Marcus's classic study of Victorian pornography, *The Other Victorians*, presented a more nuanced account of the period, it too subscribed to the image of a veneer of public respectability, barely concealing a seething underworld of sexual guilt (Marcus, 1966). Pornography was the disruptive reverse image of public Victorian culture.

These stories of modernity, and their concomitant frameworks for discussing sexuality, still continue to exert considerable influence, both on academic historians and in more popular debates. Michael Mason's recent two-volume work on Victorian sexuality (Mason, 1994a; 1994b) displays a characteristic mixture of chaotic empirical and statistical research, dedicated towards unlocking the 'meaning' (in the singular) of nineteenth-century sexuality. His historical account is implicitly set against the sexual consensus of the 1990s, which Mason characterizes via a series of familiar tropes – liberation, emancipation, freedom, disinhibition and hostility to taboos and censorship.[2] While at a more popular level two television programmes, Steve Humphries' series, 'A Secret World of Sex' (see Humphries, 1988), along with the more recent 'Ruling Passions: Sex, Race and Empire' (see Gill, 1995), also worked with the idea of sex as the illicit underside of domestic and imperial histories of the nineteenth and twentieth centuries. Contemporary viewers of these stories of Victorianism are usually positioned as voyeurs uncovering a dark secret. The long-term influence of progressivist histories of sexuality continues. Their appeal lies in the persuasive power of a teleological narrative. None the less, recent research and scholarship has profoundly destabilized those confident narratives and chronologies

SEXUAL POLITICS AND DISCOURSE

Central to that process has been the rise of feminist, gay and lesbian historiographies and the continuing impact of the work of Michel Foucault. In the context of the progressivist accounts which we have reviewed, one of the most important contributions from feminist historians of sex has been their problematization of the very notion of sexual enlightenment itself. Challenging a linear and developmental narrative, feminist perspectives have brought into focus the troubled and unstable history of sexual modernization. There is here no smooth unfolding of sexual progress. Indeed, the concept of sexual progressivism is now itself frequently understood to be the problem. Feminist history has paid meticulous attention to the multifaceted power relations governing sexuality, power relations between the sexes which did not of course disappear with the rise of modernity, nor indeed with the 1960s so-called 'sexual revolution'. Gay and lesbian histories have interrogated sexual modernity rather differently. But the insistence that homosexual identities and experiences have been an integral part of the making of urban forms of masculinity and femininity has also disrupted some of the simpler assumptions of modernization theses. Histories of the modern city, for example, together with urbanism's most celebrated persona, the male *flâneur*, appear more nuanced and differentiated when metropolitan space is re-mapped to include homosexual and homosocial ways of being and acting (D'Emilio, 1983; Chauncey, 1994; Mort, 1996; Bech, forthcoming). Feminist and lesbian historians have also undertaken detailed research into the sexual lives of women – women who until recently were nothing but shadowy figures in mainstream history, merely objects of the gaze, if within the historical gaze at all. In doing so they have not only produced a new field of inquiry; many of them have also raised critical methodological questions about how sexual practices and desires, and sexual identity itself, are to be conceptualized. Simple appeals to an infrastructure of the physical body, or to common-sense understandings of sexual acts, fail to grasp the complex ways in which language and culture furnish the raw materials of erotic life. Taken together, feminist, lesbian and gay historiography has opened the space for the expanded treatment of the social and historical construction of sexual identity and experience.[3]

An emphasis on social and historical construction was of course central to the project of Michel Foucault. Reviewing Foucault's writing on sexuality from the vantage point of over a decade since his death, we can attempt to identify those aspects which were most significant about his historical interventions. Here we concentrate on the first volume of his *The History of Sexuality*, because it is this text which most explicitly discusses the relationship between power and modern sexuality. In the context of the earlier traditions we have outlined two themes stand out most prominently in this text: first, the break Foucault initiated with the progressive chronology of sexual modernity; second, the problematization of the very meaning and status of the category of sexuality, both as an object of social investigation and as an issue for historical research. For Foucault, the central issue was not whether societies say yes or no to sex, whether they permit or prohibit, but that both of these positions are part of the way in which sex is put into discourse. What matters in consequence is why sexuality is spoken about; who speaks and from what positions. This concept of the discursive rendering of sexuality was not as original as Foucault himself appeared to claim. Many of Foucault's insights had already been anticipated by feminists; sociologists working within the traditions of role and labelling theory also recognized sexuality's social construction and indeed its history (McIntosh, 1968; Plummer, 1975). But Foucault's interventions crystallized and developed these concerns. The concept of putting sex into discourse also opened up a greater space for those cultural historians who were seeking to explore the part played by particular practices in the formation of sexual identities. For example, rather than seeing Victorian visual or literary discourses as merely passive reflections 'of the age', or as supplements to the dominant narratives of social history, such forms could be assigned a more active role within the production of sexual identities (Jordanova, 1989; Nead, 1987). Combined with insights derived from work on the social dimensions of language, Foucault's discursive emphasis raised a critical point for the treatment of all historical material. This is the way in which historically-specific languages play an active role in the construction of objects of historical inquiry. In consequence the representational and symbolic quality of sexuality becomes a key concern.

In positing sexuality in this way Foucault profoundly and irrevocably questioned common-sense understandings of what a history of sexuality could be about. Foucault's approach uncovered sex in the most unlikely places, as well as in more familiar areas: within sanitary science, household manuals and psychiatric principles. Sex intruded into the circuits of government and inflected the tables of statistical classification, in addition to signifying bodily acts, identities and desires. Modern sexuality is, in short, a *dispersed field*, not a restricted one. It continues to be organized around multiple points of reference.

Recently a more polarized codification of sexuality has emerged from the work of a group of cultural and literary writers associated with the concept of queer theory. The notion of queerness has privileged the idea of transgression and perversion as cultural dominants in the organization of modern Western societies. Eve

Kosofsky Sedgwick's account of the complex rendering of male homosexuality within late nineteenth-century literary milieus in the *Epistemology of the Closet* has been a recurrent point of reference for this type of writing. Rather than claiming familiar minority status for the homosexual theme, Sedgwick's account is premissed on a much more all-encompassing trope, namely, that 'many of the major modes of thought and knowledge in twentieth century Western culture as a whole are structured... by a chronic, now endemic crisis of homo/heterosexual definition, inductively male, dating from the end of the nineteenth century' (Sedgwick, 1990, p. 1; see also Dollimore, 1991; Bristow, 1992; Sinfield, 1994). This reading of the 'perverse implantation', the understanding that perversion is endemic to modern societies, was familiar from Foucault's own history of sexuality. But in the work of cultural critics such as Sedgwick the idea is elevated to a much more problematic status, as a quasi-anthropological principle of human culture. Literary analysis of a series of modernist texts facilitates her dehistoricization. Sex is not now grounded in the family, or in moral law, nor is it a function of capitalism, but is grounded according to the binary principle of homo- as opposed to heterosexuality.

Such accounts have delivered important insights for our understanding of the historical mechanisms whereby perversity and the norm are mutually dependent and reinforcing. But like the 1960s account of Victorianism, they also carry with them the burden of a binary reading of modern sexual regimes. Queer theory has tended to elevate the principle of sexual dissidence as *the* epistemology of sexuality, in such a way that the perverse as against the norm becomes the motif of sexuality. Sexual theory is littered with such reductionisms. They have proved unproductive precisely because they fail to grasp the plurality of sexual systems, forcing disabling choices around polarized oppositions. Rather than restating binary dualisms, it is important to grasp the multiple points of construction of modern sexuality. Delimiting sex to a single principle of choice, such as queerness versus normality, offers an over-prescriptive reading of the sexual.[4]

Two case studies attempt to explore concretely the problems faced by historians in accessing the dimensions of language and subjectivity in work on sexuality. The first, from the late nineteenth century, relates to the difficulties in analysing the emotional and sexual forms of expression of certain women and men who were in the vanguard of sexual politics during this period. The second example, from a century later, illustrates the way in which ethnographic work with young men highlights the extremely unstable formation of heterosocial and homosocial identities within contemporary culture. The two vignettes, a century apart, are further divided by status and social register. While the former focuses on a relatively elite grouping, the latter centres on an aspect of popular culture. What unites the two examples is a common endeavour: to situate subjectivities historically.

THE MEN AND WOMEN'S CLUB

Our first example is drawn from research carried out for Lucy Bland's recent book *Banishing the Beast: English Feminism and Sexual Morality, 1885–1914*. This is the case of the Men and Women's Club, which met in London in the second half of the 1880s and which has been analysed by several other historians, most notably and suggestively by Judith Walkowitz (1992). The club, composed of radicals, socialists and feminists of both sexes, and instigated by the future eugenist and statistician Karl Pearson, met to discuss 'all matters...connected with the mutual position and relation of men and women'. The primary sources available to the researcher, housed in the Pearson Collection, University College, London, are rich and various: brief minutes of the club's monthly meetings, copies of many of the papers given, an unpublished, autobiographical account of the club by its secretary, Maria Sharpe, and, in great abundance, many items of correspondence. Unfortunately, while much of the correspondence to Pearson is preserved, as well as correspondence to Maria Sharpe (Pearson's future wife), we have few of the letters sent *by* Pearson – save to Maria. Nevertheless, the letters clearly demonstrate that club debate extended beyond the boundaries of official meetings; they also give some sense of the passions, conflicts and grievances of club members, including incidents of romantic intrigue. Judith Walkowitz suggests that the archives, in their variety, allow the historian to 'present the club discussions stereophonically, in multiple voices', permitting an interpretation of the silences as well as the interventions at club meetings (Walkowitz, 1992, p. 136). While agreeing that much can indeed be surmised from reading between the lines, as it were, it is still often difficult to fathom club members' sense of their selves, especially their sense of their sexual selves – their desires, their longings, their fantasies, let alone their sexual practices. At one level one could read the club as composed of individuals holding a range of competing knowledges and understandings of the world: Social Darwinism, social purity, radical individualism, state socialism, various religious stances, and so on. But the way that these individuals spoke and activated the different discourses cannot be apprehended simply through analysis of the discourses themselves. While Foucault centres on the production of discourses, it is clearly necessary to focus too on discourses' *reception*. And the whole process of analysis is made yet more complex when one recognizes the difficulty for individuals, then as now, in *speaking* their sexuality, and when one appreciates that individuals are not unified subjects, with stable unified psyches, but, in different contexts and periods, live out different aspects of their selves, or rather of their multiple selves.

Here we focus briefly on the troubled love affair of two of the club members: the spinster and feminist Maria Sharpe and the most dominant of the club members, Karl Pearson – attractive yet cold, rationalist, suspicious of feeling, but later desperate to express, in acceptable terms, his desire for Maria. This was a relationship which shifted gradually over the four-year duration of the club, from one of teacher and pupil, through to that of wooer and wooed, and finally, a year after the club's closure, to that of husband and wife. But the transition was not without tribulations. Maria had gained much from her experience of the club, not least, a new intellectual confidence, a conversion to socialism, and, perhaps less positive for her, a crisis of religious faith. She agonized over Pearson's offer of marriage for many months. Many of her letters for this period are missing, destroyed later at her request, but one gathers something of her emotional turmoil from Pearson's anxious replies, and from the reflections sent to Pearson by Maria's sisters and friends. Part of her deep ambivalence may have related to her fears of self-surrender. In an earlier letter to Pearson, before his marriage proposal, she had written that 'the purely physical side of [women's] sexual desires... is so closely connected with the desire for self-surrender' (Sharpe, 1889), yet self-surrender was an enemy of women's emancipation. This was why women striving 'to realise their own individuality' frequently renounced their sexuality. Elsewhere, she had asserted that women entered marriage with 'repulsion toward the exercise of the sex function' (Sharpe, 1885). Did she fear that the sexual side of marriage would entail *her* self-surrender and thus loss of her individuality? She must certainly have dreaded the loss of independence. Her involvement in the Men and Women's Club had prompted her to explore her politics, religion and intellectual potential. Now she faced a choice of continuing with her state of spinsterhood and her newfound freedom, including the various recent openings into writing and research, or marrying, acquiring respectability, but also economic dependency, the loss of legal and political rights, and the possibility of having to relinquish her intellectual pursuits for the duties of housewife and mother. She wrote: 'I am more paralysed than I can say, but seem to see clearly that I cannot now give you love.' She told him that she had a dread that she would 'wreck his life'; perhaps she also dreaded that he might wreck hers (Sharpe, 1890).

After a seven-month period in which Maria refused to see him, Pearson and Sharpe met again several times in April 1890 and at some point in this month she agreed to marry him. Gaps in the correspondence leave us frustratingly unclear as to why she changed her mind. Back in September 1889, Maria's sister Elizabeth Cobb, an old friend of Pearson's, had inquired of him whether or not he had 'won her'. Thirty-seven years later, the question was finally answered in the form of a long, tragic letter to Elizabeth which he asked her to destroy, but which, it appears, he never finally sent. He sadly and movingly reflected on his marriage:

> As I look back on it now I think life has been largely a failure. I have sacrificed everything – Maria would say wife and children included – to the idea of establishing a new tool in science [eugenics] which would give certainty where all was obscurity.... I have made many enemies and few friends.... It is not so much the waste of mine but of others' lives, in particular Mia's. She has been a splendid wife, if you mean by that, she has ever worked for her husband's purposes. But she has done it from her inbred sense of duty.... I have never actually won her.... Marrying as we did after what happened previously, I ought to have realised that I had still to win her, but I spent my life over my work and she sacrificed her life in looking after home and children.... I cannot let you of all people believe that our marriage has been an ideal one. It wanted delicacy of handling to make it so, and I have given too little of my time and thought to it. I have never won Mia, and that is the tragedy of it, when it is too late to remedy.
>
> (Pearson, 1927)

Pearson's lament is poignant. A complex mixture of emotional and sexual registers, it combines longing, frustration and arrogance. Drawing on the confessional structures of the epistolary form, it assumes an intimate language of male–female friendship to produce a retrospective on the destructive interrelationship between his professional and his married life. Written at the time his wife was dying, his marriage is relegated to the past tense, as part of an earlier set of temporal relations. Narrated as a domestic tragedy, it passes through a range of emotional timbres – sacrifice, failure, duty and the sentimental regret which comes from an awareness that the world might have been different. Set in the context of the broader stories of late nineteenth-century feminist struggles, it also provides a late twentieth-century reader with a bitter-sweet sense of an ending. Satisfying because knowing what we do about the power struggles between Karl and Maria in the 1880s, it seems just that she does manage to elude his grasp. Tragic because as more humanistic subjects we hope for a happy conclusion to this affair.

The passage is worth analysing in detail because it draws attention to the range of psychological and social factors which confront the cultural historian who attempts to engage with the emotional and sexual life of subjects of past periods. Narrative structures, a strong sense of temporality, the fiction of a centred self all play their part in Pearson's account. They form part of a set of ongoing problems concerning the nature of identity, agency and affective life which are central to the embryonic field of cultural history.[5]

HOMOSOCIAL IDENTITIES

We conclude by moving the chronology forward almost exactly a hundred years to consumer culture in London during the 1980s, drawing on Frank Mort's recent book *Cultures of Consumption*. This was the site for an ethnographic project focused on an exploration of the identities of young men, particularly in relation to their participation in the rituals of personal consumption. Recent strategies of promotional culture, as displayed in the campaigns of advertisers, marketers and retailers, have concentrated their attention on specific groups of young males in the 16–25 age range (Mintel, 1988; Euromonitor, 1989; Marketing Direction, 1988). Part of a more extensive programme of niche or placement marketing, one effect of this mode of address has been to render the bodies and the psyches of young men available for discussion, dissection and public display (Nixon, 1992; Mort, 1996). This commercial treatment of masculinity is usually discussed under the rubric of lifestyle marketing; the floating of a series of representations which are suggestive of secular rituals of the good life (Shields, 1992; Tomlinson, 1990). Anthony Giddens, addressing the characteristics of late modernity, has offered an expanded treatment of lifestyle practices (Giddens, 1991; 1992). Within contemporary Western societies, Giddens has argued, identity has become integrated into decisions made about the self. The net effect has been to produce social selfhood as a reflexively organized endeavour. Increasingly, Giddens has insisted, forms of social regulation are conducted less via the traditional public agencies and are transferred to an internal process of self-scrutiny.

This particular excursion into the field involved a set of loosely structured, taped interviews with young men undertaken by Frank Mort. Individuals were recruited by the deliberate selection of particular urban locations, especially those in Soho, in London's West End, which were associated with the aggressive promotion of the new rituals of masculine consumption. Shops, bars, restaurants, cafés, nightclubs, as well as the street, were the principal sites for the research. There was also an attempt to nominate a sexually and ethnically mixed constituency of young men.

Much recent debate on the methodologies of ethnographic research has revolved around the two-way nature of the interview transaction. The interaction, or the collision, of personalities resulting from these encounters has been seen as a significant part of the research outcome in its own right (Grossberg, 1988; Clifford and Marcus, 1986; Smith, 1988). The most sustained insistences in this area have come from feminist practitioners interviewing women (McRobbie, 1982; Radway, 1988). But the issue of fieldwork as a conversation between subjectivities is also thrown up when men meet men. Here the dynamics of what might be termed the research contract are very specific indeed. In my own experience, the interviews were organized around a version of a 'gentlemen's agreement'. In the brief period prior to the opening question, a number of unwritten rules were laid down by both parties about the boundaries of what was to follow. They were usually implicit, established by such signifiers as body posture, look and gesture, or verbal style. They related crucially to what could and could not be spoken about and the room for manoeuvre within this domain.

Many of those interviewed defined their identities and their sexuality with the aid of consumer culture. But markers of this kind did not produce a wholly unified account of subjectivity. The personal testimonies of these young men frequently displayed a fragmented and nomadic character. Their autobiographies appeared to wander through a range of social and sexual terrains, rather than projecting wholly coherent identities.

There was one particular incident when these issues surfaced in an acute form. They involved my dialogue as a white man with David, a black actor and model, who was one of my interviewees. The interview was going well; David's manner was confident and mildly flirtatious. Asking a standard question about London and the opportunities for employment, I pressed him about the types of work he did. His response, full of ambiguity and innuendo, led us both into dangerous territory. Egging the two of us on, he bragged that he would do anything for a sufficient reward: 'I'd do anything for money, strip naked, so long as there's cash involved, anything. And I have done.' Excited by a fruitful research lead, I tried to push him further. His response became hostile. Abruptly, he terminated the interview with an aggressive rejoinder. David's parting remark deftly overturned the balance of power: 'Do you think I'm queer or something?' With these words the contract between us was broken. The reasons for the collapse in communication were complex. In microcosm they condensed a number of issues about the contemporary organization of masculinity. For my part, I had pressed David too hard. I had disrupted one of the most important elements in our agreement; the pledge to tread carefully on the personal dimensions of sexuality. I also felt awkward about race; in particular about reproducing a pathologizing gaze in relation to this young black man as a sexual object. The sense of guilt made me hesitant about questioning him again. David's response was to reaffirm the fixity of his own position with heterosexuality, after a conversation which had been much more fluid. This reinstatement of boundaries was designed to force me to take up a stance on one side or other of the sexual divide. His interrogative question, 'Do you think I'm queer or something?' demanded a double reply. It asked me to state my views about his identity, but it also probed my own. Henceforward any conversation between us would take place across this fault line. Our dialogue was at an end.

Paul Willis has suggested that such small moments in the interview transaction are actually quite momentous in terms of their significance. They are essentially incidents when the researcher is taken by surprise and the subject temporarily hijacks the project (Willis, 1980). In my work in Soho most of these experiences occurred when the dialogue touched on a number of cultural flashpoints. Most of them also forced some explicit reflection, from myself and my respondents, about our sexual identities as men. One way of interpreting these tense encounters would be to rehearse a familiar argument about the limits of masculinity. In other words, to insist that the reason for my restricted conversation with men such as David was a consequence of the deep structures separating men; in this case the binary line dividing homosexual from heterosexual behaviours and the divisions of race. While this argument is tempting, it tends to simplify what such episodes revealed about current forms of masculine identity. My research uncovered more than the established boundaries organizing and regulating men. It pointed up the ways in which the languages of homosociability constitute an important and developing ingredient in the social relations of masculinity. This category is unstable; the discourse of the homosocial is continually slipping among and between more established identities. Nor is it wholly new. But contemporary forms of consumer culture do exhibit forms of masculine identity which are frequently in some degree of flux, and temporarily rather than more permanently fixed.

CONCLUSION

What can be deduced from our excursions into the historical and contemporary dimensions of sexuality? At the outset we raised the questions of language and identity as being central to a new project around sexuality. The public 'objective' voice of traditional historiography and elements within sociology fail to apprehend the intimacies of personal and sexual life. The impact of linguistics and discourse analysis on the practice of history writing has reinvigorated the stories we are able to tell about sex, while sexual politics has problematized a simple chronology of modernity. Currently, much of the debate about these issues is pitched at the highest level of abstraction. Consequently, when it came to the writing up of our own research, we found ourselves lacking the effective means for framing and speaking about questions of subjectivity. What is therefore needed is the development of a set of middle-range concepts, capable of engaging with the constructed nature of sexual identity and the languages through which selfhood is lived out. While historical appropriations of Freudian and Kleinian psychoanalysis has provided one framework through which to address these questions, concepts drawn from literary modes of analysis have provided another productive route (for example, see Steedman, 1986; Dawson, 1994; Alexander, 1994). The search should not be for a new master-narrative, but for a series of experiments in historical method. In the light of the issues which we have raised, two agendas seem particularly pressing. First, the development of an expanded set of interdisciplinary concepts which are capable of grasping the historically variable manifestations of sexual and affective life. Second, a way of approaching subjectivity which not only takes account of historical subjects in process, but which also grasps the fiction of subjectivity itself. This does not imply an abandonment of interest in individuals. Rather it involves a mode of history writing which refuses the comfortable fixities of a unified social and sexual agency. The project for cultural history turns on precisely these concerns.

ACKNOWLEDGEMENT

Many thanks to Laura Doan and Merl Storr for their very helpful comments.

NOTES

1. See Scott (1988), Riley (1988), Newton (1990) and Canning (1994).
2. It should be pointed out that Mason himself appears to favour not 1990s morality but what he terms the 'progressive anti-sensualism' of the nineteenth century.
3. See Vicinus (1985), Jeffreys (1985), Hall Carpenter Archives, Lesbian Oral History Group (1989), Faderman (1992), Kennedy and Davis (1993), Bland (1995) and Davidoff (1995). It should, however, be recognized that there are differences between some of these accounts, especially in the interpretation of historical sexual identities and practices.
4. Queer theory is ambiguous about what queerness encompasses. On the one hand, it is perceived as one side of the homo/hetero polarity; on the other, it appears far more inclusive of different sexual subjectivities.
5. See Steedman (1990), Walkowitz (1992) and Alexander (1994).

3 Psychoanalytic Challenges: A Contribution to the New Sexual Agenda
Stephen Frosh

INTRODUCTION

Since the publication in 1974 of Juliet Mitchell's book, *Psychoanalysis and Feminism*, psychoanalysis has been drawn upon by many theorists attempting to articulate a new vision of gender and sexual relations – a 'new sexual agenda'. This does not mean that Mitchell's defence of psychoanalysis has gone unchallenged. Indeed, psychoanalysis's conservatism in this area is well documented: in theory and in clinical work it has rarely supplied convincing recruits to the ranks of sexual revolution. Those who have tried using psychoanalysis in this way – for example, Herbert Marcuse (e.g. 1955) – have usually been outsiders to the movement itself; the exceptions – most obviously Wilhelm Reich – have risked having bitter ends. Moreover, classical psychoanalysis, with its emphasis on repression and hence on the difficulties of finding outlets for sexual 'tension', now appears dated, out of touch with the concerns of people in contemporary society. Where the nineteenth-century hysteric was defined by problems of control and sexual expression, the late twentieth-century narcissist is consumed by the problem of being a 'self' and of forming meaningful relations with others (Lasch, 1979; Frosh, 1991). What, therefore, might be the most promising way forward for a psychoanalysis committed to furthering the new sexual agenda? Putting sex on the map was a great achievement of the late nineteenth century, and Freud certainly contributed to that, but what is there to be said about psychoanalysis's 'newness' now? Does it really have a challenge to offer?

The unconscious is where psychoanalysis starts and ends. Psychoanalysis's great claim, the one idea shared by psychoanalysts of all schools, is that some – probably the most important part – of our mental functioning occurs outside of conscious awareness. It just happens, it seems to have causal properties yet not be willed, possess intentionality without being intended. It is the 'other' within us, the speaking voice through which we are spoken, the 'Mene, Mene, Tekel, Upharsin' aspect of experience, as Lacan (1954–5) puts it in his commentary on Freud's Irma dream. The unconscious catches us napping, catches us catching our breath. In the field of sex and sexuality, the unconscious works harder than anywhere else, having fun at the expense of every attempt at order: everywhere something unexpected slips out.

Once this might have been a genuinely radical challenge to a vision of human nature as something static, ordered and rational, but is it now not so well known as to put us all to sleep? What does it mean to say that there is an unconscious, that each of us speaks the language of the other and knows not who we are? Postmodernism has made this a cliché and defused the challenge that psychoanalysis offers when showing us that we are not 'master in our own house', as Freud roughly put it. If anything, knowing about the unconscious may act as a relief to those burdened by the struggle to become an autonomous self, something which has become rather hard to achieve in the technological society. Relaxing from the obsessional impulse to develop some kind of character, to have integrity, we are at home in the excess which once characterized only that which was not allowed us – the unconscious again. It is comforting to see this 'at homeness' as a cultural achievement, but perhaps the apparent challenge of the unconscious is just another appeasement, a resting point for tired revolutionaries, a true 'social amnesia' in Jacoby's (1975) memorable phrase. It is noticeable, after all, that so many ex-revolutionaries have become therapists, at this time.

If psychoanalysis is to offer some kind of significant challenge within the context of the sexual agenda, it is important to hold on to something new and provocative in the psychoanalytic project, something off-centre enough to make us look awry at ourselves and at our sexuality. This notion of 'looking awry' is compatible with the radical elements to be found in the whole history of psychoanalysis, but it is also a simple reference to Slavoj Žižek, whose book *Looking Awry* begins as follows:

What is at stake in the endeavour to 'look awry' at theoretical motifs is not just a kind of contrived attempt to 'illustrate' high theory, to make it 'easily accessible', and thus to spare us the effort of effective thinking. The point is rather that such an exemplification, such a mise-en-scène of theoretical motifs renders visible aspects that would otherwise remain unnoticed.

(Žižek, 1991, p. 3)

Žižek turns to the work of Jacques Lacan for a mode of entry into this off-centredness; indeed, the book called *Looking Awry* is sub-titled, 'An Introduction to Jacques Lacan through Popular Culture'. For Žižek, Lacan's appeal seems to be only partly because of the content of his theory; it also arises from the dizzying style of the work, its 'idiotic enjoyment' – a phrase Žižek uses about popular culture but which might easily apply to his own rendering of Lacan. Many of the most avant-garde writers on psychoanalysis, particularly psychoanalysis and feminism, have shared in this delirium over Lacan (see Brennan's 1989 collection), even if with some ambivalence. Trying to look awry at psychoanalysis and the new sexual agenda, Lacan's maddening style has been a constant provocation and irritant, a place somewhere off-centre, promising something unexpected. Of particular interest in this respect has been his insistence that psychoanalysis works only at the level of the symbol – that it is not 'about' anything else – and that the symbolic dimension of experience is always deeply infiltrated by the construction of sexual difference.

One argument that will be developed in this chapter is that evoking Lacan might lead to a more rigorous, less sloppy and sentimental use of psychoanalysis than can be derived from, for example, object relations or even Kleinian theory. Not everyone agrees, however, and it is worth noting that the opposition to the Lacanian influence comes not just from more traditional schools of psychoanalysis, but also from feminists who once worked with him (notably Luce Irigaray) or who derive their critical perspectives from a more activist politics or approach to social theory (e.g. Segal, 1990). To some extent this critique derives from a dislike of Lacan's famous 'ladies' man' masquerade – his coquettishness, his mystifications, his certainties which evoke uncertainty. They are also, however, built upon a more marked antagonism towards the content of Lacan's theory, to the extent that it seems to demonstrate an authoritative and unequivocal allegiance to patriarchal (usually expressed as 'phallocentric') orthodoxy. The question of whether Lacanian theory does offer something innovative and constructive to a 'new' and, by implication, non-phallocentric sexual agenda is the focus of the latter part of this chapter. However, one suggestion I would make here is that criticism of Lacan's certainty may be part of the whole muddle in and about psychoanalysis – the muddle of where something so slippery as an exploration of the unconscious can be understood to be. There are many claimed certainties in psychoanalysis, but none of them is certain – how can they be, when the procedure of psychoanalysis reveals so clearly that everything, even its own claims and rational formulations, are imbued with the seductions and irrationality of emotive, flamboyant, unconscious impulses? If Lacan flamboyantly displays his seductiveness, even when an old man, it is not difficult to understand that he may be meditating on some kind of hurt, some loss; psychoanalysis reveals that this is true of all theory, all claims to knowledge, certainty and truth. These things are built upon the gap between where we are and where we would like to be. Like sexuality and the new sexual agenda, no doubt.

For the new sexual agenda, then, it may still be possible to find a place for Lacan, even if he is neither new nor on everyone's agenda any more. If we are talking of psychoanalytic challenges, there is still one to be found in the suggestion, present in much psychoanalytic work but formulated most insistently by Lacan, that the organization of our sexuality comes in an important way from outside – in the terminology of this chapter, that the sexual agenda writes us, rather than the other way around.

The suggestion here, therefore, is that there is something in psychoanalysis which can still be a challenge to any agenda for sexuality, new or old. It is a challenge because it refutes certainties – pre-given categories or complete understandings, fixed ways of being or final comings-to-term. Lacan reveals this in some of his work, but he is not the only source. In fact, doing what comes naturally in psychoanalysis, I shall start elsewhere, with a particularly rich and important piece of non-Lacanian writing on gender and sexual identity, and then ask if Lacanian ideas can add anything to this at all.

POLYMORPHOUS IDENTIFICATION

In a recent paper, the American psychoanalyst and feminist Jessica Benjamin (1995) makes an appeal for a more complex understanding of gender development than is available either in psychoanalysis or in contemporary gender theory. Criticizing what she sees as the tendency continually to reproduce masculine identity and feminine identity as two opposed poles, she suggests that the psychological mechanism of *identification* is one which makes it possible to incorporate loving relationships both with those with whom we are ostensibly the 'same' and those from whom we are 'different'. Openness to the plurality of available identifications is a way of transcending or transgressing the conventional rigidity of masculine *versus* feminine:

> If sex and gender as we know them are oriented to the pull of opposing poles, then these poles are not masculinity and femininity. Rather, gender dimorphism itself represents only one pole, the other pole being the polymorphism of the psyche.
> (Benjamin, 1995, p. 120)

The 'polymorphism of the psyche' is an appealing notion: that, psychologically speaking, it may be possible to take up multiple positions, built around fluid identifications with others, in the areas of sex and gender as well as anywhere else. Benjamin, basing herself on recent psychoanalytic theorizing and observational work such as that of Fast (1984), offers a developmental account of how this might come about, emphasizing the significance of identificatory love (particularly, in children of both sexes, for the father) and criticizing traditional psychoanalytic renderings of the Oedipus complex as contributing to a focus on difference at the expense of links across otherness. Her general moral and political stance here is to hold that while the acceptance of difference is an important developmental achievement, *by itself* it is a formula for the preservation of rigid dimorphism. She lays out the general point elegantly as follows:

> The implicit assumption in differentiation theory is that acknowledging difference has a higher value, is a later achievement, is more difficult than recognising likeness. The neglected point is that the difficulty lies in assimilating difference without repudiating likeness; that is, in straddling the space between the opposites. It is easy enough to give up one side of the polarity in order to oscillate towards the other side. What is difficult is to attain a notion of difference, being unlike, without giving up a sense of commonality, of being a 'like' human being.
> (Benjamin, 1995, p. 106)

In Benjamin's version, the classical account of the Oedipal father as a prohibitive force produces a gender dimorphic theory (and practice, one might add) in which paternal and maternal principles are opposed. The only way forward with such a theory is to emphasize difference, eventually validating one pole (usually the masculine) over the other. By contrast, exploring multiple identifications, particularly in what is conventionally termed the pre-Oedipal period, leads to a recognition of the existence of a plurality of subject positions, out of which each human subject is built. This serves to undermine any claims to fixedness in identity, here specifically and particularly gender identity. Benjamin suggests that it is to the degree that the pre-Oedipal child has 'lovingly incorporated through identification' (ibid., p. 114) the characteristics of the other, that loss can be managed and the Oedipal child can avoid repudiating or idealizing the other. That is, if cross-sex identification based on love has been possible early on, later absolute differentiation from the other need not occur; theories and practices based on such absolute distinctions are consequently markers of failed identificatory processes, not descriptions of necessary or even healthy development. Such theories and practices also lead to a rigid vision of gender identity as something fixed, stable and homogeneous, when in fact the prospects for decent human relationships rely on it not being like that – on, for example, it being possible for a man to imagine what it might be like to be a woman, in the sexual relationship as well as in parenting and other aspects of life.

Benjamin's description of recent psychoanalytic work on gender development and her critique and revision of Oedipal theory offer an important and empirically grounded route into the study of gender polymorphism. In particular, her emphasis on the fluidity of subject positions is one which is commensurate with much contemporary feminist thought and with the insights, such as they are, of postmodernism. If there is a challenge to be found in this it is to any approach that marks out the terrain of difference as something incommensurable or incompatible; Benjamin's paper suggests that much of our browbeating about the difficulty of taking up the position of the other is itself in the service of that difficulty. Careful thinking about and observation of the way infants develop, how identifications occur and make available objects which can be taken in to form the infant's mental world, suggest that the widespread configuration of sexual difference as something compelling and irrevocable need not be maintained.

Can Lacanian thinking add anything to this? There is a question over whether formulations such as that by Benjamin do resolve the problem of gender categorization: do they not just move it back to an earlier developmental stage? It seems logically and empirically likely that identification might be the crucial psychological process out of which identity – including gender and sexual identity – is constructed. But what does 'identification' mean here: a love-relation between a pre-existent ego and a nominated object? Possibly, but Lacan asks some pertinent questions here, which are worth following up, albeit again in a roundabout way.

NEUTRALITY AND THE LETTER

I want to explore the question of what lies behind or beyond identification by referring to one of Lacan's most famous seminars, the 1955 discussion of Edgar Allan Poe's story, *The Purloined Letter*. On the face of it, Lacan uses this story to project a vision of the psychoanalyst as master-investigator, able to enter into and then release himself from the circuit of desire at will, with profound self-consciousness and some humour. However, there are a number of complications that call into question Lacan's integrity here, but that also highlight the problematic aspects of identification and invest-ment, particularly as they drift across sexual difference.

Poe's tale is told by a narrator, a Watson-like figure who is foil to the investigator/analyst Dupin and who extracts from him his philosophic musings and his account of how he outwitted the minister who had stolen – in broad daylight – a potentially com-promising letter from the Queen. Reading the Poe original with a psychoanalytic but not-yet Lacanian eye, the issue of identification stands out as a crucial theme. The police fail to find the stolen letter because their ludicrously exact investigation is couched at the wrong level. They can act only according to their own beliefs about how a thief might behave. Dupin, on the other hand, imagines himself inside the mind of the minister, identifies with him and thus comprehends what his course of action is likely to have been. He understands that the thief's actions will have been determined not by reason alone, but by something more imaginative, rigorous and compelling, which Dupin suggests is made possible by the minister being not just a mathematician, but also a poet. Dupin himself, arch-analyst, also writes verse, giving him a capacity to transcend the simple logic of those who follow only the rules and to enter into the mind of the other, eventually to trick him and recover the lost object.

Lacan makes use of the story in a variety of ways, appropriating it as an illustration of his argument that 'From the start, and independently of any attachment to some supposedly causal bond, the symbol already plays, and produces by itself, its necessities, its structure, its organisations' (1954–5, p. 193). Also, more specifically, it illustrates the 'inmixing of subjects', the way each subject is penetrated by something else, and thus speaks from a position off-centre to itself – a reminder of the fragmentary status of the ego which is one of the themes of this book of the Seminar. In Lacan's reading, it is the letter itself that penetrates the subject, a causal signifier producing effects: wherever it goes and whoever has it in her or his possession, some gap or relationship is produced. For Lacan, the letter represents the 'pure state' of the symbol, the 'original, radical subject': 'One can say that, when the characters get a hold of this letter, something gets a hold of them and carries them along and this something clearly has dominion over their individual idiosyncrasies' (ibid., p. 196).

Reading the journey of the letter in this literal way, Lacan is able to argue that the impact of the circuit of exchanges documented in the story is to demonstrate how the unconscious disrupts the fixed identity of 'character' or even 'sexual attitude' (ibid., p. 205) – how each subject is impossible to place. 'Everything which could serve to define the characters as real – qualities, temperament, heredity, nobility – has nothing to do with the story.' It is the position of the letter that is crucial – who has it and to what use it might be put. Moreover, this position defines not only the status of the subjects, but their sexual identity. So the minister is feminized in the story when he disguises the letter by putting his own seal on it and addressing it to himself in a feminine hand. Furthermore, when he becomes the duped one from whom the letter is stolen, he takes up the position previously occupied by the Queen:

> The Minister is in what had been the Queen's position, the police are in that of the King, of this degenerate King who believes only in the real, and who sees nothing. The step-wise displacement of the characters is perfect. And simply because he interposed himself in the rest of the discourse, and came into possession of this little nothing of a letter, sufficient to

wreak havoc, this most cunning of foxes, this most ambitious of climbers, this intriguer's intriguer, this dilettante's dilettante, doesn't see that his secret will be pinched from under his nose. (ibid., p. 203)

The power of the analyst lies in standing outside the game; once one becomes part of it, as the minister does when he takes the letter, one is caught up in the network of loss and desire through which every subject is structured. Lacan links this with a description of the excessive nature of the anxiety surrounding the letter and of the impossibility of speaking of it; its threat both creates something between minister and Queen and feminizes them both. Why should this thing produce such anxiety, such a sense that if it is lost, one's whole position and identity go with it? In Lacanian theory, anxiety of this kind is always referred back to the castration complex, understood not just as a configuration of ambivalent emotions, but also as a passage from one psychological register to another. Through the castration complex, the subject takes on the weight of culture, thus experiencing the power of an external structure to rupture the fantasy of wholeness and potency around which subjectivity might otherwise be organized. The phallus acts as primary signifier of this state, a source of effectivity which is coveted by all but belongs to no one. At all moments of desire and loss, this shimmering ambiguity is recalled: that that which is most desired is always out of reach. It is, therefore, not surprising to find here too, in the passage of a compromising letter from hand to hand, an evocation of the castration complex as that which sets the Symbolic game in motion. The letter creates excessive anxiety because of the effects of its loss; its impact is most potent where it itself is not.

Here Lacan seems to be pursuing the idea of subjectivity – including a primarily sexed subjectivity – as something produced by the position taken up by the subject in the circuit of exchange. However, a different light is thrown on this issue by consideration of what has several times (e.g. Gallop, 1985) been noted as the most striking feature of Poe's story *omitted* in Lacan's reading, the function of the narrator. Lacan seems to identify Dupin with the position of the psychoanalyst, for example, when discussing the issue of payment for services rendered – for advice. Dupin escapes from the game (gives up the letter) when he is paid. Lacan notes that this is also true for the analyst: prices 'have the function of neutralising something infinitely more dangerous than paying in money, namely owing someone something' (Lacan, 1954–5, p. 204). Yet while Dupin has the capacity for imagining another's thought which might be regarded as a necessary underpinning of analytic practice, he is also *motivated* in a way one would not conventionally ascribe to the psychoanalyst. In fact, all the characters in the story have a motive impelling them to act in a certain way. The Queen wishes to preserve her position in the eyes of the King. The minister is a schemer who uses his possession of the letter – and the Queen's knowledge of this possession – to gain political advantage. The Prefect of Police, who seeks Dupin's advice, is interested in the reward. Dupin, too, is interested in payment, but the end of the tale reveals that he is also motivated by competitive admiration and hatred of the minister (who once did him an 'evil turn'). He is thus a full player in the game, with an investment in its outcome. This motivated consciousness is also true of the psychoanalyst Jacques Lacan: he had a teaching career, he was involved in psychoanalytic politics, he was no pure observer of the scene. Only the narrator of the tale is neutral, the one who, in Lacan's words from elsewhere, 'does not make you speak'.

On the other hand, true neutrality lies only with the medium, the system itself. The problem for the minister is that he believes he is immune to the circuit produced by the letter – he can hold on to it. This is the source of his defeat. Dupin, on the other hand, knows he cannot hold the letter, so gives it up on payment. In terms of sexual difference, this suggests that when we strive to be at one with our masculine or feminine being, to find ourselves in a sexed identity, however polymorphous, we risk being duped. We are always in a provisional place, about to be moved. More formally but equally paradoxically, the belief that it is possible to comprehend and master the Symbolic keeps one in the Imaginary; only full awareness of how one is structured within the Symbolic order allows it to be transcended.

The seminar on the *Purloined Letter* thus raises numerous questions concerning the structural role of desire, the derivation and motivation of action, and the place of the psychoanalyst. It evokes the castration complex as something which does not fix masculinity and femininity in place so much as undermine the possibility of fixedness – it opens a space into which both male and female fall, becoming interchangeable as the letter of desire leaves them grasping after it. In Lacan's reading of this tale, identifications are mobile and multiple, and as each character takes up his or her position, so they are disrupted by some further movement of the circuit. More-over, no one is neutral; each of us is infiltrated by what we have to say. The fiction of identity is undermined by the indefatigable pressure of this speaking voice.

IDENTIFICATION AND THE PROVISIONAL

My argument here is that psychoanalysis can be used to undermine claims to fixedness or authenticity, in sex and gender as in every-thing else. Sexual identities, like ascriptions of mastery, are always invitations to dismemberment: as they are declared, so something enters in to disrupt them, to suggest an identification with some-thing else, or an origin somewhere else. Psychoanalysis, at least when used in this way, suggests that all our identities are at most 'provisional', held as something around which fantasies are built, projections located and held; but ready to dissolve and re-emerge if only we can let them. Benjamin refers to identificatory love as a way forward into recognizing the multiplicity of subject positions which are possible, thus undermining the fixed divide of difference. Lacan shows that difference – specifically, sexual difference – is contra-vened by the fragmenting impact of the 'letter of the unconscious', the presence within the human subject of something which is non-sexual, yet produces the effects of sexuality. Benjamin focuses on the creative promise of the polymorphism of the psyche; Lacan focuses on its threat. Nevertheless, in their very different ways, both demon-strate that within the desiring space with which psychoanalysis deals can be found a great uncertainty, a rich equivocation concerning what each of us may come to be. Ambiguous as psychoanalysis is, in this provisional, equivocal uncertainty lies its enduring challenge.

NOTE

A version of this chapter will appear in the journal *Human Relations* in 1997, and is reproduced here by permission of the publisher.

4 Sexual Values Revisited
Jeffrey Weeks

THE QUESTION OF VALUES

The question of 'values' has for the past decade been seen as part of the ideological baggage of the New Right. When referring to issues of sexuality it has become a code term for challenges to the changes that have shaken the sexual world: deep and visceral hostility to changes in family life, the impact of feminism, the rise of lesbian and gay politics, and passionate opposition to open sex education, changes in lifestyle, and in the United States in particular, to women's access to abortion and the 'right to choose'. When the British Prime Minister Margaret Thatcher spoke of the need to return to 'Victorian values' in the early 1980s, few had any doubt what she meant, even if her history was a little shaky. Similarly, when her successor John Major spoke of the need to go 'Back to Basics' it was not hard to detect a moral agenda, even if, typically, it soon disintegrated when faced by the realities of most people's (including politicians') lives.

More recently, the question of values has become an issue on the Left, as it attempts at fill the vacuum left by the disintegration of traditional leftist discourses. The British Labour Party, we are now told, is a value-based party or it is nothing. As it happens, I very much welcome this development. In the fluid politics of the post-modern world, values are important for gluing together disparate political aims and objectives, and for providing a focus for the clarification of principles and policies. But there is a constant danger that the values articulated will slip back into nostalgic evocations of stable families and strong neighbourhoods at the expense of validating the diverse social and erotic patterns that have emerged over the past generation. The current interest in the 'communitarianism' of Amitai Etzioni (1995) is an index of this. His work has been influential among those on the Centre Left who seek a value system that goes beyond the possessive individualism which dominated cultural as well as economic life in the 1980s, but its essentialist conservatism about family and sexual life militates against a wider appeal. My argument is that an effective articulation

43

of values must take account of the dramatic changes that have occurred in people's lives, and should seek to validate the diversity of individual goals, identities and belongings that now exist.

So the fundamental question is not about the relevance of key concepts which stress the necessary links between the individual and society, such as the partnership between rights and obligations, or the importance of responsibility as an essential element of human relationships, or choice as an essential aspect of freedom. The really crucial debate should not be over the importance of such terms, but over their *meaning*. There is a need, I would argue, to develop, or perhaps better, to articulate, a value system that respects diversity and choice within a context of common human values.

This chapter begins with a discussion of three developments that have focused the question of sexual values most sharply, at least for me: major developments in the theorization of sexuality; the challenge of postmodernist theory to the legitimizing narratives of the 'sexual tradition'; and the radical changes in the erotic world itself over the past generation, not least the impact of the HIV/AIDS epidemic. The result of these changes, I argue, is that we have the potential to move away from a morality of acts – that is, a moral position reliant on whether a sexual practice in itself is right or wrong – to an ethics of relationships, which is concerned with the context and meaning of actions. It is not so much what you do but how you do it that should concern us. These changes provide, I shall suggest, the opportunity for the development of a 'love ethic' that respects both individual autonomy and our responsibility for others (see Weeks, 1995, for a more detailed discussion of this argument).

THREE DEVELOPMENTS

The world we live in is deeply historical, in the obvious sense that it is a product of history, and perhaps even more important, it is deeply historicized, as the evocation of golden ages suggests; and it is complexly new, in the sense that we have to face the challenge of dramatic changes in personal life, the collapse of traditional legitimizing narratives, the threat of new diseases such as HIV/AIDS, and the real challenge of inventing moralities for ourselves. We live, I have argued elsewhere, in a world of uncertainty, where good guides and firm guarantees that we can reach any particular destination are in short supply, and where the goals themselves are nebulous and indeterminate. Nowhere is this uncertainty more acute than in the domain of sexuality, which has been the subject in the recent past of numerous panics, controversies, anguished moralizings and the rekindling of an overt concern with values (Weeks, 1995).

It is not that sexuality has ever been absent from social, cultural and political debate. In fact, anxiety about sexuality has shaped many of our public debates for a long time, from the fear of national or imperial decline at the end of the nineteenth century to the structuring of welfare provision from the 1940s to the present (see Mort, 1987; Weeks, 1981/1989). What is new, however, is the way in which worries about changing sexual behaviour and gender and sexual identities have become the explicit focus for debates about the current shape and desirable future of society. And if, as I believe, we can no longer rely on pre-existing narratives to shape our hopes, then what we believe to be desirable, what we value for now and for the future, matters acutely. 'An existence without a script written in advance', suggests the sociologist Zigmunt Bauman (1992, p. 194), 'is a *contingent* existence.' The debate around sexual values is a response to a growing sense of our contingency, where nothing but uncertainty and death is certain.

Let me now go on to offer some thoughts on how the question of values has become so central. In terms of my own intellectual biography, three developments have been crucial.

The first is the question of what has become known as social constructionism, essentially a historical approach to sexuality. The fundamental assumption of this approach has been that sexuality cannot be seen as a purely natural phenomenon, outside the boundaries of society and culture. We have all too readily believed that sexuality is the most natural thing about us, that our drives are fixed and inherent, that our identities are dictated by that nature and those drives, and that a history of sexuality must therefore be no more than an account of reactions to those basic biological givens.

Over the past 20 years most of the assumptions behind those positions have been profoundly challenged, building on a century of challenges to essentialist modes of thought (Weeks, 1985). As a result we increasingly recognize that sexuality can only be under-stood in its specific historical and cultural context. There cannot be an all-embracing history of sexuality. There can only be local histories, contextual meanings, specific analyses. The core of the historical argument has been that we can only understand sexuality through understanding the cultural meanings and the power relations which construct it (see Foucault, 1979). This does not mean that biology is irrelevant, nor that the body has no role (Giddens, 1992). Nor does it mean that individuals are blank pieces of paper on which society writes its preferred meanings. Take, for example, homosexuality. To say that lesbian and gay identities have a history, have not always existed and may not always exist, does not mean that they are not important. Nor should it necessarily be taken to imply that homosexual proclivities are not deeply rooted. The real problem does not lie in whether homosexuality is inborn or learnt. It lies instead in the questions: What are the meanings this particular culture gives to homosexual behaviour and identities, however they may have arisen? And what are the effects of those meanings on the ways in which individuals organize their sexual lives? These are historical questions – questions that are highly political, which force us to analyse the power relations that determine why one set of meanings are hegemonic, and to pose the further question of how those meanings can be changed.

There are, however, difficulties with this theoretical approach. Many find it too abstract, detached from their own experience of deeply entrenched desires and strongly affirmed identities. People seem to need a sense of belonging which they conceive as rooted in the imperatives of nature or of all time. They fear that if identities and the values associated with them are conceived of as historically contingent, then they will lose all solidity and meaning. This position has underscored recent efforts to discover a 'gay brain' or a 'gay gene' (LeVay, 1991; Hamer et al., 1993). Such 'discoveries' would provide a natural basis for claimed rights and legitimacy. Better, it seems to rely on the truths of science that confront the challenge of clarifying why we value what we do.

This points to a real problem, one that goes far beyond questions of identity and embraces all aspects of sexual ethics. Social constructionism has no political belonging. It does not carry with it any obvious programme. On the contrary, it can be, and has been, used recently as much by sexual conservatives as by sexual progressives. In the attempt to ban the 'promotion' of homosexuality by local authorities in Britain in 1987/8, culminating in the passing into law of the notorious Section 28 of the Local Government Act, the Act's proponents explicitly argued that homosexuality could be promoted and learnt – hence the Act's justification (Smith, 1990). Of course, the logical corollary of this is that heterosexuality could equally well be learnt, and is in fact promoted all the time by the institutions of our culture. But as Carole Vance (1989) has pointed out, by and large heterosexuality has not been subjected to the same vigorous enquiry as homosexuality. Very few people are interested in tracing *its* social construction. It is still regarded as the natural norm from which all else is an unfortunate perversion (on this see Katz, 1995).

Essentialist positions are tempting because they offer certainty instead of doubt, fixity rather than the anguish of personal decision, but they depend, I would suggest, on absolutist positions that cannot begin to deal with the complexities of value choices, let alone the lessons of our own experience of change and ambiguity. In the case of Section 28, and similar moral and political controversies, the arguments of one side cannot be resolved by appeals to reason, science, truth or tradition precisely because all these terms are contested. Different moral and ethical positions are being staked out, and in a heightened moral climate, where opposing positions are being staked out, theoretical perspectives alone cannot promote a particular outcome. They only have meaning within specific contexts, in particular power relations, and in the arguments over time embodied in ethical traditions. So the effectiveness of theoretical approaches in the end is not dictated by their truth but by the meanings they glue together. Sexual values are important, not because they are either rooted in the 'natural' or some revealed truth or foundational given, but because they provide the basis of social and cultural identification which makes possible a meaningful individual and social life, and, where appropriate, moral-political struggles.

That puts squarely on the agenda the question of values (see essays in Squires, 1993, including Weeks, 1993). What the historical approach to sexuality has achieved is to make us more aware of the complexity of forces that shape erotic life, and to sensitize us to the power relations which organize the meanings we live by. Far from sexuality being the least mutable of forces, it is probably the most sensitive to social influence, a conductor of the subtlest of changes in social *mores* and power relations. If that is the case, then we need to be clearer than ever before of the values that motivate us, and the choices we have to make.

If social constructionism poses acutely the question of value, so does its distant cousin, the postmodernist challenge, the second key development. However, I do not intend here to enter into the debate about the meaning of the postmodern; rather, I want to use it as a convenient trope. 'Postmodernity' is clearly a relational term defined by something that came before, or at least is passing, 'modernity'. It carries with it a sense of an ending which haunts many of our cultural preoccupations as we approach the *fin de millennium*. We can debate its implications endlessly, as many have done, and doubtless will continue to do. But however we characterize the age, there can be no doubt of its sense of fundamental change with all its resulting uncertainty. This sense of change, of being on the edge of time, has been compounded by the weakening of the legitimizing traditions and master discourses of high modernity. The twin processes of a secularization of moral values and of a gradual liberalization of social attitudes, especially towards what has traditionally been seen as 'the perverse', have begun to dissolve the old verities (Weeks, 1995). The narrative comforts of the Christian tradition have long suffered the corrosive effects of scepticism and critique, creating the space for fundamentalist revival alongside liberation from superstition. Now even the 'Enlightenment project' of the triumph of reason, progress and humanity, the sense that science and history were leading us inexorably to a more glorious future, has been subjected to searching deconstruction, and its roots have been shown to be murky. The universal aspirations and foundational givens of modernity have been radically challenged (see essays in Weeks, 1994).

There are striking parallels between such positions and recent challenges to the dominant discourses of sexuality, especially of sexual progressivism. The rationalistic triumphalism of the nineteenth-century sexologists is itself now under assault. A number of feminists have seen the science of sex as little more than a cover for the recodification of male power, imposing a male-oriented 'sexual liberation' on women (for example, Jeffreys, 1990). Foucault (1979) has famously challenged our illusions concerning the very notion of sexual 'liberation', and by many others sexual liberalism has been denounced as little more than a new garb for the incessant process of sexual regulation and control. Alongside these there has been a radical undermining of the original basis for the enlightened hopes of the pioneers of sexual reform at the end of the nineteenth century, and which by the mid-twentieth century had come to dominate sexual thinking, even among the most conservative: the triumph of science (Weeks, 1985). In his presidential address to the

1929 Congress of the World League for Sexual Reform, the pioneering sexologist Magnus Hirschfeld declared: 'A sexual impulse
based on science is the only sound system of ethics.' His Institute for
Sexual Science had inscribed on it the words, 'Through Science to
Justice' (see Weeks, 1986, p. 111). Part of that hope died as the
Institute's books burned under the Nazi torch. Much of the rest
faded in the succeeding decades as the sexual scientists squabbled
over their inheritance and disagreed over everything from the
nature of sexual difference, female sexual needs and homosexuality
to the social consequences of disease (see Bullough, 1994).

Behind this was the more subtle undermining of the sexual
tradition which had been defined in the nineteenth century, in
sexology, medico-moral practice, legal enactments and personal life.
The narrative of sexual orthodoxy has been vigorously challenged,
to be complemented if not replaced by a number of new historical
narratives, many by those hitherto disqualified by the would-be
science of sex. As Gayle Rubin (1984) has famously put it, a
veritable catalogue of types from the pages of Krafft-Ebing has
marched onto the stage of social history, each new sexual subject
claiming its legitimacy and place in the sun. If the hallmark of the
nineteenth-century pioneers of sex reform and the sexual sciences
was a belief in the efficacy of science and the revelation of the laws
of nature, the characteristic note of modern sexual activists (despite
an occasional dabble in sociobiology or genetic determinism) is self-
activity, self-making, the questioning of received truths, the con-
testation of laws which elevate some and exclude others. Scientific
sexology has been challenged by a grass-roots sexology; reform
from above by community organization from below; and a single
narrative of sexual enlightenment by a host of separate histories,
from women, lesbians and gays, racial minorities and others (see
Plummer, 1995).

We are seeing in these developments, I would argue, a profound
weakening of sexual modernism. The sexual order, with its fixing of
sexual identifications under the banner of Nature, Science and
Truth, has all but gone, reflecting a fundamental shift not only in
theory but in what theory is attempting to grasp. The contemporary
sexual world appears as irrevocably pluralistic. There is no longer a
dominant discourse telling us how we should behave, and the
absolutist moralities which attempt to fill the vacuum may have
their listeners, but cannot affirm an ultimate legitimacy. As a result,
sexual behaviour, sexual identity and sexual mores have increas-

ingly become matters of choice, at least for those who have the freedom to choose. There is greater freedom of choice than ever before about the age of first sex, whom we do it with, how often, in what sorts of relationship. We can choose how we wish to identify ourselves and what our lifestyles should be. Even gender, apparently the most reliant of natural divisions, is now seen as more a performance or masquerade than something we are born with. Choice has become the ruling morality both of the political Right (at least in economic matters), and of the liberal Left. The idea of choice has become deeply embedded in the liberal ethos of Western societies, but under the conditions of postmodernity it has assumed a new significance. But how, and with what criteria, we should choose is less clear.

This absence of narrative comfort and legitimizing certainty is itself a consequence of profound changes in personal relations themselves, what Giddens (1992) calls the 'transformation of intimacy', and which in turn is an aspect of the growing democratization of everyday life. This is the third major development. The radical individualism that appears the dominant theme of our age, in sexual and ethical values as much as in economic, is an ambiguous phenomenon. On the positive side it undermines the solidity of traditional narratives and relations of dominance and subordination. A discourse of choice is a powerful dissolvant of old verities. In the 1980s, as New Right administrations in the United States and Britain attempted to combine a radical emphasis on a free economy with a social and moral conservatism, it was noticeable that the individualism of the first constantly seeped into and fundamentally undermined the second. By the 1990s, it was clear in both countries that the loosening of the bonds of sexual authoritarianism associated with the 1960s was continuing, even accelerating, despite haphazard attempts at moral rearmament. Individual freedom cannot stop at the market; if you have an absolute freedom to buy and sell, there seems no logic in blocking a freedom to choose your sexual partners, your sexual lifestyle, your identity or your fantasies.

But on the negative side of this is a sexual libertarianism that puts a premium on individual satisfaction, that makes individual pleasure the sole yardstick of sexual ethics. The vast expansion of choice opens up but simultaneously undermines the possibility of individual development and social cooperation (cf. Wilson, 1985). It makes possible escape from dying and repressive traditions, but it places a new, sometimes unbearable, burden on those who are the victims of careless and selfish choices. This provides a strand of plausibility in the jeremiads of cultural conservatives about a prevalent 'narcissism' in contemporary behaviour (Lasch, 1980; 1985). When the cultivation of the self is pursued without care for the other, without a sense of mutual responsibility and common belonging, it can lead to an ethical desert.

Carol Gilligan has noted as a paradoxical truth of human experience that 'we know ourselves as separate only insofar as we live in connection with others, and that we experience relationships only in so far as we differentiate other from self' (Gilligan, 1982, p. 63). In striving for that balance, however, we need to escape the imprisoning limitations of the essentializing individualism of which we in the West are heirs.

The sexual tradition was complicit with these individualistic assumptions. If in the past 200 years, as Michel Foucault (1979) has argued, sex has become the 'truth of our being', it is precisely because the erotic has been conceived of as the core of an essential self, a, sometimes *the*, defining element of our unique individuality. The paradox is that this essentializing of our sexual natures has gone hand in hand with a hierarchical ordering of sexual norms (cf. Rubin, 1984): the male definition of heterosexual normality has been at the apex, with female sexuality and the perverse at the base. Choice was limited because only normal men had the real freedom to choose their sexual tastes.

Developments during the twentieth century have fundamentally questioned this picture (Weeks, 1985), challenging, in theory as well as in cultural practice, the idea of the unitary individual, with a nature-given destiny. We can no longer hunger for the sovereign self, with his (usually his) earth-making will. Instead, we search out the possible identities we can feel at one with: class and national identities, religious identities, gender and sexual identities, racial and ethnic identities, consumer identities. And none of them is straightforward, for we are simultaneously shaped by all these influences, each of them making differing claims, pointing to different priorities, offering sometimes radically conflicting ways forward. Identity has become more of a process than a given, offering a choice of beings rather than the truth of ourselves. The unity of the human life, as Alasdair MacIntyre (1985) has suggested, is the unity of a narrative quest.

Of course, none of the choices is absolutely free. They are constrained and limited by relations of power, by structures of domination and subordination. Identities are drawn into the mesh of economic need, social discipline and cultural conformity. Some identities, however, are a product of struggles, battles against definition by others and for self-definition. This is the case above all in relation to contemporary dissident sexual identities, especially lesbian and gay identities. And it is around these that the social movements and communities of identity have evolved. These movements and communities are largely networks of small groups submerged in everyday life. Though frequently erupting into the public domain with major interventions (for example, campaigns for abortion, equal rights, against anti-gay legislation) their focus has been the local or functional group, loosely connected confederally with others, forming a community of interests. But within such groups and networks there is an experimentation with and practice of alternative frameworks of sense, producing alternative definitions of self, which sometimes contrast with, and sometimes mesh into, the consumerized identities being shaped and reshaped alongside them. The result has been profoundly influential in reshaping our thinking about the private sphere, especially with regard to the possibilities of democratized relationships. The links between the social and the personal are constantly being defined and redefined, while at the same time the power relations in the domains of everyday life are being made visible, and the spaces for individual inventions of self are being expanded (Weeks, 1995).

But in this they are only the more visible signs of an even more profound change. The fragility and hybridity of modern personal identities forces everyone in highly developed societies to engage in experiments in everyday life: to define themselves, their identities and their needs against a shifting landscape. The transformation in relations between men and women during the past century, however limited and constrained it has been in some areas, is a strong marker of this. Women's claims to sexual autonomy represent the strongest undermining of the traditional narratives of the sexual order. It is not surprising that this has also produced signs of a 'male backlash' and 'flight from responsibility' (Ehrenreich, 1983). Not only is a sense of self being remade, but there is also a fundamental unsettling of relationships (Giddens, 1992).

The postmodern recognition of the instability of the self, of openness in the choosing of identities, seems to many to reduce everything to flux: there are no fixed boundaries between people, only arbitrary labels. Identities are relativized, and therefore it seems to some diminished. Yet we cling to them. In a world of constant change, people apparently need fixed points, points of alignment. Identities, personal and social, are both precarious and essential, historically shaped and personally chosen, affirmations of self and confirmations of our social being. We construct narratives of the self in order to negotiate the hazards of everyday life, and to assert our sense of belonging in an ever more complex social world. But that puts on the agenda the sort of lives we want to live – and in a world of multiple ways of life this question can become a powerful focus for thinking about values.

PRINCIPLES

Sexuality is at the heart of contemporary anguishing about values. The moral Right has long grasped this. The Left has for too long assumed that the value-laden discourse of the morally conservative did not deserve a considered response from liberals and radicals, because such ideas were self-evidently ill-intentioned. I believe, on the contrary, that the failure of progressive thought to counter effectively the values of the Right has left a vacuum which thwarts an effective defence of what I believe in: the values of sexual diversity and freedom of choice.

So what are my values? As I have already hinted, I believe that the hope of the new lies in the everyday experiments in sexual life which are transforming personal life. These range over a variety of issues which shape contemporary sexual politics: questions of individual freedom ('autonomy') versus social involvement; transgression versus sexual or 'intimate' citizenship (Plummer, 1995); the right to public openness and the right to privacy (and to other rights of everyday life). Our responses to these are often muddled and confusing, marked by the uncertainty which governs public and private life today. But they also contain within them evidence of care, mutuality, responsibility and love which make it possible to be hopeful about our human future. The essential point I want to insist on is that such values are not the prerogative of any particular type of relationship, least of all a mythical and heavily mythologized traditional family. They exist in many forms of life, many ways of being, which need to be nurtured and valued for what they are, not feared for what they are not.

To illustrate this I want now to outline four principles which I believe to be central to the rethinking of sexual values and the development of what I shall call a 'love ethic' (see Weeks, 1995 for a more detailed discussion). These are 'care', 'responsibility', 'respect' and 'knowledge' (cf. Fromm, 1971).

'Care'

Care involves an active concern for the life, hopes, needs and potentialities of the person or people we love: parents or carers for children or dependants, partner for partner, carer for those who are ill or dying. The term 'carer' itself has become an almost universal signifier for the combinations of involvement and trust that such relationships require, though in Western cultures it is still seen as overwhelmingly a female responsibility.

Yet we also know that 'caring' is an ambiguous activity. There are many forms of destructive care: the smothering love of the over-possessive parent or lover, or the love that crushes the hope and life out of those we claim to love, or the symbiotic love where the pair give up everything for each other. The structured inequalities that still shape our lives, of age, or race, or gender and sexuality, make genuine caring relationships an often perilous achievement, enforcing dependencies that make love a duty, a punishment or a trap. Women particularly, as Coward (1992) argues, are victims of their 'treacherous hearts'.

Care can be a trap. There is the care we do out of a sense of weary obligation and duty to the helpless, while all the time we resent the intrusion into our own sense of self of an enforced altruism (Finch, 1989). There is also the private care that covers for a wider lack of communal care for the marginal and ill. Cindy Patton (1990) has vividly described the 'new altruism' that has arisen in the response to HIV and AIDS, whereby the 'immune' (often well-meaning middle-class women in a passable revival of nineteenth-century philanthropic intention) have sometimes taken responsibility for caring for the 'vulnerable', as part of a prolonged process of state avoidance of, or disengagement from, caring for people with a feared disease, and where 'self-help' has become a motto for privatizing concern.

There is, no doubt, 'love' in all these activities, but it is a love where an active concern for the lives of others impedes care for the self, and in certain situations threatens to obliterate the autonomy of others, to crush their sense of self and self-worth, and to deny the possibility of, and need for, more complex involvements.

A truly loving care can only be built on a recognition of the autonomy of the other, the equality of carer and the person cared for, the mutual, reciprocal needs thus addressed, and ultimately on the recognition that the autonomy of oneself is dependent on the autonomy of others. Love as care, in other words, implies an act of imagination, an ability to enter sympathetically into the life of others. But that in turn requires that we love responsibly.

'Responsibility'

Responsibility as a term carries with it a powerful echo of prescription, of enforced duty. It also now appears to be well on the way to becoming a code word for returning to 'traditional values'. If only, the ideologues of conservative values argue, we could build in our youth a sense of responsibility to authority, if only parents could be more responsible for – that is, more disciplining – of their offspring, if only we could return to the tranquillity and decency of that golden age somewhere in our past of self-control and decency and discipline, then the pathologies of our age would gently dissipate: the young would cease to take drugs and steal cars, teenage women would not become pregnant to scrounge on the welfare state, adults would not neglect their children, adultery and divorce would diminish, families would grow in strength and become again the building blocks of our society.

The clock cannot be turned back, and it is folly to try to do so. Yet, the concept circulates as a political cliché because it resonates with a sense that a selfish commitment to self does destroy not only the individual and his or her relationships, but also the wider culture. A culture of individualism, of personal freedom, puts responsibility firmly on the agenda. Individual freedom implies that people are made more self-responsible, and that means responsibility for sinking lower or climbing higher. The difficulty, therefore, does not reside in the idea of responsibility, but in the various meanings caught up in it.

Responsibility as duty, as a must, is bound up with sanctions, with enforcing the laws of behaviour laid down by others or by traditions, which often means the same thing. There is, however, a more valuable sense to the term: responsibility as a voluntary act, expressing our response to the needs, expressed or unexpressed, of others; and receiving in return the responsible behaviour of others. A responsible love is one based on mutual obligation, and on the recognition that what I do has consequences for the other.

In her influential book, *In a Different Voice*, Carol Gilligan (1982) underlines the conflicts between an ethics of justice and rights, reliant on a strong sense of individual separation, and an ethic of responsibility, which assumes mutual dependency between individuals. She argues that the first concept of morality essentially reflects the masculine experience of psychological growth, while the second reflects the feminine. Her researches on how the moral psychology of individuals develops suggest that while men might indeed find it necessary to subordinate relational responsibilities to the needs of autonomy and achievement, women are more likely to espouse values associated with sharing, caring and obligation. In a male-dominated world, it is the masculinist ethic of rights which dominates the culture, confining ideas of mutual responsibility to the private, 'feminine' sphere.

There is no reason to assume, however, that these qualities are exclusively 'male' or 'female', whatever the historical associationsmay be. Both are necessary for a good society, balancing the qualities of justice and compassion. Nor is there any reason to suppose that these cannot at the same time be both private and public qualities, with a fuller sense of private responsibility to others being the real building block of a more humane and just public culture. The discourse of 'safer sex' in the context of the HIV/AIDS epidemic provides a useful illustration of this.

In the gay community, safer sex became a means of negotiating sex and love, of building a respect for self and others, in a climate of risk and fear. From this point of view, safer sex was a way of recovering the erotic, not a defensive reaction to it, based on the minimization, if not the complete elimination, of risk, in relationships of mutual trust and responsibility (Weeks, 1995). I take this as a powerful example of the ways in which a responsibility for the self requires a responsibility to others, in a web of reciprocity that takes for granted that a small concession of absolute freedom to do as you desire guarantees a wider freedom. Safer sex, despite the difficulties that make it often problematic, can be taken as symbolic of a wider need for a sense of caring responsibility which extends from sexual behaviour to all aspects of social life. Love as responsibility means accepting that we are not isolated monads, sufficient unto ourselves. Our humanity is dependent on our caring and responsible involvements with others. This in turn means respecting the other.

'Respect'

People are worthy of respect when they strive to achieve their life-plans in ways that do not harm others, that express care for and responsibility to others in the pursuit of individual goals. Our culture, however, denies worth and respect, even full citizenship, to many categories of people: because of their colour and ethnicity, their gender or age, their class or status, and because of their sexuality. Respect for individuals, in their individuality and their diversity, already therefore implies a cultural and political programme which seeks to eliminate institutionalized discrimination and domination.

Respect involves taking seriously the dignity of the other: both their autonomy as a person and their needs for you and for others. Dignity is lost when the possibilities of autonomy and of mutual respect, of achieving an appropriate balance between full subjectivity and reliance on the other, are thwarted by false polarities and hierarchical relations.

Respect for the dignity of the other is impossible when men and women 'do' emotional work differently. Duncombe and Marsden (1993) speak of 'gender asymmetry in emotional behaviour'. Women's responsibility for caring and responsiveness is balanced against male fear of intimacy and male non-disclosure in the context of family responsibilities where emotional work is solidified into gendered expressions. The tensions in all of us, between the need for autonomy and the need for others, become solidified into poles of gender. The challenge is to recognize the paradox while avoiding the polarity. That, ultimately, requires much more than an act of will, but rather a working through of the transformations of personal relationships that have already fundamentally undermined the basis of gender relations. Respecting the dignity of the other is a necessary first step.

'Knowledge'

That implies knowledge, an openness to understanding both your own needs and the needs of others. The democratization of love

that is implicit in the broad developments of the culture assumes
that human relationships should be based on what Heller (1987)
describes as 'symmetric reciprocity', or what Benjamin (1990, p. 16)
calls 'mutual recognition'. This in turn suggests that knowledge of
the other has to be based on an awareness of the complexities of
human subjectivity and social belongings. Reciprocity and recognition suggest an attention to the lives of others, which Foucault and
others have termed 'curiosity' (see White, 1991, p. 92): not a heavy
wish for total knowledge of others, which is a denial of the privacy
of the other, but a delicacy of concern, which is sensitive to the
needs of our partners, creating a space for understanding where
difference can flourish while solidarity grows.

CONCLUSION

Love in its broadest sense, based on care, responsibility, respect and
knowledge, is not an escape from a life without meaning, but a
recognition that we make our individual lives meaningful through
our involvements with others. We cannot retreat from the contingency and arbitrariness of the world, but we can make life meaningful if we face it with a recognition of our mutual need for one
another. Those who strive for a meaningful life may recognize the
inherent limitations of life's strivings, while all the time seeking to
make sense of them, to develop their capacities to live, and live with
and because of others. The individual who is attempting to live a
meaningful life, Heller (1984, p. 267) argues, 'is not a closed sub-
stance but a developing one who shrinks from no new challenges...It is a process to which death alone sets a term.' Self-
development in these terms is not simply about cultivation of the
self; it is concerned with developing one's abilities, to transform
one's contingency into destiny (Heller and Feher, 1988, p. 27).

The language of self-fulfilment, self-determination, autonomy
and authenticity, the 'motivating ideals' (Taylor, 1992) of our culture, contains within it some concept of our being-with-others. But
the introduction of a word like ideal presupposes that what we have
are goals to be achieved, values that we can struggle to realize,
rather than the current givens of everyday life. The discussion of
care, responsibility, respect and knowledge, has already suggested
the ambiguities of their meanings and the barriers to their realization. A love ethic starts with these individual experiences and their

hazards, but ends with a sense of the indissoluble link between the individual and the social.

NOTE

This essay was presented as an attempt to explain the underlying rationale for my writing my book, *Invented Moralities* (Weeks, 1995). I have obviously drawn on the material in that book to illustrate my argument, but this essay is not a summary of the book. I refer interested readers to the book if they want a more fully developed presentation of the case made here.

5 Sexual Revolution
R.W. Connell

THE RISE AND FALL OF THE SEXUAL REVOLUTION

The idea that social progress means greater sexual freedom has been a theme of European radicalism for more than a century. It was common, though not universal, among socialist and feminist intellectuals before the Great War. The same idea was held by their opponents: feminism was denounced on the grounds that equality would lead to sexual licence, and Freud in his day was reviled as a pornographer and moral anarchist.

The theme took a definite conceptual form in the 1920s in the work of radical educators and psychoanalysts in Vienna and Berlin. Among them Reich (1972) went furthest in conceptualizing sexual revolution as both a social process and a political programme. Reich saw the struggle against sexual repression as an essential part of the social revolution, and sexuality therefore became a key element in socialist strategy.

Reich's astonishing attempt to develop a mass politics to liberate the sexual potential of working-class youth broke up in a few years. The fascists came to power in Germany, and Reich himself was expelled from the communist movement. But some of his ideas stayed in circulation, especially through the Frankfurt School's attempts to synthesize Marx and Freud. Marcuse's (1955) concept of 'surplus-repression' held that class domination produced a level of sexual repression over and above what was needed for society to exist. With the concept of 'repressive desublimation' Marcuse (1964) proposed that a basically authoritarian though apparently liberal social order might capture sexual drives for its own purposes, by a controlled relaxation of pressure on sexuality.

From these sources the idea of sexual revolution entered the culture of the New Left in the 1960s and circulated widely among youth in the metropolitan capitalist countries. In the student movement, breaking down sexual inhibitions was felt to be part of the general project of overthrowing authority and disrupting social control. More, it was an essential part of the New Left idea of 'living your politics'. The sexual revolution was not an expert prescription, as it had been with Reich. It was a democratic utopia to be realized in the present – something one *did*, here and now (Segal, 1994).

This conception was taken up by the new feminism and the new gay politics, with crucial amendments. Pointing out that sexual freedoms for men were being gained at the expense of women, Women's Liberation defined freeing women's sexuality as another and altogether more radical project (Valverde, 1985). Gay Liberation theorized heterosexuality as part of a repressive social order (Altman, 1972). Sexual revolution required the overthrow of heterosexual dominance, and homosexual desire was the harbinger of a liberated world – a concept that would have made Reich's blood run cold.

Since the mid-1970s, enthusiasm for sexual revolution has vanished so completely that the term itself seems quaint. Sex became a very fraught topic in feminism, with pornography, rape and incest becoming more prominent concerns than pleasure or freedom (Segal, 1987). New Right movements mobilized around sexual politics of a very different stamp: anti-abortion, anti-homosexual, anti-sex education, anti-pornography. The growing popularity of Foucault's critique of Freud and Reich discredited the idea of power 'repressing' sexuality, replacing it with the idea of sexuality as a cultural formation produced by power. By the later 1980s the idea of sexual revolution was good mainly for a horse-laugh, or a nano-second of nostalgia in the world of the New Puritanism.

Yet something did seem to have changed in popular sexual practice, as academic research on sexuality in the United States persistently showed (see below). Something seemed to have changed in sexual culture, the 'post-feminist' young women of the 1990s (visible numbers of them, at least) being assertive about their own claims to sexual pleasure. The most successful AIDS prevention approach, the 'safe sex' strategy, showed that a sexual liberation current in gay communities was alive and well.

The idea of a repressive power impinging on sexuality is far from irrelevant today. No one can examine contemporary sex education (Sears, 1992), or the 'porn wars' (Burstyn, 1985), without being aware of the vehemence of attempts by the political Right to channel sexuality narrowly. At the same time, corporations in the global markets of the 1990s sexualize their advertising as much, or more, than they did in the Cold War Keynesian economy that

Marcuse studied. There seems to be relevance still in his idea of repressive desublimation. Witness the marketing triumph of Madonna in the United States, and the even more astonishing figure of the blonde television star Xuxa in Brazil (Simpson, 1993).

I think, therefore, that the idea of sexual revolution is due for resurrection. But the old formulations will not do. To reconstruct the idea, we need to make a critical examination of the concept of sexuality that underpinned sexual revolution theory and the conception that replaced it, and then examine the pattern of social change in sexuality in recent decades. This leads to an approach that preserves the radicalism of the original idea of sexual revolution, while breaking decisively with its nativist assumptions.

MODELS OF SEXUALITY

Reich drew from Freud what Freud drew from Darwin, the idea of sexuality as part of the realm of nature. Darwin had theorized 'sexual selection' as a key mechanism of evolution. In the second half of the nineteenth century, evolutionary biology displaced religion as European culture's main framework for understanding sex. Freud's 'psycho-analysis', like Ellis's contemporary 'psychology of sex', operated within this frame. His key notion of *Trieb*, usually translated as 'instinct' but perhaps better translated as 'urge', 'pressure' or 'drive', always conveyed the idea of a natural force at work in human life. The drama of *Civilization and its Discontents* was supplied by the tragic incompatibility of natural impulse and the limits required by social life.

This conception of natural impulse and social repression was widespread in twentieth-century sexology, even among thinkers who took their distance from Freud. The pioneering ethnographers of sexuality, Malinowski and Mead, were acutely conscious of the diversity of social forms, but nevertheless presupposed a biological impulse which the social forms expressed. Even the arch-empiricist Kinsey, who replaced Freud's subtle analysis of desire with a mechanical analysis of physical performance, shared the notion of a robust, hedonistic, natural urge, which found varying expression according to social prohibition (see the excellent analysis by De Cecco, 1990).

Reich and Marcuse, then, were drawing on a widespread nativist view of sexuality and its relation to society, in viewing the revolutionary impulse as a matter of breaking down social controls. This view was no monopoly of 'Freudo-Marxism'. Conservative ideology typically places sex at the boundary of the social, as the quintessence of what is irrational, uncontrollable or animal in human life. Readings of sexuality as 'natural' or beyond the social have provided cultural feminism and New Age religion with images of women's sexuality outside of patriarchy (e.g. Argüelles and Argüelles, 1977). Yet another such reading provides Bersani (1987) with a means of rejecting complicity with the 'murderous judgment' against gay men in the political context of AIDS.

The whole nativist framework was dramatically rejected in the 1970s, by the sociologists of the Kinsey Institute in the United States (Gagnon and Simon, 1973), and by Foucault (1978) in France. Foucault's critique of the 'repressive hypothesis', somewhat vaguely addressed but with Reich evidently in view, has become classic. It marked a decisive shift towards social constructionism and has been followed by a flood of research on discourses of sexuality and the production of sexual identities, which still shows little sign of abating.

The contest between essentialism and social constructionism in the study of sexuality has been set up at times as if it were an academic fist-fight (Stein, 1990). I am reminded of the great 'nature vs nurture' fight over IQ. That fight turned out to be spurious, not because the true explanation is 'interaction' (the undergraduate textbook solution), but because measurements of intelligence always consist of social judgements of social performances. We are, from the start, in a social domain; there is not an independent Something that can be partitioned between social and natural causes. (This has not prevented crypto-racists from pursuing the fight, and getting spectacular publicity for 'proofs' that inferior races inherit stupidity.)

Social constructionism has displaced scientific nativism not as an alternative explanation of the same object, but because it has brought into view a wider object of knowledge. This includes the social practices and relations in which bodily processes occur, which had mostly been written out of positivist sexology (Connell and Dowsett, 1992). We are, from the start, in a social domain.

But whether the social constructionists have yet produced a satisfactory account of that domain is open to question. They face, as a group, difficulties about the bodily dimension of sexuality.

Bodily processes and products – arousal, orgasm, pregnancy and birth, menarche and menopause, tumescence and detumescence, semen, milk and sweat – seem to underpin the nativist sense of sex as a domain of eternal repetition. Placing an emphasis on the historicity of sexuality, as Foucault and his followers do, often marginalizes these matters.

Social constructionist approaches to sexuality, as Vance (1989) observes, risk drifting away from bodily experience altogether. There are ways of talking about the politics of AIDS, for instance, which treat the matter as a problem of language, the power of medical discourse to control debate about the issue (e.g. Gilder, 1989). There is a strong tendency in poststructuralist theory to treat bodies as the surfaces on which social meanings are inscribed, as a neutral substratum for the play of identity and signification.

It is important, then, to insist that the bodily processes and experiences conventionally taken to be outside history are elements of social process. Sexual practice is body-reflexive practice, focused on people's erotic and reproductive potentials.

Bodies are in play in social relations, they are not surfaces or landscapes. We have no difficulty in accepting the social character of labour, which involves bodies as much as sexuality does. A sociology of bodies now exists which shows the varieties of ways bodies are drawn into social process and historical change. Glassner (1988), for instance, traces the rise of the body-culture industry, and its connection to American moral ideologies. Theberge (1991) shows the range of ways bodies are regulated and reconstructed in competitive sport. Sport itself undergoes constant institutional and cultural change, as shown in Gruneau and Whitson's (1993) striking analysis of ice-hockey in Canada.

The interpretation of sexuality as social behaviour that follows normative 'scripts' was developed by Gagnon and Simon, and produced the most sophisticated general survey of sexuality in recent history, the National Health and Social Life Survey in the United States (Laumann et al., 1994). This is the most flexible form of social constructionism and is particularly effective in addressing the learning of sexual behaviour.

Yet its very flexibility limits its capacity to provide a social analysis. Gagnon and Simon's theory provides no *social* account of what links the diverse scripts together, what makes them all 'sexuality'. The NHSL Survey provides important evidence about the prevalence of particular forms of sexual practice. But its very interesting documentation of the diverse 'normative orientations toward sexuality' among American adults (ibid., ch. 14) – i.e. marked differences in attitudes towards sex – undermines the theoretical idea that the structuring of sexual practice flows from normative scripting.

The idea that a more powerful social dynamic is in play is certainly present in Foucault. But the dynamic he recognizes arises from a structure of social relations constituted outside sexuality, *class* relations. Here Foucault remained on the same ground as the Marxism he rejected. The power active in power/knowledge, in the discursive constitution of 'sexuality', is precisely a class power, the power of a professional and property-owning bourgeoisie. Foucault's recognition of the social terrain of sexuality is surprisingly limited.

A third version of constructionism has picked up Foucault's idea of sexual 'speciation' and has focused on the social creation of diversity in sexual practice (Weeks, 1986), often in the form of sexual subcultures studied ethnographically (Herdt, 1992). A significant tension has arisen around this interpretation, particularly in relation to gay identity: whether this is a source of strength for challenges to heterosexual dominance, or, as queer theory suggests, is itself a form of social discipline that must be challenged (Plummer, 1992).

A focus on the formation of sexual subcultures as the path of social change has serious problems. It focuses the argument on relatively small avant-garde groups, and emphasizes what distinguishes them from the masses (a tendency built into the very concept of a 'subculture' and the method of ethnography), not what links them to the rest of the people. One result is getting trapped in implausible claims about how big the subculture is – for instance, the much-debated 10 per cent estimate of the number of 'homosexuals'.

Social constructionism, I would suggest, is limited because it is (in the forms we have seen so far) *not social enough*. It has not pursued the implications of Rubin's (1984) argument that sex is in itself an 'arena of social practice', the locus of a distinct form of politics, or – to generalize the point – a structure of social relations. It is only by analysing this structure and coming to some understanding of its dynamics that the concept of sexual revolution can be renovated.

CHANGES IN PRACTICE

Analysis of the structure of sexual relations must begin by recognizing its historicity. Of all the arguments of social constructionism, the claim of historicity has been the hardest to swallow. In proverb, poetry and mass culture, sexuality is precisely what does *not* change, what remains eternally the same. So it is necessary to consider the evidence of change. I shall briefly review four bodies of evidence: mass surveys focusing on heterosexual practice; community studies of gay sexuality; the emergence of new sexual categories; and postcolonial transformations of sexuality.

Sample survey research in the United States, whose population must be the most surveyed in the world, gives us a unique view of large-scale change in sexual practice. Taking the Kinsey studies as a benchmark certainly limits the breadth of understanding of sexuality, as De Cecco (1990) argues, but allows comparison of national data from the 1940s, 1970, late 1980s and early 1990s (Turner, 1989; Laumann et al., 1994).

With all the difficulties of comparison between studies using different questions and sampling methods, two broad trends in heterosexual practice are clear. One is a rising rate of sexual contact outside of marriage, most notably a greater number of partners in youth. The other is a gradual but far from complete erosion of the double standard, with women's patterns becoming more like those of men. (This still has a long way to go: in the latest of these studies, women are less than half as likely as men to report coming to orgasm in heterosexual intercourse, and more than five times as likely to report an experience of forced sex.)

These trends in broad population studies are also seen in more specialized studies, for instance of adolescents (Diepold and Young, 1979) and of college students. The student survey by Robinson et al. (1991) is notable because it traces change at five-year intervals from 1965 to 1985 at the same institution. Here the percentages engaged in premarital coitus and in heavy petting rose over the period, though levelling off in the 1980s, with women still reporting lower frequencies.

Robinson et al. report that by the early 1980s oral-genital sex had become acceptable among the students, and Laumann et al. report a longer-term generational shift in this direction in their national study. A study of working-class families in California by Rubin (1976) showed the social struggle this involved. She found situations where husbands had begun to introduce oral-genital sex into the repertoire, but some of the wives were resisting it as degrading, as the kind of thing prostitutes, not wives, might do.

Equally conscious changes in practice are involved in the response of gay communities to the AIDS/HIV epidemic. This has been documented in studies such as Kippax et al. (1993), in Sydney. Here a community-based survey examined the social conditions for adopting new patterns of sexual conduct, and followed up to see how far they had been maintained five years later.

An overlapping range of strategies developed within this community. They included changes in the structure of relationships; changes in sexual techniques, towards those generally known to be safer; and negotiations over safety for specific situations, such as HIV-concordant partners. Changes at a personal level were stimulated and supported by a collective process in which information was disseminated by word of mouth and by the gay press, organizations and networks were created and strategies debated. In effect the whole sexual culture was taken in hand and reworked around the issue of prevention. One result was falling rates of new infection.

The changes made by this and other gay communities involved mobilization around an existing sexual category. Another pattern of change involves the historical production of new categories of sexuality and new erotic objects. Weeks (1986) has emphasised this process in his account of erotic diversity. It is possible to trace in fine detail the construction of particular sexual subcultures, their venues, styles, leading personalities, economic and political histories, as Gayle Rubin (1982) does for a particular SM venue in San Francisco.

This kind of transformation affects heterosexuality as well. Studies of fashion (Wilson, 1987), and conceptions of beauty (Banner, 1984) chart the changes over time in the object of heterosexual desire − especially men's heterosexual desire.

Further evidence shows the contradictory and mutable character of this desire. The very recent creation of the 'transsexual' as a category (King, 1981) was supposed to provide a surgical route from membership of one gender to membership of another. But some were delayed en route, so to speak, and found they could survive as prostitutes (Perkins, 1983). Their customers are not other transsexuals − this is not an erotic subculture in the sense of the leather scene. They are straight men, who are excited by the gender contradiction embodied in the transsexual prostitute. In the last few years, some transsexual activists and cross-dressers, especially in the United States, have come to speak of a 'transgender community' or identity.

The most widespread changes in sexuality at present are not, however, in the rich metropolitan countries. Murray's (1991) study of street traders and prostitutes in Jakarta provides an example of the major change in contemporary sexuality, the transformation of sexual categories and practices during dependent capitalist development in poor countries.

One type of prostitution in this case involves the servicing of the Westernized sexuality of businessmen by lower-class women, who use this as an entry point to the modernized sector of Indonesian society. Another involves middle-class housewives, excluded from useful employment by the policies and ideology of the Suharto dictatorship. Different class sexualities, as Murray puts it, are produced despite a homogenizing official ideology of womanhood.

The impact of global capitalism also affects sexuality among Javanese men. Javanese society traditionally provided a space for *waria*, cross-dressing men who typically had sex with straight men. This pattern is now being displaced by a new sexual category, gay men, modelled on the gay sexuality of European/North American cities (Oetomo, 1990). There is a striking parallel on the other side of the world, in Brazil. Here another pattern of male-to-male sexuality, this time involving a fundamental distinction between insertor and insertee (rather than cross-dressing), is also being displaced by a gay sexuality on the European/North American model (Parker, 1985). Altman (1995) rightly observes that this is not a simple displacement of a 'traditional' sexuality by a 'Western' sexuality. Globalization involves an enormously complex interaction between sexual regimes which are in any case diverse and divided. The result is a spectrum of sexual practices and categories, formed in contexts of cultural disruption and massive economic inequalities.

It is this kind of interplay that has produced the new pattern of international sex tourism. The reputed passivity of Asian women is marketed as a fantasy not only by the prostitution industry, but also by airlines. In reality an extreme disparity of wealth allows the tourists to command sexual services that are hard to get elsewhere, the most important being condom-free penetration. The current result is a high level of sexually transmitted disease in the prostitute workforce and a looming AIDS disaster in Thailand (Bonacci,

1992). As fear of AIDS spreads, extreme youth in the prostitute becomes more valued (as a sign of being 'clean'). The prohibition on sex with children is progressively overwhelmed.

SEXUAL SOCIAL RELATIONS

Though these changes certainly involve the structures of class, imperialism and race, they are not reducible to them. We are on another social terrain, that of the relations constituted *through* sexuality. There are, as the Red Collective (1978) argued, systematic relationships between the sexual relationships between people; that is to say, there is a social structure in sexuality. This structure defines inequalities and gives rise to oppression, as Rubin (1984) argued; that is to say, there is a sexual politics not reducible to any other form of politics.

To name 'sexual social relations' is not to imagine a separate sphere of life which one enters, like walking through a door. It is to identify a logic of practice, a course which social action may take in any of the settings in which practice does occur. It is clear that sexuality is not confined to the bedroom, nor to any other restricted set of venues. What Hearn and Parkin (1987) call 'organization sexuality' is a ubiquitous feature of life in offices and factories. The broadening issue of sexual harassment makes it abundantly clear that sexual politics is not confined to special settings.

Particular aspects of sexual social relations, of course, have particular institutional settings. The cultural politics of sexuality is played out in mass media and in churches, and also in schools. If sexual practice is social practice, then as scripting theorists argue, it is learned; and the occasions of learning are important. Trudell's (1992) remarkable ethnography of an American sex education class demonstrates the complexity of the social processes and the active cultural politics at work in the production of the dismal curriculum of contemporary schools.

As I have emphasized, this social practice does not float free from the material world; it is embodied. Sexual practice is distinctively embodied, since bodies are not only engaged in the practices but are also their objects. Sexuality involves bodily arousal and pleasure, bodily processes such as pregnancy and childbirth, bodies as objects of desire. Sexual practice, then, is body-reflexive practice, even in its most refined cultural forms.

But it is also *social* practice, governed by social structure as well as by the possibilities and limits of bodies. Personal practice encounters organized limits and organized enablement, in an ordering of sexual social relations. Of the very extensive evidence that goes to show this, the most striking is the organization of desire through gender: heterosexuality and homosexuality considered not as opposites but as a couple.

Structure always involves constraint. Developmentally, this is what distinguishes adult sexuality from the flux of infant sensation, in the process of repression and re-ordering mapped by psychoanalysis. Constraint is not necessarily a question of group power; but it can be, when the enablement of one group constitutes limitation for another. In that case the structure is one of inequality. The positions in a structure of inequality define conflicting interests. The struggle of interests over the possibility of structural change is politics – 'sexual politics', in a sense reasonably close to Millett's (1972).

Perhaps the most profound result of the historical and ethnographic research on sex in the last two decades is the proof that the whole structure of sexual practice is liable to mutation. Sexual categories as well as sexual mores, the forms of cathexis as well as the objects of cathexis, the patterning of sexuality through the life history, the practices through which pleasure is given and received, all differ between cultures and are subject to transformation in time. (For examples of this work see Herdt, 1981; Caplan, 1987; Greenberg, 1988; Laqueur, 1990.)

The possibility of mutation in the structure of sexual social relations is what makes the concept of sexual revolution meaningful. But the two ideas are not equivalent; revolution implies political purpose and mass action. So we need to define the political content of change in sexuality: what are struggles for justice in this realm about?

SEXUAL POLITICS AND JUSTICE

Young's (1990) critique of the 'distributive paradigm' in philosophy defines justice in terms of the social conditions for two goals: self-expression (which may be collective as well as individual), and participation (citizenship, very broadly understood). Injustice, conversely, is the denial of these conditions and the blocking of these goals. There are, thus, two broad forms of injustice: oppression and domination.

This is a useful starting-point for the politics of sexuality, which is hard to understand in terms of the distribution of goods, but in which both oppression and domination are lively issues.

The 'speciation' of sexualities (Rubin, 1984) within a hierarchy of power or legitimacy involves a politics of self-expression and oppression in Young's sense. Through institutions such as state, church and mass media, a legitimate form of sexuality is defined, and others are declared to be perverted, deviant, sinful, degenerate, etc. Those people who engage in stigmatized sexual practice are oppressed through the hierarchy of sexualities, whatever their social position in other respects.

The oppression of gays by straights, and resistance through the formation of a sexual subculture, is the paradigmatic case. A striking feature of current sexual politics is the way other stigmatized groups are now following this path. The concept of 'queer', incorporating transgender as well as gay and lesbian identities, is an attempt to name this wider movement.

Sexual politics also involves domination, the constitution of inequalities through sexual practice itself. The most familiar cases are within heterosexuality, where the gendered object-choice brings into play the structure of gender inequalities. Research on marital rape (Russell, 1982), for instance, shows sexual violence by husbands occurring in a continuum of coercion, intimidation, claims of ownership, claims of right, claims of need, economic pressure, persuasion and customary interpretations of marriage. That this is not just a local issue is shown by Laumann et al.'s (1994) finding, for a carefully constructed national sample in the United States, that the experience of forced sex is much more widespread among women than among men.

The state is deeply involved in both oppression and domination. Governments attempt population policies directly regulating sexuality, and sometimes they work. Governments attempt public health measures, which often bear on sexual practice and the structure of sexual relations. A historical example is the intervention which created the modern socio-legal category of 'the prostitute' (Walkowitz, 1980) and a current one is the attempted regulation of homosexual practice through AIDS education. Institutions at the national level thus attempt the 'regulation of desire', as a Canadian study put it (Kinsman, 1987).

Of course, attempts to deploy state power do not always work. One of my treasured possessions is an official publication of the New South Wales government, entitled *Notice Under Section 14 (1) of the Indecent Articles and Classified Publications Act, 1975* (Waddy, 1975). A Conservative government of this Australian state had brought in a censorship law, establishing three categories of publications which were to be sold under various restrictions. To make this system work, they needed to list the publications in each category, for the use of booksellers and the police, and duly issued the list as a government document. The resulting 92-page booklet, which lists items alphabetically and classifies them by degree of lewdness, must be the only user's guide to pornography ever published by government. It cost 96 cents and rapidly became a best-seller.

Most discussions of justice, and most discussions of sexual politics, operate at the local or national level. There is also a global politics of sexuality, which has only just begun to be recognized. We could hardly understand the post-colonial transformations in sexual practice discussed above without acknowledging the power of global markets, global communications and international agencies.

If we look at this global process historically its political character is inescapable. It has regularly involved a violent appropriation of bodies, social disruption and indeed mass death. Colonial occupation commonly meant the taking of indigenous women for the sexual service of settlers, the occupation force being mainly men. In Australia, as in the United States, aboriginal children were liable to be seized from their parents to be 'civilized' in missions, boarding schools or white foster-homes. Venereal disease followed the flag: European sailors were the vector for the spread of syphilis as well as Christianity around the globe. The coercive sexuality of the colonial frontier is now eerily replayed in the postcolonial global market with the growth of sex tourism.

Beyond the patterns of oppression and domination defined by Young, there is a third dimension of sexual politics where the distributive paradigm of justice seems more relevant. This concerns the way in which the practice of one person or group represents constraint and enablement for another. In Sartre's (1976) analysis of this problem, the underlying condition for structural antagonism is material scarcity – not natural scarcity but historically produced scarcity.

The argument seems apt for sexuality, where scarcity is a familiar condition and is socially produced. Monogamy, compulsory heterosexuality, prohibitions on adult/child sex, rules against premarital sex and rules against sex with kin all involve the social denial of possible gratifications. A compound of these denials, the incest taboo, was central in Freud's analysis of the making of personalities. A sense of their total weight fuelled both Freud's and Reich's critiques of modern civilization.

Yet scarcity is not inherent in sexual practice. Indeed one of the most striking things about sexuality is its social amplification, the way in which an increase of pleasure for one partner need not decrease, but generally increases, the pleasure of the other. Stepping outside the Western discourse of sexuality, Ram (1991) notes how the very language in which sexual matters are spoken of among the Mukkuvar people of south India makes women's sexuality inseparable from questions of auspiciousness, fertility, a kind of social prosperity.

It is the denial of plenitude that marks the operation of repressive power in sexual intercourse, where one partner 'takes' pleasure from the other. Cases range from the real-life demand by American husbands for oral-genital sex from reluctant wives, mentioned in the previous section, to the fantasized extreme of *Histoire d'O*, remarkable in modern SM literature in emphasizing the *lack* of gratification for the heroine in a diet of whippings and anal rape (Charney, 1981). The feminist critique of the 'sexual revolution' of the 1960s accurately focused on its repressive moment, in which men's gratification was increased at the expense of women. But as Segal (1994) argues, this critique does not rule out the more authentic goal of pursuing pleasure for both.

There is, then, a contradiction between the social production of plenitude and the social denial of its possibility (for all, or for some). In this sense sexual politics, while taking quite specific forms, are not fundamentally different from the other kinds of politics which shape human possibilities and the creation of our shared future.

The concept of sexual revolution as the liberation of sexuality, or the liberation of people via sexuality, can now be replaced by a concept both more mundane and more political: the democratization of sexual social relations. I have tried to spell out this idea in another paper (Connell, 1995). Briefly, it means the pursuit of justice in the whole sphere of social life being discussed, ending the patterns of oppression and domination that are found across this sphere. This is a revolutionary enterprise in the sense that it requires the overthrow of a powerful institutional system and a major structure of social inequality. The course of events is unlikely to resemble the familiar models of revolutionary politics; there is no Winter Palace of the sexual Tsars to be stormed. But in thinking about the project of democratizing sexual social relations, it is equally necessary to appraise the state of the structures being contested, the historical moment in which we currently act.

THE PRESENT MOMENT

The metropolitan countries of the global system at present have a sexual order dominated by institutionalized heterosexuality, structured by men's power and women's subordination. While marital heterosexuality is hegemonic, a great diversity of sexual practice is produced around it: homosexual, heterosexual and autoerotic.

This regime is anything but stable. It is in the midst of a historical trajectory which involves both internal transformation and global expansion on an unprecedented scale. Elements of the internal transformation have been documented above: changes in practice within hegemonic heterosexuality; the formation and internal change of sexual subcultures; the emergence of new sexual categories. These are happening under the continuing impact of two cultural forces: the commodification of sexual fantasy on a vast scale in commercial media; and the feminist challenge to the structuring of heterosexuality by men's power over women, now widely diffused and supported by women's gradually increasing economic resources. Global expansion involves both the direct export of European/American sexual practice and fantasy, originally through colonialism and now through the control of global media, and the indirect creation of the conditions in which a Western-style sexuality will reproduce itself. This has produced new complexities of sexual life in the interplay between metropolitan and colonized cultures.

Though the idea of sexual revolution differs from other models of revolution in many ways, it shares one basic point: 'revolution' is an empty idea without popular action on a mass scale. That was clear to Reich and should still be clear today.

Popular action has clearly driven some of the recent changes in sexual practice and culture in the metropolitan countries. The widespread use of the contraceptive pill by Catholic women despite the Pope is impressive proof of the failure of regulation. The increase in numbers of youth having heterosexual genital intercourse and the resulting increase in births to unmarried mothers equally defies official ideology. The collective coming out of urban gay communities in the 1960s and 1970s, and their shift towards safe sex practice in the 1980s, is perhaps the most striking case of popular action breaking through systems of prohibition and control.

Looking back to the benchmarks provided by the Kinsey studies, it seems reasonably clear that popular action in countries like the United States over the last five decades has loosened the control of sexual practice by church and state and diversified the available forms of erotic life. The patriarchal structuring of heterosexual practice has been challenged, but there has also been a vigorous backlash. Overall, what has been accomplished has been deregula- tion more than democratization. This has made sexuality more open to commercial exploitation and thus, ironically, has increased the possibilities of control by corporations.

Little in popular culture immediately disputes this control, which is after all based on gratification through fantasy and the consumption of products. This produces the paradox seen from *Playboy* to *Cosmopolitan* to MTV: corporate entrepreneurs apparently promoting liberation. At a deeper level, however, there are impulses in popular culture that contradict the commodification of sexuality and, in however inchoate a way, reassert the human relationships involved. They include demands for privacy; the enjoyment of smutty jokes and sexual folklore; dislike of the pornography industry; scepticism about the celebrities of the media.

The current prospects for the democratization of sexual social relations depend a great deal on whether this popular contradiction of commodification can be connected with the radical agendas for sexuality now mostly confined to marginalized groups. Such connections were made in the 1950s and 1960s, in culturally surprising ways. No earlier experience would have suggested that music was to be an important vehicle of political change, but rock music undoubtedly was. We should not be surprised by another cultural mutation of this kind.

While the goal is the democratization of sexual social relations, we must contemplate the possibility that the outcomes of social change will be far from democratic. Struggles are not necessarily won. The most powerful trend in sexual social relations in recent history is the pulverization of indigeneous regimes of sexuality under the impact of globalization. This is not, on the face of it, a democratic triumph.

Lyotard (1984) was right in observing that the intellectuals of the rich countries can no longer believe the grand narratives that presented a logic of history guaranteeing the triumph of reason or human freedom. In that sense we live in a world of necessary disillusion, deeper than the provisional pessimism of the generation that encountered Nazism and Stalinism. Reich's kind of utopia is truly dead and gone.

But Lyotard was wrong in measuring our possible purposes by the depth of our disillusion. The most severe realism must admit the possibility of constructing purposes larger than our particular interests. We have the possibility of speaking across boundaries, the possibility of conjoint action. These are all the bases we need for reinventing revolutionary sexual politics as a democratic movement.

6 Feminist Sexual Politics and the Heterosexual Predicament
Lynne Segal

'There is feminism and then there's fucking,' declares the bulimic literary critic Maryse, in the Canadian film *A Winter Tan* (1987), based on the published letters of Maryse Holder, *Give Sorrow Words*. Maryse tells her audience that she is taking a holiday from feminism to indulge herself and her 'natural sluttishness' with young Mexican men, one of whom eventually murders her. After gloomily absorbing this narrative, I found it hard to decide whether it was Maryse's notion of feminism or her own (and her killer's) predatory view of sex which was the more depressing in this sad tale of one woman's neurotic self-destruction. The fact that many feminists would confidently endorse Maryse Holder's dual depiction of feminism as anti-heterosexual pleasure and heterosexual pleasure as anti-woman (a dangerous, if not deadly pursuit) only adds to my sinking spirits. Some of us expect cautionary tales warning women of the price we must pay for sexual pleasure to come from our would-be patriarchal 'protectors', determined to stamp out the rich and hopeful dreams of women's liberation. It is harder to know what to think when the same message comes from our own side. (*A Winter Tan* was produced, written, directed and performed by Jackie Boroughs, a leading feminist in Canadian film and theatre for the last 25 years.)

One thing is clear, however, at least to me. The way to fight the continuing victimization of women cannot be to abandon notions of sexual liberation, or to make women's pursuit of heterosexual pleasure incompatible with women's happiness. It was not only the generation that came of age in the affluent 1960s that discovered that the fight against sexual hypocrisy and for sexual openness and pleasure could inspire both personal and political enthusiasm for creative and co-operative projects of diverse kinds. Such sexual openness lay at the root of the politicization of women and gay people in the 1970s, suddenly fully aware that pleasure was as much a social and a political as a personal matter; well before they discovered Foucault, and his genealogy of the cultural institutions and discourses dictating the norms and regimes of 'sexuality'. It was seeing and hearing the dominant language and iconography of the joys of sex focused on the power and activity of straight men, while subordinating and disparaging straight women (as 'chics'), lesbians and gay men (as 'queers'), that inspired the women's and the gay liberation movements to engage in a battle against both sexism and, after a few early skirmishes, heterosexism as well.

The ramifications of this battle take us all the way from opposing gender hierarchies to challenging the very conception of 'gender' itself. From the extensive debate about the care and treatment of women in relation to fertility control and childbirth, alongside pressure on men to share the full responsibilities of household tasks and parenting, to the subsequent highly successful 'safer sex' strategies pioneered by gay communities against the spread of HIV and AIDS, the struggle for sexual liberation has played a crucial role in changing patterns of life in Western countries. Indeed, it was the repression of any moment or movement of sexual liberation in the former Eastern European 'state socialist' countries that constituted the most significant aspect of the oppression of women there. Despite greater access to childcare facilities and extensive participation in the workforce, Eastern Europe saw almost no politicization of interpersonal relationships or sexual experience, making sexism, violence against women and exclusive maternal responsibility for childcare and housework as unchallenged as it was ubiquitous (Einhorn, 1991).

Today, however, feminist sex radicals (who in these times are almost always lesbians) have repeatedly challenged heterosexual feminists 'to come out of the closet'. We're still waiting, they tell us, wearily, for you to discuss your sexuality, stop generalizing and get specific: 'Is domination and subordination a clear-cut issue in heterosexual sex? Do heterosexual feminists have thoughts on SM? Has anyone sighted a butch-het woman and femme-het man together? Answers in a *Feminist Review* article please.' (Ardill and O'Sullivan, 1989, p. 133.) Silence, as usual, greeted their challenge. *Feminist Review* is still waiting.

It is a silence I have come to expect. Straight women have been on a bumpy ride for some considerable time. But in many ways it has been bumpiest for those closest to feminism. In recent years it has been feminist polemic, rather than male backlash, which has done most to confuse and discourage new thoughts on sexuality in feminist texts. Heterosexuality has been coupled consistently with male violence, and presented as both the cause and enactment of men's power over women. How, we might well wonder, did a movement which came out of, and drew its initial strength and inspiration from, the assertive sex radicalism of the 1960s manage to produce so many who would end up so silent about their own sexuality? It is a concern, clearly, which was not only central to the genesis of feminism, but remains central to the majority of women.

The first impediment was, of course, men. Men as they are; and 'manhood' as it is figured in the inescapable discourses and images of masculinity in language and culture. 'Masculinity' in Western culture means, at least in part, the sexual pursuit of women, expressed in a type of sexist *brogadaccio* which betrays both a fear of real intimacy and a horror of 'weakness' or 'effeminacy'. Challenges to its presumptions can motivate men's rage and violence – often towards women or gay men – through attempts to shore up a flagging sense of personal power. But it may also encourage rebellion against oppressive forms of male identity, albeit with still limited success.

The second restraint, holding back discussion of women's erotic desires, came from within feminism itself. It was the attempt to identify authentically 'female' bodily experiences. These were to serve as alternative images, to be contrasted with the 'custom-made woman' designed only to please and titillate men. But the search for some fully autonomous, self-directed sexuality (only to be found in masturbation) would lead some women to abandon, and others to say no more, and certainly to write no more, about their longings for the admiration, desire and physical intimacy of men.

The many insecurities and uncertainties women feel about their bodies leaves little space between reclaiming sex and the setting of norms. For a while, it was only a small group of defiant lesbians who felt confident enough to question the Utopianism and growing prescriptiveness in feminist accounts of a distinctively 'womanly' desire for benign, sensual, egalitarian relationships. They spoke instead of the complexity, ambivalence and unsettling elements of power and submission present in all desire – female as well as male (Vance, 1984, p. 21).

The final impasse was thus the inescapable contrariness of sexual passion itself. Some level of confusion was inevitable in rethinking women's sexual agency, given the crucible of contradictions at the heart of sexual desire – triggering emotions that make us feel both powerful and defenceless at one and the same moment. This was further complicated by a change in the political climate. All kinds of social anxieties are easily displaced onto sexuality, and the Right knows just how to orchestrate hostility against sexual 'permissiveness' as the cause of social 'decay', seen most recently in their virulent attacks on single mothers. Retreat from optimistic feminist hopes for women's sexual liberation was always likely to accompany the defeat of broader attempts to build a more caring and equal society. And so in the 1980s it did.

Yet even as Catharine MacKinnon gains a popular readership for her own particular brand of sexually repressive feminist rhetoric, telling women that feeling good in sex with men is merely enjoying the seeds of victimhood, something is clearly awry (MacKinnon, 1987). For feminism's greatest influence came from its campaigns in the name of the sexual liberation she denounces. Demanding women's control over their own bodies and seeking changes in their relationships with men brought more responsive and respectful gynaecological provision and made it possible to identify and object to sexual harassment, redefine rape and prioritize violence against women. 'Part of my attraction to feminism involved the right to be a sexual person,' one North American feminist ruefully recalls. 'I'm not sure where that history got lost' (English et al., 1982, p. 42).

What is more, the current thrust of feminist criticism of heterosexuality is at odds with what most women are saying about their sex lives. No longer ahead, but *out of step* with many women's dreams and desires, feminism in the 1980s became pessimistic or silent about straight sex just when women themselves were displaying much of feminism's former enthusiasm for sexual (and social) independence. Reflecting a new liberal aceptance of women's sexuality outside wedlock, marriage rates in most Western countries were declining, divorce rates rapidly rising and many women were choosing to cohabit. Parenting was being postponed until careers were established and, overall, women were having fewer children by the 1980s than in the 1960s.

Married women, it seemed, were also receiving greater satisfaction from sex with their husbands. Morton Hunt's survey of sexual behaviour in the United States in the 1970s reported far greater variety and frequency of sexual activity compared with Alfred Kinsey's a generation before: 90 per cent of wives claimed to be happy with their sex lives, three-quarters were content with its frequency, with one-quarter wanting more. Blumstein and Schwartz reported much the same from their extensive survey of couples a decade later. Women and men were displaying similar sexual preferences, desiring frequent sexual activity, happiest when initiating or refusing sex equally as often, and – whether heterosexual, gay or lesbian – became discontented if sex was infrequent (see Segal, 1994, p. 67).

British surveys agree. They show women initiating more sexual contacts and married women having more affairs, reflecting their heightened expectations and sense of sexual agency. Contrary to conservative hopes or feminist warnings, the most recent survey of sexual behaviour here (the one Margaret Thatcher tried to abort by withdrawing promised funding) concluded that sex is both far safer and less fraught for women today than ever before. The overwhelming majority use contraception during their first sexual intercourse, and three out of four women felt that it occurred at about the right time, for the right reasons.

There is thus a dramatic lack of fit between what one very visible group of feminists have been saying about women's experience of sexual victimization, and what most women have been reporting about their experiences of sex and its importance to them. Nevertheless, while the gap between women's and men's sex lives is narrowing, and marriages seem happier, this is probably *only* because of the high rates of divorce. One in two marriages in the United States and over one in three in Britain ended in divorce in the 1980s, the majority initiated by women unhappy with the 'unliberated' behaviour of their husbands – behaviour that includes significant amounts of abuse against women and children.

When women's frustrations do lead to separation or divorce, they are economically disadvantaged. A woman may be just a divorce away from poverty. Nevertheless, contrary to the backlash stories broadcasting the bleak situation of women after divorce as a warning to them to stay married, it is actually men who most fear and try to prevent marital break-ups – sometimes with more of the violence which provokes it. Teenage pregnancy (though far from the spiralling problem conservatives denounce) can leave young women and their children impoverished. Around a quarter of adolescent girls still complain of feeling pressured into having sex with boys, and most report little physical pleasure from their early sexual experiences, finding it hard to talk about sex with their partners.

In fact, when Lillian Rubin set out to discover the impact of the sexual revolution in the United States, she found that both men and women typically spoke of being 'disappointed' with their first encounter with genital heterosexuality. But whereas almost all men saw it as an important achievement on the way to manhood (sowing the seeds for men's frequent resort to sexual coerciveness), no woman saw it as definitive of womanhood. (Menstruation conventionally serves as the far more ambivalent marker of entry into womanhood.) Women's most frequent regret was feeling cheated of the 'romantic fantasy' they had hoped to fulfil. Even so, most contemporary reports on teenage girls and their culture show them as much tougher and more in control of their lives than the previous generation (Rubin, 1991).

More women are feeling satisfied in their sex lives with men. Yet they still suffer disproportionately from (and pervasively fear) sexual assault from men. How can we shift the sexual codes which encourage coerciveness from men, endorse compliance from women and continue to serve as barriers to change? *Only by rethinking the very idea of heterosexuality*: pursuing a long and arduous cultural journey with endless setbacks on the way.

At the heart of the problem is the way in which 'masculinity' and 'femininity' tie in with the cultural symbolism of the sex act: masculinity as activity, femininity as passivity. As the lesbian theorist Judith Butler argues, following Foucault, gender contrasts gain much of their meaning through this more basic image of heterosexuality: 'The heterosexualization of desire requires and institutes the production of discrete and asymmetrical oppositions between "feminine" and "masculine", where these are understood as expressive attributes of "male" and "female"' (Butler, 1990, p. 33). Such oppositions inevitably obscure the diverse initiations and activities which actually do take place between women and men. It is this symbolism which we need to keep on challenging if we are ever to turn around the idea that sex is something men *do* and women *have done* to them – with all its oppressive spin-offs, for both women and gay men.

The first way to do this is to talk more, not less, about the diversity and fluidities of heterosexual experiences and bodily contacts. But neither feminists, nor anybody else, have found this easy to do. When feminist-inspired research, like that of Shere Hite, reported that only 30 per cent of women reach orgasm during penetrative sex, this was quickly transformed, by Hite and by others, into the spurious announcement that most women did not like penetrative sex (against the grain of the complexity of feelings Hite herself uncovered) (Hite, 1976). Before long the coercive message of much feminist sex advice literature was that wise women, in touch with their 'authentic' needs, would avoid penetrative sex. (*'Hmn ... do I put it somewhere?*?' a feminist cartoon muses, depicting a strong, naked woman, looking dubiously at a penis-shaped vibrator. She moves it around a bit, only to fling it down in horror, repeating in outrage the absurd suggestion, *'In my CUNT?!'*: Meulenbelt, 1981, p. 100.) Yet, any feminist insistence upon the significance of clitoral over vaginal, 'active' over 'passive', self-directed over self-shattering, sexual engagement, not only ignores the unruliness of desire, but reflects, more than transcends, the repudiation of 'femininity'/'passivity' in our misogynist culture.

The repetition of this repudiation is easy to understand: even the most recent feminist encyclopaedia on sexuality in Britain, *The Sexual Imagination*, has no entry under 'vagina', although the history and meaning of the 'clitoris' is boldly covered by its presiding editor as playing 'a disproportionately major role in women's sexual pleasure' (Gilbert, 1993, p. 56). It did not go unchallenged, but when affirmed, the reproductive resonance of vaginal iconography as 'birth canal' always threatened to override or undermine any pleasure-encoding signification. It was the pioneer of postwar Western feminism, Simone de Beauvoir, who affirmed, with reference to the vagina, that 'the feminine sex organ is mysterious even to the woman herself... Woman does not recognise its desires as hers.' Her own description of this 'sex organ', so often 'sullied with body fluids', tells us why:

> woman lies in wait like the carnivorous plant, the bog, in which insects and children are swallowed up. She is absorption, suction, humus, pitch and glue, a passive influx, insinuating and viscous: thus, at least, she vaguely feels herself to be.
>
> (de Beauvoir, 1988, pp. 406–7)

There is no vagueness in this description. It is a perfect illustration of the horror of what Kristeva has elaborated in her (currently much over-used) conception of the 'abject' object. Kristeva describes abjection as the process whereby the child takes up its own clearly defined ('clean and proper') body image through detaching itself from – expelling and excluding – the pre-Oedipal space and self-conception associated with its improper and unclean, 'impure', connection with the body of the mother. The mother's body, having been everything to the child, threatens its engulfment. On this view, entering the symbolic space of language brings with it a horror of (and fearful attraction to) everything without clear boundaries, everything which suggests a non-distinctiveness between inside and outside (Kristeva, 1982). Elaborating Kristeva's thoughts, Elizabeth Grosz explains that her notion of an 'unnamable, pre-oppositional, permeable barrier, the abject requires some mode of control or exclusion to keep it at a safe distance from the symbolic and its orderly proceedings' (Grosz, 1990, p. 95). However culturally-specific this psychoanalytic narrative of the child's entry into the symbolic may be (and Kristeva, with unconvincing but characteristic Lacanian grandiosity, takes it to be universal), it would seem to resonate with the place of vaginal iconography in our culture, and its absence from respectable discourses and contexts). The vagina has served as a condensed symbol of all that is secret, shameful and unspeakable in our culture.

The question which Grosz raises is whether it is discourse itself which confers the horror of 'abjection' onto female bodies, and whether there might thus be other ways of registering, or resignifying, the sexual specificity of female sexual bodies (which may include, but would not reduce to, reference to the mother's body, however conceived). Neither de Beauvoir nor Kristeva addresses this question. It is indeed a formidable task. That some interference, shift or resignification in standard perceptions and meaning are possible, however, when old images are repeated in contexts where they may be seen in new ways (always involving contention, and fears of recuperation), is evident from the battles which have already been fought around women's film and art-works involving female genital anatomy.

When Anne Severson started showing her short silent film, *Near the Big Chakra*, assembling close-up, colour photographs of women's 'cunts' or vulvas, back in the early 1970s, she incited extraordinarily strong reactions of both pleasure and disgust. Women fought over it, one supporter telling Severson, 'I would kill for your film.' Some women saw the images as powerful, teasing and pleasurable, suggesting energy and activity, 'an active passivity'. For them the intricate delicacy, complexity, varied shapes and different hues making up the 'whole' female genital (vaginal opening, pubic hair, mons, outer-lips, inner lips, clitoris, magnified pores, secretions, occasional tampax string, and so on), can mock and reverse the

'hole' male discourse has made of it – as sheath for the penis. Cathy
Schwichtenberg explains its subversive effect as follows:

> the absence which is not an absence, gazes back at male
> viewers producing a double-bind of fear and desire which
> alternatively sucks them in, pushes them out; and asks for more
> than a penis/phallus closure. These vulvas ask for textural/
> sexual caresses – a pleasurable foreplay and a questioning of
> ideas.   (Schwichtenberg, 1980, p. 81)

They may well ask. Schwichtenberg is right to suggest that these
new images of the female body, which some women (and perhaps
even men) may find pleasurable, especially in cultural contexts
where viewers are already hoping to stir up trouble for traditional
meanings, can begin a slow process of resignification. But with
other women rejecting Severson's art-work (and those which would
follow it, with similar intent), as disgusting, demeaning and 'pornographic' (one man vomited at a London screening), we have a lot
more stirring, and a lot more explaining to do, before female
genitals exist securely in language as more than 'manholes'. Many
other women writers, poets and artists (like the late Helen Chad-
wick, especially in her 'Piss flowers') have since continued to provide
us with a supply of new and subversive images, but these works
have so far had little impact on what became the orthodox feminist
theorizing of heterosexuality.

Yet, for all the psychic and cultural pull of dominant binaries of
heterosexuality, its codings have never been secure. Because it has
always been in desired sexual encounter, of whatever kind, that the
presumed polarities of gender can most easily be felt to falter and
blur. Sexual pleasure – taking us all the way back to the fears and
longings of childhood attachments – is as much about letting go and
losing control for men as it is for women. Nor is there any inevitability about either the occurrence or the preferred form of heterosexual bonding. As any prostitute knows, straight men are both
terrified of, yet passionately attracted to, powerlessness and loss of
control. Many men like nothing better than a good spanking,
although it bores the pants off *Ms Whiplash*. Sexuality can be as
much a place for male as for female vulnerability (though any
physical coercion men face is almost always from other men). This
is precisely why men, more than women, so often remain so fearful
of physical closeness, denying themselves the pleasures of passivity
which, in the end, is what much of joyful sex is all about. Men,

much like women, long for what they also fear and dread: the intense vulnerability which accompanies the embraces, enclosures and penetrations of another – whether rythmically stroked by fingers, tongues, lips, teeth, arms or that most fragile and fluctuating of all appendages, the penis. The distinction between inside and outside breaks down as fingers, lips, nose or tongue wander over, in and between the flesh of the other.

In contrast with texts (whether mainstream or feminist), which suggest that women can never escape the 'subordinating' meanings of heterosexuality, it is actually harder to insist upon its strictly gendered oppositions. *There are many 'heterosexualities', and all sexualities, including lesbian and gay ones, are 'hetero' in one way or another.* There is diversity and 'otherness' in same-sex encounters and relationships, and there are pluralities of cross-sex meetings. It is usually assumed that we consolidate our gender identity and endorse male dominance through sex – heterosex: 'A man can become more male and a woman more female by coming together in the full rigors of the fuck,' cocksman Norman Mailer crows (Mailer, 1971, p. 171). But do we? Sex is often the most troubling of all social encounters just because it so easily *threatens* rather than confirms gender polarity. The merest glimpse of the complexity of women's and men's actual activities suggests that straight sex may be no more affirmative of normative gender positions (and in that sense no less 'perverse') than its gay and lesbian alternatives. In consensual sex, when bodies meet, the epiphany of that meeting – its threat and excitement – is surely that all the great dichotomies (activity/passivity, subject/object, heterosexual/homosexual) slide away.

Indeed, as Leo Bersani (1987) suggests, we can see much of men's phallic swagger as not just about denying power to women, although it certainly has that corollary, as the denial of the reality, the pleasure and the assertive pull of men's feelings of passivity and dependency. Even mainstream surveys on health, happiness and sexual patterns have been highlighting for some time now that, as a recent US study puts it: 'What most men really need is to develop their "feminine" side and become more focussed on relationships, more emotionally expressive and more comfortable with being dependent' (Segal, 1994, p. 285).

Men's dangerous anxieties over power ('manhood'), and for some the accompanying resort to sexual coerciveness, will only fade away with the passing of their general social dominance – which was always the motor of 'phallic' symbolism. But within the diversity of heterosexual encounters and relationships, some are compulsive, oppressive, pathological or disabling; others pleasurable, self-affirming, supportive, reciprocal or empowering. Many move between the two. Taking note of the self-display and barely covert homoeroticism currently thriving (and selling commodities) as never before in images of men in the media, any insistence that male sexuality is simply predatory becomes little more than a new way of affirming what it pretends to deplore.

I am not suggesting, however, that the struggle to break the codes linking active ('masculine') sexuality to cultural hierarchies of gender will ever be easy. Sex and gender hierarchies have survived despite their increasingly obvious contradictions. It is a trap to assume (with the *Cosmopolitan*-led, fashionably feminine layer of mass culture) that we can ignore both the symbolic dimensions of language and the existing relations of power between women and men. In *Cosmo* and its ilk, women are presented as already the equal sexual partners of men, and told how to obtain and please their men, as if men were all seeking much the same advice. Such rhetoric nonchalantly neglects the extent of men's general power over women, and its defensive façade of endemic misogyny: apparent from the merest scratch on the liberal surface of sexual equality. Who's afraid of women's independence? Of the single working woman? The single mother? The sexual female? Watch your local cinema for clues.

We must also take on board the mass-cultural images of women, especially in romance fiction. We imbibe it from our mothers' fantasies and daydreams and our own enjoyment of most popular film or novels, where we see ourselves reflected only in the *waiting* female heroine. Many studies of young women's sexual experiences point to the disabling aspect of this heritage. Defining sex in terms of love and romance is the main reason young women offer for allowing their male partner to dictate their sex lives. It also explains their frequent disappointment, even though the pervasive games with power in such narratives reveal some of the contradictions of 'feminine' identifications.

Yet however powerful the iconography of sex and the conventions of romance, their effects are diverse. If the first trap for sexual radicals is to ignore the constraints of symbolic codes and social hierarchies, the second trap is to declare them fixed and immutable. In fact, they are chronically fragile and unstable, easy to subvert or parody – however equally easily recuperated. There have always been men who could consciously delight in being the object of a woman's (or a man's) desire; and who could see the penis as merely a penis. Just as there have always been women who are lusty, aggressive and sexually dominating, and everything in between. Many already suspect that it is precisely the icons of masculinity who can barely conceal the 'woman', the 'faggot', inside. The more rigid the sexual norms people feel they must affirm, the greater the threat of all those experiences they struggle to exclude. Was there ever more than masochistic pleasure for men to gain from *Rambo*'s muscled display of grunting, passive, patriotic flesh – repeatedly wounded, in pain, humiliated and tortured with his own knife?

As I have indicated, it is lesbians and gay men who have played the critical role in revealing the artifice of the gender and sexual oppositions constructing heterosexual norms. These norms not only provide repressive accounts of heterosexual experience. More destructively, they impose themselves on homosexual experience too, producing our lasting images of the 'effeminate' male and 'butch' lesbian. Today, 'queer' activists turn traditional symbols on their head. Whether insisting that penetration is no more heterosexual than kissing, waving the lesbian 'phallus' or asserting the power of 'passivity', they subvert the heterosexual norms which have tried to imprison them.

What I want to suggest is that straight women (and men) should also play a part in this subversion. Instead of guilt-tripping heterosexuals, we would do better to enlist them in the 'queering' of traditional understandings of gender and sexuality, questioning all the ways in which women's bodies have been coded as uniquely 'passive', 'receptive' or 'vulnerable'. But we must also look at *male* heterosexual desire (and how their bodies become 'receptive' and 'vulnerable') since the two are inextricably linked.

We all, and young people especially, need new sources of sex education, new erotic narratives and images which depict both women and men asserting *or* surrendering control in situations of mutual esteem, safety and pleasure. Surveying the diversity of heterosexualities enables us to affirm those encounters which are based on trust and affection (however brief or long-lasting), and to wonder (because it is never easy) how best to strengthen women to handle those which are not.

There is still a long way to go in creating a radical sexual politics that includes heterosexuality. When Joan Nestle wrote her moving recollection, 'My Mother Likes to Fuck', other women picketed the

London magazine which published it. In it she had dared to protest: 'Don't scream penis at me, but help to change the world so no woman feels shame or fear because she likes to fuck' (Nestle, 1987). Quite so. Straight women, like gay men and lesbians, have everything to gain from asserting our desire to fuck if (and only if), when, how and as we choose.

7 Conservative Agendas and Government Policy
Martin Durham

In recent years much has been written about the relationship between right-wing politics and sexuality. Some of this has been historical, for instance examining the Third Reich or the morality campaigns that were an important part of the Ku Klux Klan's appeal to its millions of members and supporters in the 1920s (see e.g. Bock, 1984; Blee, 1991; Burleigh and Wipperman, 1991). More contemporary work has been concerned with the rise since the 1960s of what some have termed the Moral Right, campaigning organizations that seek to ban abortion, restrict sex to within the confines of heterosexual marriage and restore 'traditional values' (see e.g. Cliff, 1979; Herman, 1994; Petchesky, 1984). This body of work has been of fundamental importance in understanding how political forces have mobilized around issues of family and morality, but it has also brought us face to face with the complexities of such struggles. National Socialists, for instance, opposed abortion selectively, for those that they saw as racially fit; contemporary anti-abortionists oppose it universally. Some conservatives advocate banning pornography in the name of morality, some defend it in the name of liberty. Some moral crusaders are involved in right-wing politics; some avoid party identification altogether. The relationship between sexual morality and right-wing politics is not as straightforward as it might seem, and we not only need to differentiate within the Right but also question whether groups that campaign around particular aspects of sexual behaviour are necessarily to be identified as part of the Right.

Amidst what is a more vexed relationship than might at first appear, one argument has achieved a particular prominence – that in both Britain and the United States in recent years we have witnessed the rise of a militant conservatism that has as one of its central concerns a fundamental challenge to the legislative and attitudinal changes around sexuality that are associated, helpfully or not, with the term 'permissiveness'. Surely, it might be argued, if we are uncertain about how exactly to deploy the term 'right-wing' in struggles around sexuality, we can agree that the modern Right in Britain and the United States has been vitally concerned with sexual politics. In this chapter, I want to raise some problems with that reading. In doing so, I want to do three things. First, I want to question the assumption that modern conservatism, whether in pursuit of power or actually in possession of it, has been pursuing a moralist agenda. Second, I want to emphasize factors that are more likely to make conservatives reticent rather than enthusiastic in taking up issues of sexual politics. And third, I want to argue that there is an aspect of sexual politics which conservatives have been, and will increasingly be, concerned with, but that it is not one of the areas that most discussions of sexuality and the Right have tended to focus on. In making these arguments, I intend to consider developments in both Britain and the United States and propose first to turn to the British case.

For much of the postwar period, British Conservatism was the Conservatism of consensus. Already moving in that direction before the 1945 election, defeat at the hands of Labour convinced the Tories that commitment to extensive welfare provision and state responsibility for full employment were inescapable if they were to return to office. Instead of free enterprise, coexistence between a private and a public sector was the order of the day, and the party that returned to office in 1951 (and won the next two general elections after that) believed that they had recaptured the initiative. Labour's 1964 victory and an intensifying debate about the state of the nation cast that into question, and when the Conservatives regained office in 1970, they were already having second thoughts at what now looked like a policy of presiding over decline. The radicalism of the new prime minister, Edward Heath, was to prove somewhat short-lived, but Conservative defeat in 1974 propelled the party into a far more wide-ranging reconsideration of its assumptions.

At the heart of this re-evaluation lay a revival of a form of economic thinking that had hitherto appeared to be obsolete. Neo-liberalism, championed first by the Institute of Economic Affairs and then by the Centre for Policy Studies, held that the state needed to be rolled back and the market restored to its full glory. But if the state needed to be curbed, it still had a vital role. Not only had the realm to be defended, but the rule of law had to be reasserted both against over-mighty unions and mollycoddled criminals. This was argued not only by neo-liberals but by a different strand of the Right, the so-called 'traditionalist' or social conservatives, and as what came to be called the New Right grew in importance during the 1970s, it brought together different themes and different groupings in a single offensive against what it saw as the rise of collectivism since the war.

Within this overall argument, criticism of the legacy of 1940s Labourism was welded together with criticism of 1960s permissiveness. Shop stewards and social workers were both to blame for the woeful state of Britain and a phrase that was later to become popularized, 'Victorian values', captures the sense of a golden age of economic liberty and moral responsibility that had been lost but could yet be regained. This phrasing, of course, was associated with Margaret Thatcher, and it is she, along with Sir Keith Joseph, who was to be crucial in bringing the ideas of the New Right to bear on the battle to renew Conservatism first in opposition, then in office. What came to be known as Thatcherism was a particular rendering of New Right ideas in the context of a party that needed to negotiate resistances, both within and without, to the full-blown carrying out of a New Right programme. In this negotiation, economic questions were to the fore. But social issues were also important, both as a problem and as an opportunity, and some of the Conservatives' rhetoric both on the road to power and after its attainment suggested that such issues, particularly as they impinged on sexuality, had a special prominence in the party's concerns.

In 1974, for instance, Joseph made a much publicised speech in which he argued that young women in the semi-skilled and unskilled working class urgently needed to be discouraged from having children outside of marriage. In 1986 the then Conservative Party Chairman, Norman Tebbit, calling for an end to 'the poisoned legacy' of permissiveness, denounced rising divorce, births outside of marriage and 'demands for deviance ... to be treated as the norm'. And in 1989, Margaret Thatcher accused 'the proponents of the permissive society' of creating a generation of children in danger of 'seeing life without fathers not as the exception, but the rule' (*The Times*, 21 October 1974; Tebbit, 1986, pp. 9–10; *Guardian*, *Daily Mail*, 18 January 1990).

Nor was it simply a matter of rhetoric. In 1986, the government decided that sex education should be taught so as 'to encourage ... pupils to have due regard to moral considerations and the value of family life' (Thomson, 1994, p. 48). The following year, it supported the introduction of a new clause – clause 28 – of its Local Government Bill (subsequently Section 28 of the Local Government Act 1988) by which local authorities were forbidden to 'intentionally promote homosexuality' or promote the teaching of its acceptability as 'a pretended family relationship' (Smith, 1994, p. 183).

Both for its pronouncements and its legislation the Thatcher government has often been seen as concerned not only with a new economic order, but a new sexual one too. Thus, for Tessa ten Tusscher (1986, p. 78), the Thatcher government should be seen as having launched an 'attack on women's sexuality' as part of a project to restore a threatened male domination. According to Stuart Hall (1988, p. 90), the government was 'all too willing' to take up a moralist agenda on abortion, homosexuality and sex education, while for Tim Newburn, 'the Thatcherite New Right' during the 1980s was engaged in an 'ideological battle over the nuclear family and legitimate sexual expression' (1992, pp. 187–9).

A closer examination of the Thatcher government's record, however, suggests a more complex picture. (For a more detailed discussion, see Durham, 1991.) On sex education, the decision that it should be taught in the context of family and morality came about because of a long-term campaign by Christian moral campaigners, and they remained highly critical of the government for refusing to allow parents to withdraw their children from sex education altogether. Clause 28 likewise came about as a result of pressure on the government, and those who greeted its introduction were somewhat less pleased by the government's support of an education campaign on AIDS which refused to condemn homosexuality. In other areas, the government declined to follow the moral crusaders' lead altogether. Throughout the 1980s the Department of Health and Social Security insisted that doctors had the right to give contraception to girls under the age of 16, leading Victoria Gillick, the leading campaigner against this policy, to declare that the Thatcher government merely paid lip service to 'traditional values', but was in reality locked into the values of a 'pagan State' (Gillick, 1989, pp. 250–1, 307). Similarly, for those who expected the Thatcher government to restrict abortion, the 1980s was a period of immense disappointment, brought to a head at the end of the decade when, as leading ministers had hoped, Parliament voted down the proposed 18 weeks' time-limit on abortion that campaigners sought. Majority support for a nominal reduction (from 28 weeks to 24) but with exceptions both for serious foetal abnormality and if there was a danger of grave permanent injury to the physical or mental health of the woman, was seen by anti-abortionists as a massive defeat.

As this account suggests, Britain does not lack for moral campaigners. 'Pro-life' organizations, most importantly SPUC (the Society for the Protection of Unborn Children) and LIFE campaigned against abortion, while a broader array of 'pro-family' issues was championed by such organizations as CARE (Christian Action, Research and Education), Family and Youth Concern and, from 1986, by an organization set up within the governing party, the Conservative Family Campaign. But moral campaigners neither became a powerful force within the party nor created an electoral base which Conservatives needed to appease. The Thatcher government was little concerned with sexuality, but positively resistant to rejecting the advice of civil servants and medical opinion over how to deal with abortion or how to respond to AIDS. On occasion, as we have seen, moral crusaders were successful. Particularly in matters relating to the schooling of youth, the government was happy to play the populist card or speak in the name of parents' rights against what it saw as extreme and, all importantly, electorally unpopular. But where moralists looked to Conservatism in power to take up their agenda, they were to look in vain.

British Conservatism in the 1980s was not engaged in a sexual counter-revolution. But what of the United States?

The modern American Right came into existence in the 1950s, above all around the magazine *National Review*, as a conscious attempt to pull together hitherto scattered groupings. Some were primarily concerned to stop what they feared was the inevitable advance of world communism. Some were libertarians, committed to the free market and a minimal state, while others were traditionalists, seeking a return to absolute values in place of the relativism they saw as undermining American society. From such beginnings, American conservatism by the early 1960s was strong enough to capture the Republican presidential nomination for one of its own, Barry Goldwater, even though it was not strong enough to avoid a landslide defeat at the polls. In the years that followed, the conservative movement continued to grow in strength but seemed unable to defeat either Democratic Party liberalism or the moderates who wielded much of the power within the Republicans. Central to the breakthrough in conservative fortunes was the rise in the 1970s of two linked groupings – the New Right and the New Christian Right. Where the term New Right in English usage is used to refer to the broad array of neo-liberal and social conservative think tanks, pressure groups and individuals, in the United States it has a far more specific meaning. Associated with a number of key figures, notably Richard Viguerie and Paul Weyrich, the American New Right was new not only in its commitment to the most modern techniques of organization, but in its conviction that social issues were crucial to the creation of a conservative majority. (For a fuller account of 'pro-family' politics and the American Right, see Durham, 1994b; 1996.)

One of its earliest initiatives was to approach leading figures in the white evangelical Christian community and attempt to persuade them to mobilize what was effectively a sleeping giant. Perhaps as many as a quarter of the population, white evangelicals either voted Democrat or abstained from politics altogether. Yet they overwhelmingly opposed abortion, rejected feminism and supported heterosexual marriage against the claims of the gay movement. This, the New Right argued, made them a potentially crucial factor in conservatives gaining the presidential victory which had eluded them in 1964, and the winning over of such figures as Baptist preacher Jerry Falwell brought a New Christian Right into existence, above all Falwell's own organization, the Moral Majority.

The New Right and the New Christian Right played a highly visible part in Reagan's victory in 1980, a year in which the Republicans declared themselves for the banning of abortion and Reagan give a key address to the Christian Right's Religious Roundtable. But this did not mean that the issues that the New Right had deployed and were the basis of the New Christian Right's very existence were to play a central role in the politics of the Republican Party in power. Instead, the government prioritized economic and foreign policy issues. Congress did not pass the Christian Right's Family Protection Act, a wish-list of proposals ranging from tax exemptions for children born within marriage to the denial of federal funding for educational programmes that tended to 'denigrate, diminish or deny' role differences between the sexes or presented male or female homosexuality as acceptable (Petchesky, 1984, pp. 264–6). Attempts to ban abortion by constitutional amendment similarly foundered. The government did take up some of the 'pro-family' agenda, for instance by withdrawing funding for international organizations that carried out abortions, and the Christian Right continued to support the President. By the end of the Reagan years, however, the leading organizations of the Christian Right were in disarray, and some commentators were even predicting its demise.

As we know, what happened was rather different. While Moral Majority was dissolved, and a Christian Right challenge to George Bush for the 1988 Republican presidential nomination was defeated, what was actually occurring was a transformation of evangelical politics that in the 1990s has produced a (newer) Christian Right of considerable dimensions. (For the beginnings of this restructuring, see Moen, 1992.) Bush's challenger, Pat Robertson, had represented only a section of the Christian Right (Falwell, for instance, had supported Bush). His challenge none the less had built the beginnings of an impressive national apparatus and in the years that followed, his new organization, Christian Coalition, was to become a major force in Republican Party politics. The 1992 party platform emphasized many of its issues, just as today the leading candidates for the 1996 Republican presidential nomination speak at Christian Coalition gatherings and seek to win its support. Does this, then, mean that American conservatism is prioritizing sexual counter-revolution?

If we look at the successful 1994 Republican campaign for Congress and at the much discussed Contract with America, we do not find this to be the case. The Contract, signed by over 300 candidates for the House of Representatives, pledged to bring ten Bills to a vote within the first 100 days of the new Congress. These measures, revelling in such names as the American Dream Restoration Act and the Taking Back Our Streets Act, blended an economic conservatism with social issues, most importantly crime. Social conservatives were particularly pleased by its proposals for a tax credit for families and a fundamental restructuring of welfare provision which would stop payments to young unmarried mothers. But the Contract expressly excludes both restrictions on abortion and moves against homosexuality. Every issue in the Contract was tested on groups of voters and only popular measures were included. Neither abortion nor homosexuality is seen by Republican strategists as maximizing electoral appeal or uniting the party. Abortion, in particular, is seen as a problem for the party. In 1989 Republican pollsters concluded that 35 per cent of younger voters might defect over an anti-abortion stance. Analysis of the 1992 election results indicate that an anti-abortion stance won the party more votes than it lost. None the less, leading Republicans continue to worry abortion opponents by trying to find a wording on abortion that would keep the support of both 'pro-life' and 'pro-choice' voters, and the divisive nature of the issue is well illustrated by a questionnaire circulated to supporters by the Republican National Committee in 1993 in which some 90 per cent of the 133 000 who replied were enthusiastic about economic conservatism, but only 58 per cent were in favour of banning most or all abortions (*American Spectator*, April–May 1994).

As for gay issues, while opposition to gays in the military was important in reviving American conservatism after Clinton's victory, the Contract's architect, Newt Gingrich, is not a social conservative. (In the words of the veteran New Rightist Paul Weyrich, Gingrich has 'been all over the place on homosexuals': *Spectator* 13 May 1995.) This is not to say that the Republicans are pro-gay (or pro-abortion), although some within its ranks are. Rather, it is to argue that the party finds issues of sexual politics far more problematic than might be expected.

Indeed, this is even the case for the Christian Right itself. In 1992, of course, Bush's campaign for re-election proved unsuccessful. In the 1970s, the New Right had been convinced that social issues were central to conservative growth. Some of the issues they cited, such as crime and opposition to gun control, have been important to conservative electoral gains in the 1990s. But sexual issues did not play such a role. For Ralph Reed, Christian Coalition's executive director, one of the lessons of Clinton's victory was that 'concentrating disproportionately on such issues as abortion and homosexuality' did not link up with the concerns of the mass of voters. Instead, he argued, the Christian Right needed to develop a broader agenda around taxes, crime, government spending and other issues 'but with a pro-family twist' (*Christian American*, July–August 1993). In looking at the Contract, then, Christian Coalition could see elements of such an agenda and devote much of its resources to supporting it. In a subsequent Contract with the American Family, the organization set out its own politics of the possible, which included restrictions on (but not a banning of) abortion but, despite extensive New Christian Right activity at state and local level against gay rights measures, made no reference to homosexuality. While we can conclude that the Christian Right remains vitally concerned with opposition to abortion and gay rights, sexual politics is less to the fore than we might think.

In looking both at the record of the Thatcher government and the development of American conservatism since the 1970s, it is impossible to conclude that sexual politics has been at the cutting-edge of a right-wing offensive. In Britain the relationship between 'pro-family' organizations and the Conservative Party has frequently been strained, while in the United States the Christian Right has become a major component of the Republican Party, but has been unable to convince party decision-makers that the banning of abortion or the repudiation of gay rights are practical politics or conductive to a conservative election victory. This does not mean, however, that such issues will go away. More importantly, in looking at abortion or homosexuality (or sex education) as the key issues in sexual politics, we are at risk of missing the very question whose importance is rising in conservative circles. It is a question we have already encountered in our discussion both of Britain and the United States. In Britain Sir Keith Joseph's 1974 pronouncement on single parenthood was much criticized as eugenicist, his talk of a threat to 'the balance of our population, our human stock' dealing a fatal blow to his hopes of challenging Edward Heath for the leadership of the Conservative Party (Halcrow, 1989, pp. 81–92). But the figure who replaced him as standard-bearer of the Right was also to raise the issue of single parenthood, for instance in the 1990 speech cited earlier, and it has increasingly become a major concern of neo-liberals and social conservatives alike. Thus in 1990, Lord Joseph, as he now was, declared in a Centre for Policy Studies publication that 'our child-rearing structure' was under grave threat from 'divorce... casual procreation' and 'adolescent mothers' (Joseph, 1990, p. 9).

In the same period, as she was later to discuss in her memoirs, Margaret Thatcher had become 'increasingly convinced' that much of what was wrong in the country, from learning difficulties to rising crime, was attributable to family breakdown and single parenthood and that government had to give serious attention to 'strengthening the traditional family' (Thatcher, 1993, pp. 628–9). Arguments about single parenthood were crucial to the Major government's ill-fated Back to Basics campaign too. Thus at the 1993 Conservative conference, in the days leading up to Major's declaration that the party would 'lead the country back to... basics', the Social Security Secretary, Peter Lilley, had declared that it was time to make it clear that the two-parent family was the best way to bring up children, while at a fringe meeting the Home Secretary, Michael Howard, had described the decline of the traditional family as one of the causes of crime. Three months earlier, the Welsh Secretary, the then little known John Redwood, had caused a furore in a speech following his visit to an estate in which the majority of families were without a second parent. At the time Major's call for a 'return to core values' was seen as heralding an attack on single parenthood, and in the months that followed Howard's reiteration of a correlation between single-parent families and crime and Lilley's call for a re-examination of the benefit system in order to strengthen the two-parent family fitted well with such an interpretation.

As the Back to Basics campaign unravelled, however, hit first by division in the Cabinet, then by a seemingly unending round of scandals in the parliamentary party, Major declared that the campaign had never been about sexual morality. If we turn back to his conference speech, we do indeed find no reference to sexuality or to single parenthood; instead, the nearest the Prime Minister came in his list of basics was in his reference to 'self-discipline' and 'accepting responsibility for yourself and your family'. But while some ministers were to complain that Back to Basics had been hijacked by their moralist colleagues, it is certainly the case that the campaign gave a temporary publicity to a more long-term concern in New Right circles with single-parent families. (For Major's speech, see the *Guardian*, 9 October 1993; for a fuller discussion of Back to Basics, see Durham, 1994a.)

Joseph's intervention in 1990 was not the only one of that year. The Institute of Economic Affairs, long associated with arguments about monetarism and trade union power, moved on to new ground with the publication of a pamphlet by the American conservative Charles Murray on the dangers posed to the social fabric of a growing underclass, a group whose existence he particularly linked with the rising rate of births outside of marriage (Murray, 1990). More IEA publications along similar lines followed, in part functioning as the basis for Howard's arguments about crime (Dennis and Erdos, 1992; Dennis, 1993; Murray, 1994; Morgan, 1995). Within the Conservative Party itself, Redwood's comments during his June 1995 challenge for the party leadership and his subsequent visit to meet Newt Gingrich, along with Howard's speech to the Conservative Political Centre in October, continued to keep the issue alive after the Back to Basics débâcle (*Observer*, 2 July 1995; *Daily Telegraph*, 12 October 1995; *Independent*, 11 October 1995).

As references to Murray and Gingrich make clear, this is not a matter of a coincidental concern with single-parent families on both sides of the Atlantic. The proposals on welfare in the Contract with America represent the culmination of an argument that has been developing in the United States for some considerable time and has in turn fed into the debate in Britain (for the United States, see Stacey, 1994; for Britain, see e.g. *Daily Mail*, 6 July 1993; *Independent on Sunday*, 10 October 1993; *Daily Express*, 19 December 1993). While there are significant differences in the context, in both cases key sections of the Right have turned their attention to single-parent families. The reasons are twofold. Most importantly, unlike abortion, homosexuality or sex education, an attack on single-parent families is about saving the government a significant portion of welfare expenditure. For the Right in both countries, reducing government spending has proved an elusive target; reducing the amount spent on single-parent families and, they believe, reducing the very number of such families, will bring down the amount the government needs to spend, borrow – and tax. But as we have seen, calls for restoring the two-parent family are also a way of arguing that claims of the damaging effects of conservative government policies are fundamentally misplaced. Crime, educational under-achievement, homelessness can all be dealt with, it is argued, by encouraging a family form that provides effective socialization, discipline and a male role model and by discouraging family forms that do not. Economic conservatives and social conservatives cannot agree that campaigning against homosexuality or abortion is crucial, but they can coalesce around defunding and discouraging sexual relationships that call on the state for aid. In the United States that has already happened; in Britain, there is far more hesitation, but the potential is already visible.

II
MEDICINE AND
MORALITY

8 Medicine, Morality, and the Public Management of Sexual Matters

Leonore Tiefer

INTRODUCTION

As many major contemporary theorists in sexology have indicated, we are in a period of paradigm shift in sexology. To understand where we are going, it helps to see where we are have been and where we are.

One of the most important of the prevailing sexual ideologies and management forces has to do with the relationship of sexuality and medicine, and I want to devote myself to that subject. Although not a new relationship, I do not need to emphasize that the relationship of sex and medicine is central to the current social construction of sexuality.

How medical authorities currently construct sex – what and who are included and how, as well as what and who are ignored – is fundamental to understanding the current sexual *Weltanschauung*. Medical authorities have an impact far beyond the consulting room in terms of their influence on the mass media, on legislation, on courts of law and on policy-making. In the consulting room, medical 'experts' provide certain kinds of resources and opportunities for certain groups of people, directly influencing the actual sexual lives and experiences of millions upon millions of people in the industrialized world.

MY LOCATION

Let me briefly describe my perspective on these issues. I am employed as a clinical psychologist in the Urology Department of a large New York City hospital. So I am a sexologist, but I could also be described as doing participant-ethnography in sexual medicine. As a sexologist with appropriate credentials and employment, I study the management of sexuality from inside medical practice. This participant-ethnography, I should point out, is done at the frequent peril of losing my job and offending many sexologist friends who don't see their work with a sociopolitico-anthropological lens.

My primary job is to interview men who have been referred to the Urology Department in order to evaluate and treat their sexual problems. Usually, they have been referred by their GPs. My interview is one component of a comprehensive evaluation, which also includes much physical testing. In an interview lasting from 15 minutes to an hour or so, my job is to form an impression of the nature of their problems, the probable cause or causes of their problems, and the type of treatment which might be of most benefit to them. When the patients are accompanied to the interview by a sexual partner, I interview her (only women partners have come) separately.

During the 12 years I have been doing this work I have interviewed over 2000 men and about 1200 of their sexual partners. I have observed a dozen urologists who do this work and have become familiar with the ever-changing panoply of diagnostic tests and treatments available. I have conducted follow-up research on how men and couples cope with the treatments they undertake, and I have attended dozens and dozens of professional meetings in sexology. I have published the sexological research in scientific journals, and I have published the participant-ethnographic work most recently in a collection of essays.[1]

SOURCES OF POPULAR AND EXPERT INFORMATION

The reality of contemporary society is that there are very few places to go for sexual advice or help, or just to get questions answered. Sex education is practically non-existent, and what there is usually focuses very narrowly on matters of contraception and sexually transmited diseases.

Most people get their sexual information from the mass media, and encounter four different types of message:

1. *Sexual images*: Fictional and celebrity models and images of sexual relationships emphasizing beautiful bodies, drama, passion, transgression and sexual acts. Transsexual tennis stars, lesbian

tennis stars, Hugh Grant picks up a prostitute, what Michael Jackson and Lisa Marie do; how many women John Kennedy had sex with in the White House, etc.

2. *Sexual advice for women*: Women's magazine articles and advice columns directed towards heterosexual women, emphasizing sex differences, women's needs for intimacy, the importance of technique, simple rational solutions.

3. *Sexual health news*: Health news and advice, framing sexuality in physiological terms; themes which are duplicated in men's magazines. A typical article, 'A Guide to Your Sexual Health – News You Need to Know to Keep your Body and Mind Primed' (in *Longevity*, January 1995, p. 34) begins: 'Some of the best news coming out of the lab lately is that good sex and good health often go hand in hand. We're glad to hear it, since we've always felt that a healthy sex life is a cornerstone of longevity.'

4. *Current sexual events news*: Sex news – which is always sensational, and focuses either on sex-related crimes (whether the names of parolled child sex offenders should be published in the neighbourhoods they are moving to, sex on the Internet) or marvellous medical breakthroughs (the Italian mother in her sixties, does John Wayne Bobbit's penis work? the gay gene) or political controversies (whether AIDS curricula should emphasize abstinence or condoms, new censorship laws or court cases).

Morals and mechanisms are the dominant themes in all these media categories, and one of the foundational terms is 'health'. Health *is* morality nowadays (a theme we need to explore further), and calling upon 'health' serves as a kind of mantra in popular writing and thinking about sexuality. 'Healthy' serves as the modern equivalent to 'normal' in terms of endorsing and recommending sexual scripts for what's done, why it's done, when, where and with whom it's done, etc.

I would argue that the language and social value given to health is the most significant underpinning for the dominant ideology of sexuality, the 'medicalization of sexuality', which we can define as a gradual social transformation by which medicine, with its distinctive ways of thinking, its models, metaphors and institutions, has come to exercise authority over sexuality.

THE MEDICAL MODEL

The medical model emphasizes that the body has its own empirical laws and processes that work independently of mental or social life.[2] The body is a morally neutral, self-contained unit which only physicians are fully authorized to evaluate and treat, based on their unique claims to morally neutral, objective science. The body of the medical model is basically a machine, like a piano, with functional purposes which can only be fulfilled if the body and its parts are functioning properly. 'Properly' can be determined by objective research and is subject to the natural laws of chemistry and biology.

Modern medicine sees the body as an archipelago of organ systems, with each professional speciality inhabiting an organ system island of its own: the nervous system, the vascular system, the endocrine system, the genitourinary system, etc.

Sexuality, according to the medical model, is a natural property, or set of properties, of individuals expressed in acts which require properly functioning organ systems (although there are ownership contests among the organ system island owners!). Proper sexual functioning can be assessed and studied by laboratory measures according to the medical model (this is a key element) and can be altered and corrected by familiar medical interventions (medicines, devices, surgeries), i.e. by the family of curative, rehabilitative and, less often, prophylactic strategies.

The dominance of this medical specialist evaluation is most visible in urology with regard to men's sexual complaints, as the urologic subspeciality of 'impotence' has grown exponentially over the past two decades. I shall return to the urology story below.

THE HUMAN SEXUAL RESPONSE CYCLE (HSRC)

First, however, I want to suggest a contestant for top honours as catalyst for this dominant ideology, the medical way of thinking about sexuality, and that is the physiological research of William Masters and Virginia Johnson published in the 1960s. Masters and Johnson observed hundreds of solo and coupled sex acts in their laboratory, and scrupulously recorded and reported a variety of physiological parameters. In 1966 they described a supposedly universal 'Human Sexual Response Cycle' during which various neurological, vascular and muscular events transpired in a predictable and invariant sequence. They argued that this one sexual response cycle characterized men and women, homosexuals and heterosexuals, and that this human sexual response cycle constituted the basic physical bedrock for human sexual expression. Feminists were happy about the gender equality, gays and lesbians were happy for the imprimatur of normality, sex educators were happy about the specificity, and physicians were ecstatic about the medical mandate.

This physical model of sexuality was praised from every quarter, and was immediately enshrined as the centrepiece of sexuality in academic textbooks, research and classification of clinical problems. The American Psychiatric Association has described sexual dysfunctions since 1980 as follows: 'The essential feature is inhibition in the psychophysiological changes that characterize the complete sexual response cycle.' All of professional sexual treatment is organized around making sure the sexual response cycle works properly.

Specifically, this means that normal, healthy, proper sexuality means that the vagina works properly (opening nicely and getting wet when it's supposed to), the penis works properly (getting hard and ejaculating at the proper time) and the orgasm works properly.

Regularly occurring sexual desire, which Masters and Johnson did not discuss, was later added as an element of the sexual response cycle, and became the only sexual dysfunction defined without reference to proper functioning of the genital organs. But that's been the only change. The physical model has become the medical mandate for proper sexuality – the medicalization of sexuality, the physical bedrock, the physical cycle of genital arousal and orgasm.

CRITIQUE OF THE HSRC

I have written at great length about scientific, clinical and feminist criticisms which can be made of this human sexual response cycle (Tiefer, 1995). Summarizing rapidly, close reading of their work reveals that Masters and Johnson didn't 'discover' the HSRC, they (1) selected research participants who were already experienced at coordinating their sexual activity so as to enact a smooth arousal/orgasm performance; (2) they went out of their way to find participants who had a strong interest in effective masturbation and intercourse; (3) participants underwent a training period ('controlled orientation' it was called) to help them perform in the laboratory; and (4) participants whose performance occasionally 'failed' were coached on how to avoid recurrences.

There was no investigation of the feelings or motives or fantasies or subjective experiences of the participants. No note was taken of the meaning this kind of sexual activity had for them. No discussion occurred about how these participants had developed this kind of sexual script, or even of how this sexual script operated in their non-laboratory lives.

Because the assumption was that the body has its own empirical laws and processes that work independently of mental or social life, it seemed perfectly appropriate that the only records were of genital changes and nipple changes and respiratory changes on this highly selected group of participants, and that the results be called 'the' human sexual response cycle.

So, the outgrowth of this research was perfect for the medical archipelago. Normal sexuality became defined, and remains defined, as specific performance of fragmented body parts. If the parts function normally, you cannot qualify for a sexual dysfunction; if the parts do not function normally, no matter what you say or feel or want, you have a sexual health problem.

A REAL-LIFE EXAMPLE

Let me illustrate how the unquestioning assumptions this approach to sexuality takes segues into modern medical practice.

In June 1989, a conversation took place during the annual meeting of the International Academy of Sex Research in front of a poster titled 'Healthy Aging and Sexual Function'. One of the figures depicted nocturnal penile tumescence measures for a group of 65–74-year-old male volunteers. A urologist studying the figure said to the poster's author, a psychiatrist, 'So, these men did not have rigid noctural erections; they may actually have had disease.' 'No,' the psychiatrist replied, 'they were healthy, and in fact they were having sex; their wives confirmed that there was no dysfunction.' 'But', continued the urologist, 'their wives may be satisfied, even *they* may be satisfied, but since *some* men in that age groups *can* have rigid erections, *these men* must have had some impairment.'

This is a rich illustration with many important implications for contemporary sexuality, but I just want to highlight a few:

1. The disagreement about the meaning of the data illustrates the important gap between physical measurements of the body and what they signify. High-technology measurements are subject to multiple interpretations, a fact not well appreciated by the non-medical professional. The medical model fosters the illusion that machines reveal the hidden body directly. But actually the body is silent, and many layers of mental (i.e. cultural) decision go into what is chosen to be measured, how it's actually assessed, and how the readout is decoded. Our modern wish to bypass the lies of culture and politics, and get back to the pristine truth of the natural body deludes us here – the body, like God, is a Rorschach, a projection of our ideologies!
2. What's going on in this illustration is the actual establishment of a definition of deviance. In the argument over what is a problem, the specialists are arguing over what is normal and what is healthy. Again, the body doesn't speak; authorities speak and label.
3. The urologist and psychiatrist represent different investments in the machine and the person as sources of authority and definition. This is an ongoing contest within the medicalization movement, and it may be that progressives will find themselves in an unfamiliar coalition with psychiatrists as they contest the biological reductionism of other medical specialists.

THE MEDICALIZATION OF MEN'S SEXUALITY

I could pursue the implications of this illustration, but instead I shall show you how medicalization is playing itself out at the present moment within urology, and perhaps suggest what this portends for the future.

In 1986 I published a paper titled 'In Pursuit of the Perfect Penis' in which I described how social interest groups can exert steady pressure and collude to create reality. Very briefly, these groups include:

1. Urologists, highly paid surgical specialists, who, as they are losing some of their surgical opportunities because of technological improvements, are looking for other areas of specialization.
2. Medical industries and pharmaceutical companies who are always on the lookout for new markets, and are especially alert to opportunities related to changing demographics, i.e. the ageing baby boomers of 1946–50.

3. The mass media which boost sales by capitalizing on the public's interest in health and the perennial attractiveness of sexual topics. Medical sex is 'clean sex', and thus appropriate for every kind of show and publication.

4. Various entrepreneurs such as self-help group starters and newsletter promoters who have created markets on many subjects by portraying themselves as something between consumers and professionals, but who, in the area of sexuality, promote an exclusively medical model in terms of language, recommendations, and designated authorities.

5. Insurance companies who adhere to 'objective' measurements and interventions to minimize costs.

6. Men who favour a medical model because it's face-saving, maintains phallic privilege and offers them an 'objective' and optimistic world of science to minimize their anxieties over self-disclosure and mental health. Men's socialization and masculine ideology both suport a medical model.

7. Some heterosexual women who find it congenial for a variety of reasons to define sexuality in terms of men's erectile and ejaculatory function.

The point is that the overt interests of many groups – economic, psychological, political and ideological – combine to support medicalization. Without an alternative model, itself actively supported and promoted, the need of society to understand the social forces which construct and mediate our understandings of sexuality will be filled by medical language and models.

We might even speculate that covert interests of institutions with a stake in sexual restrictiveness (e.g. conservative political and religious organizations) may indirectly support medicalization because of its potential for sexual social control through specifying norms, eliminating deviance and enforcing conformity.

And what do men get who enter the medical world of men's sexuality at the present time? They get a discourse of reified erections divorced from the body, the person, the couple, the script – erections as universal biophenomena are the focus. Once the patient cooperates in the discourse of erections, it is easy for the physician to move even further down the reductionist ladder, and start talking about how erections merely consist of filling and containing compartments in the penis. This language and construction lead the patient to agree that the next step is to measure these processes and then to repair them or replace them.

Urology currently offers three treatments – penile injections, vacuum devices and permanent penile implants.[3] They all work, i.e. they create secure and functional erections. But this type of evaluation and treatment is a little like a Soviet retail store – you go in, and you get what's there, whether you need it or not, whether you'll use it or not! The patient's sexual unhappiness combined with the usually weeks-long period of evaluation have been exhausting, and he is eager for something, preferably something simple and permanent. Yet follow-up studies generally show a decline in frequency of use and in estimates of satisfaction at the same time as the men say they would take the same path again.

In the urology setting women's interests are assumed to be central to the evaluation, the prime reason why the man is coming for treatment. Yet, women are usually omitted from the evaluation, and certainly are never invited to speak about their own sexual interests. My work has explicitly invited women to contribute as equal partners to the evaluation, 'since sex is a two-person thing'. Often, the wife's answer is that she is here merely to be supportive, and that it is clear that her husband feels bad because he can't have an erection, not necessarily because he can't have sex. Of course, she acknowledges, once his erection is restored, he (and she) will be obliged to have intercourse to make it all worthwhile, a prospect she often greets with considerable ambivalence. There are, of course, a million different stories, but the problem with the medical model is that the stories seem far less interesting to the professionals than the penis-archipelago.

CONCLUSION

I have illustrated some of the ways in which medicalization is a major player in the contemporary sexual picture. As an ideology it offers advantages and disadvantages which I can see when I speak, day in and day out, to real couples immersed in renegotiating their sexual lives. The good news is that people of little education who have lots of questions and are troubled with lots of worries about sexuality get to talk to somebody who can listen sympathetically. It's something they are grateful for. Most sites of sexual medicine, however, do not allow much time to help people find a language to talk. Usually there is a medical doctor who 'takes a history', 'makes a diagnosis' and then it's directly on to the physical fixing.

The gender politics of that medical sexual world seem deeply reactionary and misogynist in terms of the limited space for women to articulate and develop sexual capacities independent of a fixed masculinist pattern focused on genital function and orgasm. This is ironic, given the initial enthusiasm with which feminists embraced the liberatory potential of Masters and Johnson's claims that biological research proved women's sexual capacities (i.e. for arousal and orgasm) were at least equal to men's. Indeed, the point that women's bodies can orgasm is a useful one, and many women have employed this information to raise their expectations and demands of their lovers.

The larger truth, however, seems to be that biological potential has very little to do with sexual scripting for most women around the world, and that aeons of genital research will not create sexual liberation in a world of social inequalities. In fact, biological models seem to constrain options at least as much as they enhance them, especially when the biological information is shunted into a health model of norms and deviances.

Ironically, both the contraceptive revolution and the medicalization of sexuality have only reinforced a limited script for heterosexual sexual life – arousal, intercourse, performance, false universals, technical focus, mind–body dualism. We must look outside medicine if we want more than the rhetoric of sexual health.

NOTES

1. Leonore Tiefer (1995) *Sex is Not a Natural Act and Other Essays* (Oxford: Westview Press).
2. Will Wright (1982/1994) *The Social Logic of Health* (Hanover, New Hampshire: Wesleyan University Press).
3. It is, of course, only a matter of time before an oral medication is developed which can safely create a temporary erection, whereupon men will be able to treat themselves completely covertly.

9 'Yes, But Does it *Work?*' Impediments to Rigorous Evaluations of Gay Men's Health Promotion

Graham Hart

INTRODUCTION

We are in what has been called 'the second decade' of AIDS (Aggleton, Davies and Hart, 1993). Yet gay men, in whom the disease was first described, and amongst whom AIDS has taken a disproportionately heavy toll, are still becoming infected with HIV. How can we be in a situation in which 'everybody' knows how HIV is transmitted and how to avoid it, and yet there are still many hundreds of men in Britain, and many thousands in the United States, becoming newly infected in the 1990s? My view is that we are still uncertain as to how to prevent infection in gay men – the group recognized to be the longest affected by the disease – and that not enough is being done to remedy this situation.

It has generally been assumed that in the prevention field there has been a substantial amount of work specifically targeted at gay men, an impression that was corrected by an exhaustive survey of local authority provision (King et al., 1992). This identified only a tiny minority of health authorities providing or otherwise support-ing HIV-related work for gay men, despite a having a clear remit from the Department of Health to do so. Although the current situation has seen some improvement in terms of the number and range of interventions, a further problem is that remarkably little systematic evaluation of effectiveness – measured in terms of reduc-tions in unsafe sex, improved sexual health or incidence of HIV infection – has taken place (Holland et al., 1994). What we have instead is basic monitoring or process evaluations, many of which are predominantly concerned to provide descriptive data on the introduction and operationalization of projects, rather than their effectiveness in terms of the key outcomes of behavioural change and the adoption of safer sex (Prout and Deverell, 1995).

It is in this context that prevention of HIV infection in gay men, which has been vital since the outset of the epidemic, takes on ever greater significance in the United Kingdom, and in the developed world generally. What health education we have had, whether from non-statutory or statutory agencies, has been predominantly individually focused, the emphasis being on information-giving approaches, with occasional acknowledgement of the value of self-empowerment (Aggleton, 1989). While leaflets, written information and direct education have undoubtedly played a major role in increasing levels of knowledge about HIV, its transmission and the means by which to protect oneself ('safer sex'), there is little evidence to suggest a direct relationship between the provision of such information and either individual or population-based behaviour change (AIDS Strategic Monitor, 1991; AIDS Strategic Monitor – Gay Bars, 1991). Indeed, it may be that the primary reasons for the move towards safer sex in gay men lie elsewhere, with information provision a necessary but not sufficient requirement for behaviour change.

Related to this, it should be noted that absent from the practice and research literatures until relatively recently have been accounts of community-oriented models of HIV prevention. That is, prevention that depends upon the organized and deliberate harnessing of social networks to establish group norms and collective action to promote safer sex. The evident limitations of individual-based practice and research paradigms mean that community-oriented approaches are currently viewed very optimistically in terms of their potential to deliver the health dividend of protection against HIV infection. This perspective has come from community-based groups, gay men and their allies in health promotion and researchers with an interest in developing and evaluating different approaches to HIV prevention.

This is a key point. What we need to do is to establish whether such approaches actually work – can they finally deliver the outcome we seek of a reduced incidence of HIV infection in gay men? Also, do such approaches work when most unsafe sex occurs within the context of regular relationships? Are community-based interventions suited to this situation? What obstacles are there to the successful implementation of such programmes? This chapter seeks to outline a research and intervention strategy which could take us further forward in developing culturally appropriate prevention programmes for the group that continues to be most affected by AIDS. It begins with the current context of HIV/AIDS in the United Kingdom, which underlines the case for the provision of targeted prevention programmes for gay men.

BACKGROUND

The widespread adoption of safer sex on the part of gay men is one of the most remarkable achievements in terms of community-level health behaviour change ever recorded. Indeed, it is now well established from studies of gay and bisexual men in the United States, Europe and Australia that in the mid–late 1980s there was a major move towards the adoption of 'safer sex' in this population (Hart, 1989), and many thousands of men have been spared HIV infection as a consequence of the magnitude of this revolution in sexual expression. However, while the trend towards safer sex may apply on a population basis, unsafe sex remains a significant pro-blem. Early in the 1990s there was an increase in the incidence of rectal gonorrhoea (taken as a proxy marker of unsafe sexual beha-viour) in gay men in London (Singaratnam et al., 1991), a relatively high prevalence of HIV-1 infections in young gay men (Evans et al., 1993), and a continuing high prevalence of infection in gay and bisexual men in England (Hart et al., 1993). In London the esti-mated incidence of seroconversion in a cohort of 532 men who had repeat tests between 1988 and 1990 was 4.6 per 100 person years, with a higher incidence in younger gay men (Waight and Miller, 1991). A reported seroprevalence rate of 6–8 per cent in young homosexual men under 25 years of age attending GUM clinics suggests that new infections are occurring early in the sexual his-tories of gay men (Public Health Laboratory Service and Colla-borators, 1993).

It is also evident from the Day Report (Communicable Disease Report, 1993) that the epidemics of HIV infection and AIDS in the United Kingdom are set to continue, rising to an estimated annual incidence of 1505 AIDS cases by 1997 in men for whom transmis-sion occurred through homosexual intercourse. This figure is based on estimates of the number of men who are currently infected with HIV who will go on to develop AIDS-defined disease. The back projections for HIV incidence are approximately 500 per annum between 1986 and 1991. There is clearly a pressing need for effective prevention measures to reduce the incidence of new infections in gay men, with effectiveness measured by thorough evaluation, as well as basic research to understand better the current dynamics of the HIV epidemic. In the following section, community-oriented programmes that have been undertaken in the United States will be described, as this is where these approaches have been most thoroughly evaluated and tested.

COMMUNITY-ORIENTED INITIATIVES IN THE UNITED STATES

In the United States there have been the most systematic attempts both to initiate and research community-oriented approaches to HIV prevention among gay men. Two interventions in particular have generated a great deal of interest and are worth describing in some detail. They were described at the VIIIth International Conference on AIDS in Amsterdam, and subsequently at the IXth Conference in Berlin. The first is the Men's Network, a community-level approach for young (18–28 years) gay men, in California. It is taking place in three medium-sized cities sequentially; outcome data for one city were made available in Amsterdam (Kegeles et al., 1992).

The 'network' of the title is made up of young gay men recruited from each of the cities, and the entire enterprise is peer-run and the programme peer-designed. Support is provided through the research budget for advertising materials and for the events that the men organize. The network is intended to be a dynamic body, with a turnover of members as people leave and new men are recruited. The programme itself consisted of peer outreach, which included formal presentations in bars and at community events such as beach parties and discos, and by members of the network making informal contacts in popular cruising areas. Safer sex workshops were also organized.

Baseline data were collected six months before and then again immediately prior to the intervention, followed by questionnaires distributed immediately post-intervention, then six months and one year later. Preliminary findings were able to compare men 'highly exposed' (that is, who had participated in two more events, were themselves network members or had attended workshops) and those 'not highly exposed'. The researchers found that there was a population-based increase in norms supporting safe sex, an increase in reported discussion with friends and more communication with sexual partners about safer sex; all of these were higher in the most exposed group. Reported enjoyment of unprotected sex fell in the highly exposed as compared to the less exposed group.

When first described this research was at an early stage of development, but findings were promising. In particular, a major aim of the project was that it became self-perpetuating, through the constant turnover of members of the network and through the range of contacts made by the men *en masse* and individually. At the Berlin Conference Tom Coates, one of the researchers involved in the project, discussed it informally in a round table (Coates, 1993). He noted that while events such as the parties and discos had proved very popular, and were associated with increased reporting of safer sex in the target population, safer sex workshops tended to attract only those men who were already committed to safer sex and who were at least risk in the community. He favourably contrasted the effectiveness of peer-led initiatives such as the three-city study to one-off counselling in relation to safer sex, which has not been demonstrated to achieve long-term behaviour change or maintenance of safer sex (Higgins et al., 1991).

The second intervention, and one of the most impressive for gay men, was first described by Kelly et al. (1991), also in relation to three cities, but by the time of the Amsterdam Conference the programme had been extended to eight small cities in four states (Kelly et al., 1992), and by the Berlin Conference to 16 cities (Kelly et al., 1993). Cities were selected according to three criteria: they had a population of less than 250 000, were located at least 60 miles from any other city of the same or larger size, and each had a relatively discrete and identifiable gay male population, with between one and three well-used gay bars. Eight of the cities were randomly designated as intervention centres, and eight as comparators. In the comparison (control) cities high quality AIDS education materials were introduced to and maintained in all of the gay bars throughout the period of the research, with materials changed every three months to maintain novelty. In the intervention cities a social norm/peer influence intervention was introduced. The conceptual model used was that of 'diffusion of innovation' (Rogers, 1983). This suggests that social norms – in this case in favour of safer sex – can be successfully introduced and diffused through a community when modelled, endorsed and communicated by popular opinion leaders or trend-setters.

Baseline sexual behaviour measures were taken of men attending the bars in each of the cities. In the intervention cities bartenders were asked to identify gay men who were regular attenders at the bars and were, in the opinion of the bartenders, well-known, liked and respected by other men. These 'popular' men were approached by the researchers and recruited to a two-month training course on the transmission characteristics of HIV, safer sex behaviours and conversational means of introducing topics such as sexual risk reduction. They then were asked to engage in conversations with at least 14 different men attending bars, and others at private parties and elsewhere, over a five-week period, saying that they fully endorsed and had personally committed themselves to the practice and philosophy of safer sex.

After three, six and nine months of study repeat surveys were undertaken of men attending the bars in all cities. In the cities receiving the experimental intervention, there were systematic reductions in population-based risk behaviour, with decreases from baseline measures of 20–5 per cent in the proportion of men reporting high-risk sex, and corresponding reductions in the reported frequency of such behaviour. These data excluded the opinion leaders from analysis (around 10 per cent of the study populations) to determine the full effect on the target population. In the Berlin presentation the authors were able to show that this effect had been maintained over time, and further analysis demonstrated a dose-response, notably that men who attended the bars more often or participated in more conversations had greater reductions in risk behaviour than those less exposed to the conversations (Kelly et al., 1993). In the comparison (non-intervention cities) no significant risk reduction was found.

OBSTACLES TO COMMUNITY-BASED INTERVENTIONS

Despite a lot of interest in this kind of approach to prevention of HIV, and a recent flurry of activity in the United Kingdom in relation to peer-led initiatives, in both practice and research terms these have often been ill considered. I believe that there are three sets of obstacles to the introduction of community-based interventions. These are practical, structural and attitudinal. There is great overlap between these three areas, but they are distinguished here for ease of discussion.

Practical obstacles

Jeffrey Kelly's work was primarily oriented to men in bars having casual partners. One of the most striking and consistent findings of behavioural research on gay men is that high-risk sex is more frequently reported with someone described as a 'regular' partner or lover (Hart et al., 1993; Davies et al., 1993). In a study of 677 gay men, we found that the main difference between regular and non-regular relationships was the degree of emotional involvement the respondents reported (McLean et al., 1994). Three-quarters of the men were in love with their regular partner and two-thirds were committed to the relationship continuing indefinitely. By contrast, very few men reported emotional involvement in non-regular partners; unprotected intercourse in the context of a regular relationship was described as a way of expressing the love and commitment to a shared life that the men felt.

The study clearly demonstrated the significance of the affective context of the sexual encounter itself. However, what it also raises is a problem in relation to the use of community-oriented interventions, the main aim of which has been to reduce the incidence of uprotected sex with casual partners. Couples may or may not go to gay bars, and if faced by a peer educator who proselytizes about the necessity for condom use/safer sex, may be significantly more immune to these messages because of the overwhelming consideration of their relationship dynamics to consider. Men in relationships require a rather different and quite specifically targeted strategy if they are having unprotected sex in a relationship where serostatus is unknown or discordant.

Another, more research-related point relates to the issue of geographical propinquity. In order to determine whether there was any 'real' effect of the intervention, Kelly et al. put a limit on the size of the populations he investigated (cities of approximately 250 000 residents), with no more than two or three gay bars and, most importantly, that they should be at least 60 miles from any large cities. This was to reduce the possibility of what could be called contamination – that is, the confounding effects of easy movement of gay men between centres where the intervention was taking place, and large cities over which the researchers had no control.

It is possible in the United States to impose such 'restrictions' on interventions, but very difficult in the United Kingdom to achieve this degree of spatial and population segregation. Many cities that would fit two criteria (e.g. size, number of bars) are so close to other, larger cities with a thriving gay scene that it would be impossible to control for movement between centres. One of the assumptions of Kelly et al.'s work was that they would have essentially stable and relatively immobile populations of gay men. In the United Kingdom this would exclude towns like Blackpool or Brighton, which have thriving gay scenes, relying in the main on a resident population, but with massive influxes, particularly at weekends, of gay visitors from other parts of the country. This renders difficult the problem of replicating Kelly et al.'s work in the United Kingdom.

Finally, in terms of practical problems, there is the consideration of support for peer-leaders. There is a belief, which is not supported by evidence but certainly must influence the current popularity of this approach, that peer-led interventions are cheap. By using unpaid volunteers, keen to give something back to the gay community, this strongly recommends the approach to purchasers. Yet volunteers must be actively supported, supervised and monitored by paid staff if their work is to achieve and maintain a standard necessary to deliver positive health messages to others in the community. In my experience, the detailed and systematic training of volunteers along the lines described by Kelly et al. is the exception rather than the rule. Most frequently volunteers may have a day of training, with some support provided for them 'in the field', and at best there is some self-monitoring of numbers of client contacts. It may be the case that health messages, condoms and lubricant, and leaflets are being delivered by gay men to others, but it is far from clear that this has the desired outcomes in the same terms as Kelly's work, i.e. of reductions in unsafe sex.

Structural obstacles

If there are practical problems to the implementation of community-based approaches, then this in part is explained by the role of structural obstacles. One problem has been that, until recently, and only after a review commissioned jointly by the Medical Research Council and Health Education Authority (Oakley et al., 1994), there has been little funding available for any type of rigorous evaluation of community-based approaches. District and Regional Health Authorities have had relatively modest research budgets, and certainly insufficient to undertake large, randomized controlled trials of the effectiveness of one intervention over another, or over non-intervention. Indeed, the level of funding available for any prevention work on a local basis is extremely limited, rendering it even more difficult to make the case in favour of evaluations. Although it has been argued that process and other evaluations cannot determine whether an intervention is truly effective and indeed that, if one seeks answers to questions regarding changes in sexual behaviour and other HIV-related outcomes, money spent on such approaches is wasted, relatively speaking it is cheaper to fund such research than larger-scale projects.

To a great extent it is the person/institution who 'pays the piper' in research that has the power to determine the nature of the research undertaken. A second structural issue relates not simply to the total funds available, but the preferences of service providers. Even in a health service where there is a division between providers and purchasers, and it is in the interests of providers to prove that a particular treatment or intervention has the desired outcome, and in the interests of purchasers to buy health promotion which is of proven efficacy, there is often an absence of research expertise within Districts and sometimes Regions. This means that those who fund research have either not undertaken this kind of work themselves and are unaware of what is possible, or accept the advice of those intimately involved with research, which in itself may be flawed or, at the very least, limited in the range of research expertise and therefore possible approaches to evaluation (see below).

To be fair to the researchers who are involved in bidding for monies, another structural point relates to the pressure on researchers, through the Universities and the Research Assessment Exercise, to generate research funds and publications. As a result, unscrupulous (or simply naive) academics may suggest that their study will provide answers to questions of efficacy, and health authorities without access to systematic or academic peer-review may accept such claims and fund applications for flawed (in terms of behavioural outcomes) research. That this is an evident waste of public funds is often hidden by research reports which detail the difficulties of accessing and delivering such information, and/or provide good quality data on the practicalities and service (rather than strictly client) consequences of setting up prevention programmes. That they do not answer the questions they were commissioned to address is hidden by a conspiracy of silent goodwill involving all concerned – research commissioners to their researchers and vice versa. Unfortunately, the population of gay men may continue to be at risk because, while the intervention may or may not have been successful, we will never know, and other service providers cannot replicate it with any confidence that they are delivering a good prevention programme.

A fourth point relates to the training, experience and preferred methodological approaches of the social scientists who are currently most involved with health evaluations. Although the funding situation has been one where relatively small grants have been available – militating against large or long-term studies – this has suited many in the field of health service evaluation very well. There is a preference for small-scale, qualitative and process evaluations which reflects the micro-sociological interests of many of those engaged in this research. The quantitative elements of much of the health services research that is undertaken tends to be limited to needs assessments, monitoring of the characteristics of service users or descriptive social epidemiology, providing information on demographic and behavioural attributes of the populations under study. While this research is vital, and to be encouraged – indeed, without this it is impossible to undertake any thorough investigation of outcomes – it is not designed nor is it appropriate to deliver the information we require on the efficacy of particular interventions in effecting behavioural change.

The 'any treatment is good treatment' fallacy

It is often the case that those in health promotion, gay men and their allies, keen to act in the face of the situation described earlier of continuing HIV infection in the gay community, will sanction any intervention which they believe has the promise of effectiveness. That is, there is an understandable impetus to act, 'to do *something*', because of the terrible consequences for large numbers of gay men of inaction. For example, the current interest in community-based, peer-led approaches to intervention has led to a burgeoning of such initiatives.

Yet none of the research reporting on peer-led and community-based programmes identified by Holland et al. (1994) provides outcome measures such as increased condom use, reduced levels of unprotected intercourse, and reductions in sexually transmitted diseases, including HIV. The assumption is that *ipso facto* if the work is being undertaken, it must be producing positive benefits. The possibility that there are no benefits from such approaches – other than to the volunteers, because they feel good to be serving the gay community – or that actual harm might derive from their actions is simply not considered. In medicine, if a particular technique, treatment or drug dosage were proved to work, subject to it being applied according to the precise regimen used in the initial trial (or some modification thereof that had been thoroughly tested) and was then applied to a large population, but with individual doctors delivering their own preferred variation, there would be an outcry that the evidence-based treatment was being ignored. Yet this is arguably the situation in which we find ourselves because of the fallacy that 'any intervention must be better than nothing'. This fallacy dominates most health promotion, including that for gay men.

As suggested earlier, we are in a situation in which there continues to be an unacceptably high level of continued HIV infection in gay men, and it would be morally indefensible to withdraw all current interventions simply because they had not been subject to rigorous evaluation. This is because it is likely that some, and possibly many, of these interventions *are* successful and achieve the desired goal of protecting gay men and their sexual partners. The most that we can expect at the moment is a body of circumstantial evidence that such interventions do not result in any harm. There may be good information on contact efficacy (number of men contacted, and accepting condoms), and this may also have to suffice in certain circumstances. However, this is not an argument for the situation to remain this way, and it then becomes necessary to defend the use of unproven approaches. Unless one has a firm basis, through evidence which is agreed by all to be persuasive, most researchers and practitioners should have equipoise with regard to unevaluated interventions, i.e. true uncertainty that one approach is better than another, and therefore candidates for testing. Without this we simply act on faith, and this would seem to be an inadequate basis for attempting to prevent people being exposed to a life-threatening disease.

There is another, related argument for not withdrawing current provision. The very provision of financial support for safer sex campaigns for gay men indicates a commitment of health authorities to this community and, when well done, can positively demonstrate an anti-homophobic stance. The act of being non-judgemental in relation to same-sex behaviours, and of being sex-positive, accords to safer sex a privileged place as the right thing to do for gay men. However, such a positive stance cannot, in the long term, excuse bad interventions with poor or negative outcomes. When there are limits on funds and skilled personnel, we have a duty to ensure that these are used in the best possible way to realize the goals of preventing further infection and keeping as healthy as possible those who are living with HIV and AIDS.

CONCLUSION

Despite all this, we remain in a situation where it is necessary still to argue for and justify any targeted interventions, and not only those that are evidence based (Des Jarlais et al., 1994). If even the activity of delivering prevention services is threatened, then this offers little hope of improvement upon current provision. Yet if we had a body of literature that was persuasive in demonstrating the efficacy of particular approaches, the political battle for continued and indeed increased funding would have a firmer base in evidence. This is not a call for an end to basic research, including descriptive studies and process evaluations, as without these it is simply not possible to progress to experimental designs such as randomized controlled trials. It is rather a plea for a coalition of interests – gay men and their allies in health promotion, research funders, service providers and active researchers – to combine to deliver the health dividend that should be expected and demanded from health promotion. This is a positive improvement in gay men's sexual health in general, and a measurable reduction in the incidence of HIV infection in particular.

10 Trust as Risky Practice
Carla Willig

TRUST AS A DESIRABLE ATTRIBUTE

The psychological literature on trust is characterized by the assumption that trust is a good thing. Papers typically begin with a declaration of its desirability. Rempel, Holmes and Zanna (1985, p. 95) claim that 'trust is certainly one of the most desired qualities in any close relationship'. Such positive characterizations are no mere assertions. Numerous studies have investigated the correlates of high levels of trust in individuals and have consistently found them to be positive. Rotter, reviewing the literature on the correlates of interpersonal trust, concludes by painting an overwhelmingly positive picture of high trusters. Such individuals are:

> less likely to lie and are possibly less likely to cheat or steal. They are more likely to give others a second chance and to respect the rights of others. The high truster is less likely to be unhappy, conflicted, or maladjusted, and is liked more and sought out as a friend more often...
>
> (Rotter, 1980, p. 1)

The literature review I conducted identified just two dissenting voices drawing attention to possible disadvantages of trust (Garske, 1975; Johnson-George and Swap, 1982). While acknowledging these rare exceptions, it can be concluded that a consensus within the psychological literature conceptualizing trust as desirable has been identified. This positive characterization is applied equally to the two major types of trust discussed in the literature: interpersonal (e.g. Rotter, 1971), referring to trust among social agents in general, and dyadic (e.g. Larzelere and Huston, 1980), describing trust within close relationships. The present chapter is concerned only with the latter. It aims to explore the role of trust in the negotiation of safer sex practices within intimate heterosexual relationships, and it questions the extent to which trust is necessarily a healthy and desirable attribute within this context.[1]

125

THE NEGATIVE ASPECT OF TRUST

Two recent sociological studies of young adults' accounts of condom use (Holland et al., 1991; Maticka-Tyndale, 1992) provide evidence to suggest that trust may not always have desirable consequences. Both studies employed semi-structured interviews in order to obtain accounts of young people's sexual activities and choices. Maticka-Tyndale's analysis of 25 interviews with Canadian college students identified a number of individual constructions of sexual risk and safety as well as factors influencing these. Prominent among the HIV protective strategies employed by the sample was the use of and reliance on trust. Young people who constructed sexual activity in the context of affection trusted their partners. For women, this meant trusting that one's partner would disclose relevant information and for men it meant trusting that one's partner had nothing to disclose. As a result, women found it very difficult to request condom use from partners whom they knew well, but ironically 'they were most able to protect themselves from all three dangers – pregnancy, disease and emotional hurt – in casual sexual encounters' (ibid., p. 247).

In a similar vein, Holland et al. (1991) propose that trust becomes a significant aspect of sexual decision-making within the context of steady relationships. They found that among the young inner-city women they interviewed, there was a strong shared understanding that 'steady' relationships are based on trust. At the same time they identified a tendency to define a relationship as 'steady' in order to justify sex. Since discontinuation of condom use can signify increasing commitment to a relationship, condom use within 'steady' relationships is difficult to maintain. Holland et al. call for further exploration of this area in order to clarify the relations between risk and trust in long-term relationships (1991, p. 141). They provocatively conclude that 'If love is assumed to be the greatest prophylactic, then trust comes a close second' (ibid., p. 140).

Method

A series of semi-structured interviews with 16 individuals was carried out. The sample was drawn from a large employer in the South-East of England and it included equal numbers of males and females, covering a wide age-range (22–56 years). Respondents were interviewed individually, at a place of their choice and each interview lasted approximately 1 hour. The interview agenda included questions about the nature of HIV disease, its social and political implications as well as respondents' personal views about HIV and AIDS. All interviews were audio-taped and transcribed. False names are used throughout in order to protect respondents' anonymity.

The analysis of the transcripts was guided by Parker's (1992) guide to discourse analysis.

Results

The widely used discourse identified by the analysis can be described as marital discourse. This discourse constructs marriage (and its equivalent, the 'long-term relationship') as incompatible with condom use, and it employs three major categories in order to achieve this discursive objective: safety, trust and possible marital failure. Another paper has traced the ways in which these major elements of marital discourse are constituted (Willig, 1995). In this chapter, one of the dimensions, trust, will be examined in detail by exploring its construction within the context of talk about condom use.

TRUST-AS-SECURITY, TRUST-AS-SYMBOLIC-PRACTICE AND TRUST-AS-SOCIAL-REGULATION

Three distinct constructions of trust were identified. The first one, Trust-As-Security, reflects common-sense as well as psychological theories' understandings of trust. Here, it is suggested that the existing large amounts of trust within a relationship make the use of a condom unnecessary, as is illustrated by the following quotation:

C.W.: And did you ever have an affair where you didn't use a condom?
Tina: Only with Reg and I trust him.

Here, references to trust function as a warrant. They are used in order to justify and legitimate unsafe sex within a particular relationship.

However, a much more frequently deployed construction of trust stresses the symbolic nature of trusting behaviour. It is suggested that the request to use a condom would undermine trust and thus threaten the relationship. Here trust does not provide security; instead, trust must be communicated to one's partner through particular symbolic practices including unsafe sex. This construction is illustrated by the following quotation:

C.W.: ...everybody should assume that the partner is a risk and therefore everybody should use condoms even married couples who have been married for 50 years or so. What do you think about that? Do you think it is true or is it going too far?

Sam: Well, I think it's going too far personally, um...as far as I'm concerned, I, my wife and myself...we still have a very happy, um, satisfying relationship, um, but it wouldn't do that relationship any good at all if some sort of doubt was injected into it by suggesting that possibly one of us could be having an affair and to be absolutely certain we must use a condom. That would be disastrous for our marriage.

The two constructions outlined, however, are by no means mutually exclusive. Respondents deployed both constructions at different times and within different discursive contexts. Indeed, in one case both constructions were combined in one and the same response to the question about condom use for a couple who have been married for 50 years:

Ian: Oh well, I think that's pretty extreme...I am perfectly certain that she is faithful to me as I know I'm faithful to her, so I see no need whatever.

C.W.: Mmh. So you think there are people who can be sure that they're not at risk because they trust the other person enough to

Ian: | Yeah, it's a matter of trust and I think if I were to start wearing a condom, it would be a signal that I don't trust her and it would be a very hurtful thing to do.

The first part of Ian's response makes use of the 'Trust-As-Security' construction: there is 'no need' for condoms since there is complete confidence in the partner's faithfulness. Here, extreme case formulations are deployed ('I am *perfectly* certain' and 'no need *whatever*') in order to emphasize the unquestionableness of the assertions. Potter and Wetherell (1987) draw attention to the persuasive orientation of extreme case formulations (Pomerantz, 1986) which provide an effective warrant by taking their assertions to their extreme limits. However, when the interviewer introduces the notion of 'trust' as the basis for such sexual confidence ('...people can be *sure...because* they *trust...*'), thus challenging Ian's claim to absolute certainty, he deploys the construction of Trust-As-Symbolic-Practice: wearing a condom would be 'a signal that I don't trust her'. In this way, he is able to provide an alternative justification for not using condoms. This excerpt shows that respondents have access to both constructions of trust; as discursive frames shift and different rhetorical moves are required, alternative constructions are introduced.

CASUALTIES OF TRUST-AS-SYMBOLIC-PRACTICE

One consequence of adopting the latter construction of trust ('Trust-As-Symbolic-Practice') was an acceptance of the inevitability of casualties. Respondents acknowledged that trusting behaviour was not without risk. Casualties of misplaced trust were typically referred to as 'innocent victims', and their existence was seen as an inevitable by-product of the practice of trust. For example, Hanna describes 'the wife of a man who contracted AIDS and passed it on to [the wife]' as a typical 'innocent victim' because 'she is unaware of the risk she is taking'. When asked the question about condom use for longstanding couples Hanna responded:

Hanna: No, that would be terrible because of lack of trust.
C.W.: So, there would have to be some innocent victims?
Hanna: Yeah, I think that's right.

Ian, too, suggested that sexual partners must put themselves at risk in the interest of Trust-As-Symbolic-Practice and that this will inevitably generate 'innocent victims':

Ian: Somebody who marries, for example, and trusts their partner but their partner is HIV-positive and hasn't told them, then they're an innocent victim, too, because again, relationships are built on trust and maybe they asked their partner as it would be indeed prudent to do. If their partner said no, I'm clear, then they would have to believe it.

Ian spells out the imperative of the symbolic practice of trust: they would *have* to believe it.' In other words, in order to maintain the principle that relationships are based on trust, participants in relationships must act in accordance with this dictum even if this generates a personal risk.

John goes further and provides an emphatic account of the necessity of trust as social regulation:

John: Ah [sighs], I mean where are we without trust for goodness' sake? I mean we really are down the tubes if we can't trust anybody, aren't we? I mean there's got to be some sort of element of trust somewhere, unless life as we know it ain't gonna happen. Um, now that ah good grief, that's a dreadful thought, life without trust, hm, no, I don't agree with the couple that have been married 50 years [should use condoms].

John employs apocalyptic terms ('really are down the tubes'; 'life as we know it ain't gonna happen'; 'dreadful thought') in order to emphasize the urgency of the requirement. Trust is constructed as a vital necessity for the functioning of 'life as we know it'. John's plea for the maintenance of trust as social regulation has a desperate quality. Preceded by a deep sigh, it evokes the spectre of life deprived of one of its essential qualities ('life without trust, hm, no'). Such an urgent and dramatic plea is very effective in setting the scene for a subsequent sanction of the price to be paid for trust as a social practice. Having constructed life without trust as barely worth living, John goes on to acknowledge the inevitability of a certain number of casualties of trust:

John: I think there is a certain population who will get it through no fault of their own and, through deceit, you know, their partner is not telling them.

TRUST-AS-SILENCE

Another way in which Trust-As-Symbolic-Practice may increase respondents' vulnerability to HIV infection is through the way in which it structures couples' communication. For many respondents, the maintenance of trust within their relationships required strict censorship over what was communicated to the partner. Sue provides a very clear account of the limitations that Trust-As-Symbolic-Practice places upon marital communication. She explains that her husband's last extramarital affair, three or four years ago, caused a 'big, big shake-up in our life' leading to the decision to have a child. Sue and her partner did not talk about the risk of HIV infection ('And I didn't actually say anything to him about it, neither of us ever, ever talked about this in terms of ourselves'), but Sue read her husband's preparedness to conceive with her as evidence of his HIV negativity:

Sue: I felt pretty sure that if he felt there was any sort of danger, then he wouldn't have attempted to conceive with me ...

Here, preparedness to conceive becomes a symbolic act signifying sexual safety, among other things. In the same way, Sue's current reluctance to request condom use is explained with reference to such a request's symbolic meanings:

Sue: And since that time, I haven't wanted to rock the boat and it's the same reasons why now I couldn't go to him and say, why don't we wear condoms forever and ever?

Also note the extreme case formulation ('forever and ever') used here in order to underline the unreasonableness of the request for condom use within her marriage. Finally, Sue makes explicit the close link between the maintenance of trust and the limitations this places upon verbal and behavioural practices:

Sue: ... after some difficulties we have built up a very considerable degree of trust in each other, and I wouldn't want to do anything that would start to remove that.

Talking about sexual safety is an example of such limitations. As we have seen, respondents assume that within a trusting relationship talk about condom use is either unnecessary ('Trust-As-Security') or inappropriate ('Trust-As-Symbolic-Practice'), or both. Consequently, when such talk does take place, it is read as a sign of relationship change:

Jane: At the moment I feel like the future is pretty safe. How long have we been married? What, six months, so everything is sort of rosy and everything, I dunno, um, I think if things started to change we'd probably have to do some talking.

Here, talking about sexual safety is associated with the emergence of problems in a previously perfect ('rosy') relationship.

Hence, raising the subject functions as a signifier of such a development.

TRUST AS WRONG IN ONE WAY BUT RIGHT IN ANOTHER

Respondents frequently acknowledged the negative side of trust by way of disclaimers. A disclaimer, defined by Hewitt and Stokes (1975) as a verbal device which is used to ward off potentially negative attributions, functions by acknowledging a possible interpretation in order to reject it more effectively. For example, when asked whether she felt that her 21-year-old daughter could ever be justified in trusting a new partner to be sexually safe, Jill responds:

Jill:　Difficult. Yeah, that's, that's difficult to answer, um, I think I would rely on trust, but that might be the wrong thing to do, but that would probably be my feelings.

Similarly, when asked whether 'everybody should use condoms' Sue replied:

Sue:　I suppose that would be the most sensible way for us all to behave. I certainly would actually find it rather difficult to do that myself.

In both cases respondents construct trusting behaviour as not justified by rational considerations ('the wrong thing to do'; not 'the most sensible way to behave') and yet as their preferred choice. This strategy takes trusting behaviour out of the category of rational behaviours and into a separate realm. This is the realm of feelings and intuition: Jill's 'feelings' would tell her to rely on trust, and Sue would find the 'sensible way to behave difficult'. Respondents have constructed two mutually exclusive categories of behaviours: rational and non-rational. As a result, trusting behaviour cannot be judged against rational standards. In this way respondents achieve a positioning which makes their behavioural choices unchallengeable on rational grounds.

DISCUSSION

Discourse analysis of 16 interviews with heterosexual adults on the topic of condom use identified three major constructions of trust:

Trust-As-Security, Trust-As-Symbolic-Practice and Trust-As-Social-Regulation. Respondents instantiated these constructions within different discursive contexts. This resulted in a number of distinct positionings for respondents. However, all of these were characterized by risk-taking. Trust-As-Security positioned respondents outside the problem of HIV vulnerability. Respondents argued that they were safe *because* they trusted their partner. One married female respondent's reply to a question about the risks of HIV infection was 'it just doesn't apply'. Trust-As-Symbolic-Practice positioned respondents differently. Here, respondents acknowledged deliberate risk-taking in the interest of relationship maintenance. Such risk-taking included communicating commitment through unsafe sex as well as limiting verbal communication about sexual matters. Trust-As-Social-Regulation positioned respondents as taking risks in the interest of a greater social good, namely the maintenance of trust among individuals within society. Finally, a construction of trust as non-rational behaviour positioned respondents as unassailable, at least from within rationalist discourses. To summarize, it has been shown that discursive constructions of trust can facilitate or even necessitate sexual practices which increase respondents' sexual risk-taking and which undermine adherence to safer sex guidelines.[2]

It is clear that trust does not function as a cognitive entity whose presence (or absence) informs talk and action, as suggested by the psychological theories (a), but rather as something which is constructed out of talk and action (b):

  (a)   High levels of trust $\rightarrow$ Trusting behaviour
  (b)   Symbolic practices $\rightarrow$ Constructions of trust

These two contrasting conceptualizations give rise to different expectations with regard to the relationship between trust and risk-taking. According to (a), the presence of high levels of trust is a precondition for trusting behaviour. Therefore, risk-taking increases only in proportion to increasing trust within a relationship. In this way, trust is seen to provide an effective safety-net for both partners. In contrast, (b) proposes that trust is constructed out of behavioural and linguistic practices, for particular purposes. As a result, risk-taking is seen as a symbolic practice which may signify 'trust'. In addition, trust can never be 'established' since it requires constant renegotiation within specific interactional contexts. In other words, trust must always be occasioned. It follows that trust does not necessarily reduce risk-taking and that it does not always improve the quality of intimate relationships.

Research discussed in this chapter has examined the downside of trust within the context of sexual risk-taking within intimate hetero-sexual relationships. Discursive constructions of trust and their consequences in the negotiation of other joint activities, such as needle-sharing or taking an HIV antibody test, remain to be explored. Jane Kennedy, midwife counsellor with the Guy's and St Thomas' Hospital Trust in London, cautions against a hasty decision to test for HIV antibodies during pregnancy because of the test's meanings: 'An HIV test may raise all sorts of issues, not least of all the trust in a relationship. Pregnancy is not a good time to challenge such trust' (Kennedy, 1995, p. 5). Here, Trust-As-Symbolic-Practice is evoked in order to question the desirability of HIV antibody testing in pregnant women. Further research into the ways in which 'doing trust' may increase risk or harm in intimate relationships is required.

In addition, a critical examination of public discourses and prac-tices of trust is needed. Symbolic exchange theorists (e.g. Haas and Deseran, 1981) have drawn attention to the role of symbolic goods in the negotiation of relationships. Food and drink, gifts or atten-dance at important ceremonies symbolize the nature of the relation-ship between the receiver and the giver of such goods. Engagement and wedding rings are obvious examples of such symbolic tokens. They signify a willingness to enter into a formalized love relation-ship and they communicate high levels of commitment to such a relationship. Within the marital discourse (Willig, 1995) love and trust are so closely associated that lack of trust has come to signify lack of love, as represented by the clichéd but nevertheless widely used plea: 'If you really love me, trust me!' Psychologists need to be aware of the shared meanings and significations of words and deeds in order to understand the ways in which they may facilitate or constrain individuals' behaviours. In turn, this will enable psycho-logists to challenge common-sense assumptions which may (mis)in-form policy decisions. For example, the assumption that a trusting relationship, by definition, facilitates communication has informed much sexual health promotion and family planning literature in the United Kingdom.

To conclude, in this chapter an analysis of interview transcripts was presented which challenges the assumption that trust is neces-sarily a healthy and desirable attribute of intimate relationships within the context of the negotiation of safer sex practices. A reconceptualization of trust as a situationally-specific, negotiated and purposeful social action facilitated an exploration of the rhetoric and practice of sexual risk-taking in heterosexual relationships. Three discursive constructions of trust were identified, all of which were deployed in order to warrant the practice of unprotected, penetrative sex. Further research into the ways of 'doing trust', both publicly and privately, is called for.

ACKNOWLEDGEMENT

I would like to thank Timothy Auburn and Lynne Segal for making helpful comments on an earlier draft of this paper.

NOTES

1 Even though HIV infection in Britain has not spread as quickly and as widely among heterosexuals as had been predicted in the late 1980s, there are several reasons for seeing unprotected penetrative sex among heterosexuals as inherently risky. First, a relatively low statistical probability of being infected with HIV through heterosexual sex does, of course, not actually protect any one individual against infection. Infection is 'all or none', i.e. it either happens or it doesn't. Second, recent evidence suggests that the low prevalence of HIV among Western heterosexuals may be due to the fact that the HIV strain prevalent in the West (HIV1-B) grows less effectively in oral and genital mucus (as opposed to the rectum) than strains prevalent in Thailand, where the vast majority of HIV infections are the consequence of heterosexual sex (Radford, 1996). Given the ability of the HIV virus to mutate, there is no reason for Westerns heterosexuals to be complacent about their risk of HIV infection in the future.

2 Respondents did not refer to the low statistical probability of becoming infected through heterosexual sex in order to warrant their sexual practices. In other words, respondents did not make an informed choice to take a (low) risk; rather they used discursive constructions of trust (and marriage, see Willig, 1995) in order to position themselves as sexually safe. This latter strategy is much less open to revision than one based on a rational risk appraisal would be, paticularly since it is likely to be grounded in wider ideologies (see Willig, 1994).

11 Therapy as Think Tank: From a Man's Internal Family to New Political Forms

Andrew Samuels

The roots of this chapter lie in a number of recent political developments with which I have been closely involved. I have carried out a number of consultations with politicians in Britain and the United States designed to explore how useful and effective perspectives derived from psychoanalysis might be in the formation of policy and in new thinking about the political process. It is difficult to present psychoanalytic thinking about politics so that mainline politicians – for example, a Democratic Senator or a Labour Party Committee – will take it seriously. I have found that issues of gender and sexuality are particularly effective in this regard. Partly this is due to the perennial fascination and excitement carried by such topics. Partly it is due to the feminist politicization of such issues over the past 30 years which has gradually led to their presence on the agenda of mainstream politics. Partly it is because gender is itself a hybrid notion from a political point of view. On one level, in the social world of lived experience, gender and sexuality are everyday realities, suffused with experiences of power, powerlessness, vulnerability and misunderstanding. Gender has its own socioeconomic dimensions and set of electoral significances. But, on another level, gender is also an exceedingly private business as part of a story that people tell themselves and have told to them in attempts to produce, create or discover identities and relationships with others. Gender and sexuality are therefore liminal, sitting on the threshold between internal and external worlds, contributing to and partaking of both.

I have also been involved in the formation of three organizations whose objectives are relevant to the content of this chapter. Psychotherapists and Counsellors for Social Responsibility is a professional organization, intended to facilitate the desire of many psychotherapists, analysts and counsellors to intervene as professionals in social and political matters making appropriate use of their knowledge and, it must be admitted, whatever cultural authority they possess. The second organization is a psychotherapy-based think tank, Antidote. Here, the strategy has been to limit the numbers of mental health professionals involved so as to reduce the chances of psychotherapy reductionism and foster multidisciplinary work in the social policy field. Antidote has undertaken research work in connection with psychological attitudes to money and economic issues generally, and is also involved in work in the area of 'emotional literacy', but expanding the usual remit from personal relationships and family matters to include issues in the public domain. The third organization is a broad front based at St James's Church in London. The St James's Alliance consists of individuals from diverse fields such as politics, economics, ethics, religion, non-governmental organizations, the media and psychotherapy. It attempts to incorporate ethical, spiritual and psychological concerns into the British political agenda and to facilitate a dialogue between non-governmental organizations, single-issue groups and progressive political organizations. It is an experiment in gathering in political energy that is split up and dissipated under current arrangements.

It will be thought that psychotherapists and analysts such as myself are making these moves from an on-high and detached position, careless of the political issues affecting our own profession. However, all three organizations have been active in and profoundly affected by the acrimonious yet relatively successful campaign waged by elements of the psychotherapy profession to end discrimination against lesbian and gay men candidates for training in psychoanalytic psychotherapy and psychoanalysis. When psychotherapists engage in politics they need to do so with a degree of consciousness over the appalling mess in which their own professional politics are usually to be found, as well as irony or even self-mockery over the counter-intuitive and slightly mad content of much of what they have to say.

Regarding a definition of politics, I have in mind an elastic one, ranging from conventional politics in Westminster or Washington terms, to political struggles for resources and power, to a feminist-inspired reading of politics: the personal as political, the hidden politics of family life and relationships, and the politics of representation, cultural imagery and information.

There are three sets of questions that I am going to address. First, where do new political ideas come from? How are they carried psychologically in culture? How do they spread? I am wondering if there is something to consider apart from the common-sense or obvious answers to those questions: that political ideas spread by word of mouth, by spawning organizations, by people's subversive reading of texts, and so forth. But is there something else, for example, the idea of a political *Zeitgeist*, a political spirit of the time, that a psychological approach can flesh out?

One of my tentative answers to the question about how political ideas spread involves our getting a grasp on unconscious fantasies of incestuous sexuality that drive the relationships of what I want to call a man's *internal* family (to underscore the fact that I am not proposing that society is the family writ large). These fantasies and relationships, and what we think about them, may help in specula- tion about how political ideas are generated, how they transmit in culture and, to borrow a phrase of Stuart Hall's, how they have been 'sleeping in the public language' (Hall, 1974, p. 85).

The second set of questions concerns the divides that have opened up in modern political discourse between ideology, the social context in which ideology is produced, the emotions that attach to ideology, personal experience of living in the *polis*, infor- mation about what is happening at a distance in society, and political organization. My introduction of the portmanteau term 'political form' is a modest attempt to evaluate whether or not it is possible to bridge these divides.

My third set of questions reflects my interest in discussing the possibility of there being a progressive social role for therapy and analysis as a sort of think tank. For me, this role for therapy would depend on there being a progressive challenge mounted *within* psychotherapy to many of the conventional viewpoints and con- sensuses that exist. I do not think one can just take an ordinary set of psychotherapy ideas (in this instance, about developmental psy- chology) and bang them into politics. One has initially to challenge the ideas that are current and common within psychotherapy, and then take the resultant mixture and move that in an indirect way into political discourse. There is no reason why this should be of any less 'practical' use than much of what constitutes contemporary sociology, political science or cultural studies in the academy. Per- haps the opposite is true if we see ourselves as, to some extent, held back from even partial fulfilment of political desires by restrictive and pessimistic self-conceptions and definitions of 'human nature'. While I am sure that there are psychological (and economic and social and political) delimiters and constraints on political performance, process and thinking, I am not at all sure what they are. I do not see the apparent congruence between conventional psychoanalytical developmental psychology and current, existing political forms as somehow 'proving' that these are the only political forms that could – or even should – exist.

To summarize: I intend to dispute current, conventional and (in my view) one-sided readings of inner and outer relationships in which men participate by virtue of incestuous sexual fantasy. I hope to explore the sources and vehicles of new political ideas, to work the gaps between ideology, experience and organization, and to reposition the therapy room as a think tank.

INCESTUOUS SEXUAL FANTASY AND NEW POLITICAL FORMS

Let me move on to the connections between incestuous sexual fantasy and politics. Among other differences of opinion and personality, Jung and Freud split over the question of whether incest fantasies should be understood literally. For Jung, the images and symbols of incest in an individual carry a cultural meaning that goes beyond the circumstances of that person.

We usually approach incest in terms of pair relationships despite the fact that family therapists have noted the existence of incestuous patterns, atmospheres and systems in families. But what holds these pairs together in a family? For Carl Jung, the answer to that question is 'kinship libido', which, to use his phrase, is like 'a sheepdog keeping the family intact' (Jung, 1946, p. 224). My further question concerns the role of kinship libido in society. Critically examined, can kinship libido be socialized, to be seen as that which holds social organisms and political forms together? If so, then different facets of kinship libido, different kinds of incestuous sexual fantasies, will be involved in the coming into being and the destruction of different kinds of political form. At just one point, Jung hinted that kinship libido helps to hold 'creeds, parties, nations or states together' (ibid., p. 233). Here we see an enormous difference from Freud who, broadly speaking, identifies the need to protect culture and civilization from the incestuous components of eros.

Jung is arguing that kinship libido is the sheepdog that keeps an entire society intact.

A radical re-reading of highly charged relationships in the family – sexually and politically charged relationships – can inspire new ideas about political forms, as well as helping us to analyse existing ones. Although psychology never wholly creates anything, I think it is usually implicated in politics at some level. To the extent that psychoanalytical psychology is built around sexuality and gender, those aspects of relations between persons in conventional and, in particular, unconventional families may be the most alive ways of factoring the psychological into political discourse.

So, what is a political form? I mean the existence of a unit of understanding and action within a society that combines the effects of ideology, narratives of emotional experience and ongoing organizational structure. I see such a form as having a purpose or a goal, and also as having a much less tangible, more hermeneutic function. I think we talk about such things all the time when we talk about what kind of organization an institution or even a country is. We talk about an institution that is not a prison as if it were a prison. We talk about an institution that is not a madhouse as if it were a madhouse. We refer to places of work sometimes as families. And occasionally the phrase 'den of iniquity' will be used to describe a dry-as-dust organization that could not be further from being a 'den of iniquity'. What are we doing when we characterize organizations in this way? I think what we are doing is coming very close to speaking a language of political forms. We have a gestaltic image of the political form: its appearance plus its character plus our evaluation of it all held together. The idea is to add something psychological to a materialist version of the social. Jacques Lacan may have had something similar in mind when, in the seminar of 21 January 1975, he displayed a concern for form: 'Good form and meaning are akin' (Lacan, 1975, pp. 162–71). Lacan goes on to cite Charles Sanders Peirce on 'firstness' – what it is that divides things and signifiers into different qualities.

There are many uses of the term 'form' in other disciplines. In biology, form means a variant type of life, something to do with the morphology, the shape, the bodily character of an organism. In philosophy the term form can mean the essential character of something. In social theory it means, loosely, organization.

There is something about social organisms that you cannot measure or assess accurately. The scientific fantasy breaks down.

You can't weigh a political form or describe political forms in minute, empirical detail. This is true of a factory, a university or an economic system.

Another feature of form is that the same elements can lead to different forms. We learn this from biology, chemistry and sociology. Now, if the same elements lead to different forms, isn't there something more than a material factor or set of factors to be considered? Political forms involve psychological fields which are based to a great extent on incestuous sexual fantasy and kinship libido. These psychological fields influence the creation, existence and, above all, the mutability of political forms. But it is still somewhat of a mystery how political forms come into being and change over time. There is no 'egg', there are no 'genes', in most visions of the social. But I think that there could be a place for a kind of 'social vitalism' based on psychoanalysis.

Vitalism holds that living organisms are organized by purposeful, mind-like principles. Teleology may be a dirty word these days, but even a materialist such as Richard Dawkins (1982) uses its close neighbour, teleonomy, to link his Darwinism and the notion of final causes or purposes. I would argue that there may be a purposive organizing principle in the social, which creates and destroys political forms, both ones that we approve of and ones that we disapprove of. If this principle is non-material in nature, then it can include human psychology.

Political forms are also concerned with the crucial role of inform-ation. As I see it, we are dealing with fields of political information that derive their psychological shape from their location in relation to unconscious fantasies of incestuous sexuality and how these are managed in culture.

EXPLANATORY NOTE

Up to now, I have been preparing the ground for an exploration of four relations in a man's internal family: son–father, brother–brother, brother–sister and son–mother. I shall follow the same pattern in connection with all four relationships. First, I shall summarize the conventional wisdom about the problems and pathologies analysts and therapists seem to associate with these relationships. Then I shall advance some different ideas intended to challenge the consensus. Finally, I shall show how this thinking helps us to analyse existing political forms, inspires us to work towards new ones and generally enhances our political self-awareness. There is a sense in which what looks like theory or even wishfulness is nothing more than description in words of what is already going on in many external as well as internal families, not to mention in many consulting rooms. In the human sciences, one often finds this state of affairs in which theory is truly an exposition of cutting-edge practices.

SON–FATHER

Scanning basic introductory texts in psychodynamics, psychotherapy and psychoanalysis, we see that the son–father relationship is said to involve castration, the question of the absent father, father as a role model for the son, father as a law-giver for the son, father as a moral presence, father as either successful or failing in separating the son from suffocating symbiosis with the mother.

I dispute this account, which tends to overlook the benevolent as opposed to the universally malevolent aspects of paternal sexuality. The notion of erotic playback between father and son (set out in Samuels, 1993, pp. 125–75) reframes their relationship in both bodily and political terms. Erotic playback takes place via a physically carried but symbolic communication, which contains elements of admiration and even longing and yearning by the father in relation to his son; this is empowering for the son, and leads to what I call homosociality. (This term, suggested to me by Sonu Shamdasani, is one that Eve Kosofsky Sedgwick (1985) uses in a different context.) Homosociality can be illustrated concretely by the way in which the gay community has responded to the challenge of HIV/AIDS, particularly at the time when HIV/AIDS was thought to be a problem exclusively for homosexuals. So homosociality is already involved in a reframing of what we want from contemporary political organizations. But I am not only thinking about loving cooperation between men of different generations. I am also thinking of homosociality as inspiring a convenant of mutual protection between father and son in which they agree to look after, take care of, speak for and protect the human rights of the other. However, in order for this convenant to come alive, father and son have to overcome the homosexual inhibition that our culture has placed so firmly at the heart of male identity.

Overcoming the homosexual inhibition moves us towards an apprehension of what male nurturing might look like and that itself would constitute an enormous challenge to most of the conventionally accepted ideas about the son–father relationship in psychoanalysis today. One aspect of this might involve what I call 'orientation melancholia'. This is a phenomenon I have met clinically in which a heterosexual becomes conscious of his depression over what he senses to be the lost opportunity of fulfilling his homosexual desires.

In a broadly similar way, the father's body is also a forum in which son and father work together on the transformation of aggression in its destructive and anti-social forms into a more socially creative kind of self-assertion. Aggression can never be eliminated as such, but the movements within aggressive process can be tracked.

As regards new political forms which might stem from the particular set of ideas that I've been putting forward and the challenge that they mount to conventional ideas, the most important locates cooperation as an element in political form, based on homosociality derived from erotic playback. Father–son cooperation based on a convenant forged in the heat of their bodily interaction and communication – hence involving incestuous sexual fantasy – I see as being primarily about cooperation and non-hierarchical relating *between* males rather than two males relating in tandem to an external object, such as football, or against a perceived threat, such as women. The move from boyhood to manhood involves more than an evolving recognition that one is not female.

One thing to note here is the absence, both in psychoanalysis and in culture, of a gay/straight dialogue about these things. Gay men know about the giving and receiving of bodily affirmation within an eroticized, loving context. Heterosexual men know less about it and here I think there is a very important political and psychological dialogue to consider.

Western societies have to engage with the whole question of valorizing homosexuality and homosociality (which does not mean idealizing homosexuality). It means making it more possible for heterosexuals to access the homosexual radical in themselves. I conduct workshops on new approaches to fathering, wherein everybody wants to be directly involved with children and to have a passionate, intense, responsible relationship with them. The biggest obstacle is that such aspirations bring up the fear of effeminacy. And effeminacy, in our world, brings up the spectre of homosexuality because male homosexuals are not proper men and hence must surely be women. And if male homosexuals are really women, then fear and loathing of femininity also kicks in. If new political forms are to come into being which could make use of the energies in new images of nurturing fathers, we shall have to come to grips with our enormous fear of softness, effeminacy and hence of homosexuality. Psychoanalysis needs to consider the prejudicial tendency in much of its theory to perceive male homosexuals as female- or mother-identified.

The male body has received political theorization mainly as a destructive presence in society. However, the supposed vulnerability of the male body, exemplified in current emphasis on men's health issues such as infertility and 'stress', may be one important plank in the construction of homosocial political forms. Male physical vulnerability is a form of male hysteria perhaps, less real than apparent, and mimetically linked to the roles of victim, underdog and abused one, imitative of women and children, in fact. It should not be allowed to obscure the sociopolitical realities of male power often mobilized in support of 'traditional' family roles, but, as Segal (1990) has shown, the very existence of a monolith 'men' is extremely dubious.

BROTHER–BROTHER

I shall move on now to discuss the second of the four relationships, which is the brother–brother relationship. The conventional depiction of the brother–brother relationship is extraordinarily pathological. Nobody denies that it is a very important relationship, referring to Cain and Abel or Jacob and Esau – but tending not to mention Moses and Aaron (who did Moses' talking for him). The general consensus seems to be that there is something a bit odd about too good a brotherly relationship. Fraternity seems very close to pathology in psychoanalysis, as far as I can see. Everybody seems to be on firmer ground when the brother–brother relationship can be stated to be about rivalry, or the brothers depicted as receiving very opposite parental projections – if one is made into the thinker, then the other will be made into the doer. There is even a strand of imagery in the literature that suggests that the collective psychoanalytic association to brotherhood is rather bestial: we hear about top dogs, bottom dogs and runts of litters. Finally, most texts on the brother relation do not stay with its particularity but move rapidly on to position the brothers in relation to the father (primal horde thinking).

My critique of this thinking is that psychoanalysis has pathologized away a necessary deep connection between men. This has been done by equating psychic growth and psychic health with absorption of the other, the opposite, the whole hetero thing. We need to discuss whether health, or maturity, or growth always has to be in relation to something that is 'other'. The notion that we develop solely or mainly by absorbing, or relating to, or getting into a 'marriage' with the other is something that we get from society and culture, but I think that analysts and therapists have also promoted it. This is the typical pattern in which analysts and therapists are both reflecting the prejudices of a culture and contributing to those prejudices. Hence, if psychic health and growth, and, therefore, social health and growth are predicated on absorption of the other, then the brother–brother relation and brotherliness are ruled out as sources of health, whether on the personal or the political levels.

Perhaps it is time to resurrect the notion of the soulmate, but within a male frame. I am thinking of the social referents of warmth and closeness between men, homosexual as well as homosocial. We can think of this in terms of the particular psychology of the double and not solely in son–father terms. The idea is that psychological and social growth also rests on an encounter with the double. One example from Sumerian myth is the relationship of Gilgamesh and Enkidu, who appear in each other's dreams and, in the narrative, swap roles, one being bloodthirsty and out of control and the other rational and a good general, and then vice versa. This kind of metaphorical *brotherliness* needs to be distinguished from *brotherhoods* – the locker room, old boys' network, Masons, Bröderbund, secret society. Those well-known, misogynistic bastions of male solidarity and power can be usefully understood as disavowals of, or flights from, the all-but-homosexual social and personal brotherly aspects of the brother pair. Brotherliness need not necessarily be anti-female. The role of the brother–brother relationship in male friendship patterns, and hence in political organization as a whole, is a topic about which very little has been written, although one meets numerous spontaneous references to David and Jonathan (who were *not* brothers). This contrasts with sisterliness and its role in female friendship and the sociopolitical organization of women.

Rethought in these ways, the brother–brother relationship may be seen as a template for a retheorizing of the anima. In Jungian psychology, the anima is the part of a man's psyche that connects him to his unconscious potential. Modern approaches to the anima see the female forms the anima takes as symbolizing what is 'other' to the man's consciousness (Samuels, 1989, pp. 92–106) rather than as indicating 'female' or 'feminine' characteristics. So it is altogether possible that a man's anima may appear to him (in projection) in the shape of another man and it is this possibility that I see as fuelled by my 'soulmate' reading of brotherliness (anima meaning soul). Apollo and Hermes are a further example: sibling gods who function as each other's anima. This is symbolized by the way they resolve their dispute over Hermes' theft of Apollo's cattle: an exchange of gifts whereby Hermes gives Apollo his lyre, making him the god of music, and Apollo gives Hermes the cattle.

What would new political forms inspired by brotherliness look like? What do we find if we analyse today's political forms with these thoughts about the brother–brother relationship in mind? For many reasons, there is a huge contemporary silence over fraternity. We still talk about liberty; and equality is continuously discussed – but fraternity has gone missing. The decline of trade unions is a significant feature here, illustrating the ways in which fraternity and political forms inspired by fraternity have slipped off the agenda. We are much more enmeshed in the politics of leadership, and the models for leadership that we have inherited are paternal and heroic models with little place for the brotherly double.

The brother–brother relationship may well be a template for a different model of leadership. What would fraternal leadership look like? This is difficult to answer because most of us have little experience of such a paradoxical political form. It has not been much theorized. One example of leadership in a sibling vein comes from experience at a meeting of a witch's coven, a Wiccan group. Men can attend such covens. This particular coven made use of what they called a speaking stick. When a speaker had finished, she or he passed a staff to the person they had chosen to speak next. This replaced the more adversarial pattern of conventional meetings. Differences of opinion were introduced gradually and, over time, everyone present had the opportunity to speak, but within a different structure (or form) of communication.

BROTHER–SISTER

Trawling the conventional texts, the stress is once again unremittingly negative. This may be something to do with the psychopathological project of psychoanalysis. But there may be other factors to consider given that jealousy, rivalry, mutual over-involvement and incest are the overwhelmingly predominant themes in relation to the brother–sister connection. I would like to propose that the central psychopolitical feature of the brother–sister relationship is that it concerns people who are equal in some ways but unequal in other ways, yet who are permanently connected or stuck together. It is different from marriage, though it might be part of a marriage, and not only as a problem for a marriage. We should heed with caution those marital therapists who condemn 'companionate' brother–sister kinds of marriages out of hand.

Some empirical research is useful here. A study was made of both what people applying to computer dating agencies wanted in their partner and what constitutes 'successful' relationships (Wilson and Nias, 1977). It seems from both sets of material that there is a general cultural awareness that, for a relationship to survive, there has to be a mixture of sameness and difference in it. Hence my suggestion that brother–sister relational dynamics may be much more useful in marital or cohabiting relationships than we have been led to believe.

There seems to be an omnipresent sociopolitical element in the brother–sister relationship, and most anthropologists have placed the brother–sister relationship and exchange at the centre of kinship systems. It's almost as if this relationship is screaming for someone to point out its Antigone-like political significance.

New political forms inspired by a rethinking of the brother–sister relationship would have to involve organizational recognition that there are irreconcilable antagonisms and prejudices between women and men. I am not persuaded by an idealization of man–woman relations in an image of them marching off together into a socially progressive sunset. I suggest that, in terms of political process, we need to stop thinking in terms of marriage or romantic love when it comes to men and women engaging in political actions. Instead, let us consider images of alliances, coalitions and deals between men and women when there are political purposes in mind. I think that the brother–sister relationship, as I have been

depicting it, could be a psychological template for such a negotia-
tory approach to political organization and to political forms that
would rely on ambivalence-driven bargaining.

   Observation of daughter and son has also suggested to me that
there is something very important politically in the notion of a
partnership between sister and brother against repressive parents.
My children (and other children) do this well. They do not only
struggle against each other. But something politically and psychologically destructive happens when the first of a brother–sister pair
reaches the age of 10–11 years, just prior to puberty. Lively
exchanges and mutual bantering and teasing – and the alliance
against the parents that I have described – give way to mutual
ignoring and a stand-off. What happens is more than the concrete
result of their fear of incest. The mutual seduction of brother and
sister certainly assists in the formation of a social bond against
repressive parents. When culture smashes the structure of seduction
between siblings, it also smashes the structure of resistance.
Hence, in terms of political forms, anything that might deploy the
brother–sister relationship as a twinning of difference and diversity
is decidedly unwelcome. Psychoanalysis is uneasy about generational bonding against the parents on the basis of brother–sister
erotics.

   There is something also to consider here about the inevitable
eroticization of political action. This is shown to good effect in
Alexandra Kollontai's novel *Love of the Worker Bees*. She writes about
what it is like to be in love during a revolution. Saying this is not to
retreat into a Marcusian miasma. Rather, I merely want to point
out that there is something in the brother–sister relationship, in
addition to what is involved in romantic love or marriage, that
would permit us once again to explore how exciting and meaningful
it is on an erotic level for men and women to work together
politically.

   The brother–sister relationship may also be seen as a metaphor
for the political forms arising from information technology and the
Internet. I am thinking of the ideals behind the Internet, perhaps,
rather than its inevitable, disappointing fate as part of someone's
media empire. Such ideals include mutual learning, a non-hierarchical approach to communication and a respect for indigenous
knowledge. These are also the secret ideals of the brother–sister
relationship which we could consider factoring into our attempts to
construct new political forms.

SON–MOTHER

Conventionally, accounts of the son–mother relationship may be summarized like this: 'You (the boy) must separate from your mother lest you fall into a female identification. Your mother is dangerous, seductive and engulfing. You must not be a mother's boy. You must give up mother to father. You must give up mother to siblings. You must give up mother to her own destiny.' There is by now an alternative but equally conventional reading: 'You must harden yourself against the feminine. You'd better follow soccer. Take a stand against softness. Reject notions of play, imagination and relatedness. You may not grow in connection.' This critique of masculinity is, of course, a feminist critique and, as I say, it has become a conventional alternative to the notion of a compulsory separation from mother brought about by the father but – this is an important point – even this reading is not usually taught on mainstream courses in analysis and psychotherapy, and hence its radical potential is unrealized in those contexts. It has stayed as a somewhat marginal feminist contribution to psychoanalytic psychology.

The following ideas of mind about the son–mother relationship are intended to challenge the conventional wisdoms about 'suffocating' mothers, 'possessive' mothers, 'Jewish' mothers, 'Mediterranean' mothers and the whole accusatory lexicon of mother-blaming. Do males have to separate from their mothers, as the books say they must? Do they have to *slay* the maternal monster? Do they have to be such heroes? Is this the only valid path of ego development? Is it possible to get beyond a situation where the son is required always to be an active and heroic man, and the mother is always depicted as a swampy, seductive maternal monster? Unfortunately, as Jung pointed out;

'the heroic deed of slaying the maternal monster has no lasting effects. Again and again, the hero must renew the struggle and always under the symbol of deliverance from the mother. Just as Hera, in her role of the pursuing mother, is the source of the mighty deeds performed by Herakles, so Nacomis allows Hiawatha no rest but piles up new difficulties in his path. The mother is thus the Daemon who challenges the hero to his deeds and lays in his path the poisonous serpent that will strike him.   (Jung, 1911–12, pp. 348–9)

What if we were to recognize that both son and mother want to separate? What if this is the progressive *political* element in the psychological experience of maternal ambivalence, which, as Rozsika Parker (1995) has suggested, aids creative maternal thought? Moreover, I think that if we apply what we know of context and contingency to the image of St George slaying the Dragon, which is the underlying cultural image behind Western science showing how the boy scientist dissects Mother Nature, we can recognize that this is not the only political form within which science can proceed. There is what has been called a feminization of science going on in which the epistemological relations between the exploring ego and its subject matter are being completely reframed, underlying the connections that exist. These feminist-inspired new approaches to science (e.g. Keller, 1983; Rose, 1994) play into what I am proposing about reframing the son–mother relationship in a less adversarial way. We – not just we analysts and therapists – but we citizens need new images of the son–mother relation. In most classical mythology all great goddesses have a young male consort, and nothing seems odd or wrong about that at all. And does not Jesus in one sense marry his mother when he symbolically marries the Church?

Traditionally, the theological and psychological question has been how to extract spirit (intellect, autonomy) out of the earthy mother's body and preserve it. I want to extract or discuss the *politics* from her relationship with her son. What would maternal leadership look like? Could a new version of the son–mother relationship give a more realistic basis for what is involved in the New Man phenomenon? And if there is going to be a new relationship of men to the environment to set alongside ecofeminism, doesn't there have to be a new reading of the son–mother relationship? Mother can symbolize earth as easily as earth can symbolize mother, so the risk of demeaning essentialism is reduced.

Regarding political forms, what I have in mind here concerns the politics of protection and nurture and how these might be practised by others than mothers (cf. Ruddick, 1989). We could identify political forms, based on and symbolized by the caring labour of mothers, which might lead us to discover the politics and psychology of the caring labour of sons, including to what extent sons could care for the sick and elderly, and involving models of nursing and teaching appropriate for sons. Such political forms would also recognize our ambivalent temptation to smash that which is vulnerable in the world, just as, according to Parker, every mother faces the temptation so to do.

A son–mother inspired political form could certainly involve nurture and imagination. But I think it could also be a political form that eschews or gives up power and striving altogether, performing an anti-heroic move in relation to politics. There might be a son–mother inspired politics of reflection and even of depression, a depression stemming from the loss of the privileged maternal relationship. It would be a pluralistic approach to political form based on the multifaceted tone of maternal experience. We are going to have to learn, we sons, how to ·have many mothers, just like Dionysus, who was variously mothered by Persephone, Demeter, Io, Lethe, Semele (cf. Hillman, 1973, p. 182).

In general terms, I want to reframe the son–mother connection as radical, son-friendly and fair, and as inspiring political forms that reflect those qualities. What do we come up with if we analyse today's political forms with these thoughts in mind? It is not a reassuring prospect. I realize there's a danger of idealization of the mother in what I'm saying and I do not think we could ever just stop seeing mother as swamp. The charge of idealization can also be countered by remembering that there will always be a fearsome maternal element to consider. In addition, changes in social and political practices (nurturing fathers, brotherly men, political siblings, mothers and sons who remain in connection) put pressure to change on the Symbolic Order. To the extent that analysis supports such changes, therapy, too, has a radical potential as a social and political practice.

PROBLEMS WITH THIS APPROACH

There is undoubtedly a huge problem in mapping off from therapy onto society. A clear barrier exists between the individual psychological and collective/social levels of narrative, and maybe that barrier serves a useful function. Crossing it lightly might be dangerous in that psychoanalysis would seek to become a totalizing discourse, taking a position of mastery and normalization (see Samuels, 1993, pp. ix–xiii, 3–23). For example, although my intention is quite the opposite, the undeniable fact that what I have written is within a Western cultural tradition, speaks to a certain extent of white male experience and places psychoanalysis in a more central and potent location than some others would, may lead critics to assert that I have universalized and normalized these variables. My belief is that work in transcultural psychology and psychotherapy points up the mutability of most of what psycho-analysis touches upon (see Samuels, 1993, pp. ix–xii, 51–78). This actually strengthens the rhetorical strategy of this chapter which is predicated on the changeability of psychological ideas as signifying part of the process of production of new political ideas.

Some would hold that the psychological and the social levels of reality are totally different and that, on a Marxist or neo-Marxist reading, the psychological may only be seen as a derivative stem-ming from hegemonic class forces which constitute a (or the) pri-mary dynamic of the social. In similar one-sided vein, in the psychoanalytic tradition, there are those who would claim that psychic and social realities are indeed different from each other, but that this is because the psyche (or the unconscious) uses projec-tion to colour and cultivate the apparently external social world. Psychodynamics are primary. The social world is actually an en-souled world – *anima mundi*, soul in and of the world. Social and material aspects of our world, and the suffering to which they lead, are secondary phenomena.

Other thinkers, particularly in the past 20 years, have argued that there is a holistic oneness to be apperceived between the psycholo-gical and the social domains. It is an illusion to make these bound-aries between psychological and social. Similarly, a holistic viewpoint goes on to maintain that the boundary between the inner and the outer is also illusory. Moreover, following the birth of ecopsychology (Roszak, 1993), it is being disputed, perhaps too facilely, that we can maintain the epistemological boundary between the human and the non-human environments.

A dialectical approach would see psychological and social in ceaseless, unending, unsettlable, unclosable interplay, while a further possibility would be to say that the relations between the psychological and the social consist of *all* of the above. It just depends on the context, on who's talking, and on what he or she wants to do with these ideas. There would be no possible truth then; it would be, rather, a question of utility.

Finally – and this is the most challenging and difficult possibility – the relations between the individual/psychological and collective/ social levels of reality, and the relevant discourses, might not be encompassed by *any* of the above approaches. There may be a missing bit in our psychopolitical thinking and vocabulary that, were it to exist, would help us to establish a new reading of the relations between the psychological and social, one that would not fall into the difficulties with all the readings that I have mentioned.

A further problem with the whole argument of this chapter is that it courts danger because of the invocation of incestuous sexual fantasy. However, it is precisely because of the transgressive nature of incestuous fantasy (which, although involved therein, may be distinguished from actual incest, which is always destructive), that it is useful in thinking about and constructing what is frankly intended to be a transgressive politics. The whole point is to trade off and utilize the very anxiety that incestuous sexual fantasy rightly engenders.

Yet another problem is the risk that, when discussing parents, I have essentialized the parental function: mothers do *this*, fathers do *that*. I have taken some care not to essentialize parental function by grounding my work on the father in questions to do with lone mothers and with women parenting together (Samuels, 1995). The phrase with which I have become associated – the good-enough father of whatever sex – is intended to make it very difficult for me, and indeed for anybody else, to offer hard-and-fast essentialistic comments on what it is that female parents do as compared to what it is that male parents do. Briefly, I have called women who parent alone or in relationship with other women 'good-enough fathers of whatever sex' because such women have to address what it is that fathers do or are supposed to do without the possibility of recourse to the traditional authoritarianism of male fathers when it comes to issues of discipline. There is a psychological sense in which the crisis in modern fatherhood and questions around lone parenthood – both perennially fascinating issues in most Western countries today – are the same issue. It is possible to reframe lone parents or lesbians parenting together as present-day experts on fathering.

Readers may wonder why I have focused so much on the male side, especially on the figure of the 'son' and not on the 'daughter'. Aside from practical issues of time and space, my interests are presently focused on the politics of masculinity – for example, male unemployment and what that is doing to male psychology in our time. One thing that interests me is the way in which what I call the 'male deal' is being busted by the discovery by many men – not just working-class men in rust-belt industries but also by middle-class men in white-collar and technical work – that they are not wanted any more just as they are and that they are going to have to learn all kinds of new skills. Young men are realizing that they face a life in which either they will never work, or they will have to learn, and relearn, and relearn again, different sets of skills and knowledge. The male deal is my term for the bargain that the average male in our society strikes with that society (one which has become of dubious advantage to many men).

In the male deal, a boy agrees to give up play, imagination, softness, fun and an approach to life that is not goal-oriented – what is often called (although I really regret the term) the 'feminine' side of life – in order to have access to all the goodies that society can provide him with. I sometimes refer to this as 'all the woman you can eat'. This male deal has started to fall apart. Of course, inevitably, it is white, middle-class and middle-aged men who are challenging and questioning whether it was such a good deal for them in the first instance. But I think there are also certain ways in which the male deal, as I have just described it, is being challenged by other categories of men with interesting and unforeseeable political consequences.

IMPLICATIONS AND CONCLUDING REMARKS

In this chapter, I posed three questions. Where do political ideas come from, and what psychological vehicles carry them forward in culture? How do we evaluate the gaps between the effects of ideology, narratives of emotional experience, and ongoing political organizations that do or might exist? Is there a role for therapy as a kind of think tank? My tentative responses to my own questions incorporated the idea that therapy can function as a think tank if it interrogates its own conventional assumptions. The term political form was intended to be a way of linking ideology, emotional experience and organization without reducing society to a family. Incestuous sexual fantasy, usually a transgressive property of the internal or external family, reworked in the ways I have been suggesting, leads us to envisage and imagine new political forms. I suspect incestuous sexual fantasy has always done this or had the capacity to do this. Exploring such fantasies, deliberately restricting the scope of this chapter to male fantasies and foregrounding the figure of the son, and looking into how they are thought and theorized by analysts and therapists offers an unusual and effective set of tools for examining, analysing and even changing the political forms encountered in today's world.

In the son–father area of a man's internal family, I explored the implications for new political forms of a move from a focus on rivalry and castration to one on cooperation, mutual admiration and protection, and an acceptance and utilization of homosociality and homosexuality. This led to a discussion of cooperation and non-hierarchical organization and new forms of political leadership. One could envisage significant changes in the political form of corporations and large institutions based on such ideas as a valoriz-ing of erotic intimacy between men and an apperception of the vulnerability of the male body.

In the brother–brother area of a man's internal family, I explored the implications for new political forms of a move from a focus on complementary opposites falsely constructed by parents and the resultant competitiveness, to an authentic recognition of differing abilities, brotherliness as a soulmate template for male friendship (as opposed to misogynistic brotherhoods), and the idea of the male anima. The changes in political forms this might inspire could include the reinstatement of fraternity as a sociopolitical and com-munal value or good, and the restructuring of the processes via which debate and dispute are carried out so that differences are introduced gradually. Brothers (citizens) would be seen as always already in relation to each other and not only to leaders or to centres of power (father and/or mother).

In the brother–sister area of the internal family of a man, I explored the implications for new political forms of a move from a fear of incest and a condemnation of brother–sister elements in 'mature' heterosexual sexual relationships to an acceptance of the seductive and ambivalent dynamics of the relationship as non-pathological. That led us to consider new political forms based on deals, alliances and partnerships between (metaphorical) brothers and sisters rather than on (metaphorical) marriages between hus-bands and wives or (metaphorical) romantic love affairs.

In the son–mother area of the internal family of a man, I explored the implications for new political forms of a move from a concentration on the satisfactory achievement by the son of separation from the mother and his formation of a 'hard' male identity to wondering if a developmental psychology could exist that was comfortable with mothers and sons who stay in connection.

The mother would not be positioned as an abject and swampy enemy of the son's individuation but as an ally of the imagination, and the son would be more free to explore his taking on of 'maternal' roles in the family, in relationships and in society. Without idealization of the mother, new political forms could be theorized that would ground contemporary male aspirations of a politically progressive and humane kind, especially in relation to ecological consciousness, environmental politics, and economic and social justice.

12 The Case of the Lesbian Phallus: Bridging the Gap between Material and Discursive Analyses of Sexuality

Jane Ussher

Psychology has traditionally examined human experience from a realist perspective, within a positivistic framework which focuses on observable 'facts'. The psychologist's aim has been to uncover objective 'truth', and narrowly to delineate the boundaries of the scientific gaze. This is never more clear than in areas of psychology which focus on the body. Sexuality has been reduced to hormones, penile pulse amplitude or vaginal swelling; reproduction to evolutionary concepts of mating or to the physical machinations of the womb. In recent years, those working within a 'biopsycho-social' framework, or those interested in social and psychological aspects of experience, have 'added on' a psychosocial analysis to reductionist interpretations of sex, or reproduction. However, many theorists working within this field still rely on realist assumptions, failing to question the social or discursive construction of bodily experience. They also fail to address the role of discourse associated with the body in social regulation and the construction of identities – in defining what it means to be 'woman' or 'man'.

In contrast, many sociologists, anthropologists and feminists have turned their attention exclusively to the cultural and discursive aspects of 'the body', often treating it as a phenomenon virtually unrelated to the biological processes traditionally studied in psychology, regarding the physical body as essentially an object constructed within sociocultural discourses and practices. For example, in recent years, largely due to the influence of poststructuralist theorizing, critical feminist attention has shifted to the power of symbolic representations of female sexuality and their role in the construction and regulation of what it is to be 'woman'. This has led to critical analyses of how female sexuality is portrayed in art, film, popular culture, literature and pornography. The focus here has been on the regulatory power of discourse – control through that which Foucault termed the 'intelligible body'. Many of these critiques focus on that which semiotic theorists would term 'woman as sign',[1] the analysis of what 'woman' signifies or symbolizes at a mythical level[2] – the representation of woman as object, or as fetish, and the splitting of 'woman' into Madonna or whore. Representations of 'woman' are undoubtedly of central importance in the construction of female subjectivity. We learn how to *do* 'woman' through negotiating the warring images and stories about what 'woman' is (or what she should be). As one critic comments, 'one becomes a woman in the very practice of signs by which we write, speak, see .... This is neither an illusion nor a paradox. It is a real contradiction – women continue to become woman' (Blumm, 1984, p. 335). But where does this analysis leave the material body?

It is arguable that one of the factors that acts to hinder the development of coherent and pluralistic theories of sexuality, which would allow us to reconcile these different interests and concerns, is the disciplinary split between those who focus on the corporeal body and those who focus on representation – the split between analyses of the material and discursive body. Yet this is a false divide, an inappropriate separation. For to understand sexuality we need to examine both bodily processes and practices, and the ways in which sexuality is constructed in the realm of the symbolic. We cannot separate the two.

To illustrate this argument, I want to take one level of discursive representation where representations of sexuality are most openly displayed – that of mainstream heterosexual pornography – and an arena of material practice where the functioning of the flesh, the material body, has been positioned by psychology as the central issue – that of male sexual problems. I shall examine the tension between material and discursive practices in relation to sexuality by focusing on the question of the representation of the phallus, because the myth of phallic mastery is arguably at the heart of dominant constructions of heterosexual sexuality. Yet paradoxically, for a number of lesbians – women who would explicitly position themselves *outside* a heterosexual matrix (Wittig, 1980) – the phallus has also become an effective site of resistance.

MALE SEXUAL PROBLEMS: THE PRESSURES OF PHALLOCENTRICISM

Within the realist framework traditionally adopting in psychology, 'sex' is reduced to the biological workings of the body, and focuses on the actions of the penis. Male sexual problems are positioned similarly. For, with the exception of 'disorders of desire', where the problem is manifested by absence of interest or aversion to sex, the very definition of a 'problem' is signified by a dysfunctional penis. So the Diagnostic and Statistical Manual of the American Psychiatric Association (DSM) classifies male sexual problems as falling into categories of male erectile disorder; inhibited male orgasm and premature ejaculation. The very definition of these 'disorders' acts to reify heterosexual intercourse as the only 'normal' form of sexual activity, with an inability (or unwillingness) to perform this act a sign of deviancy or deficiency in man. Not surprising then that men feel anxious or afraid when they can't 'get it up'. They have 'failed' as real men: something that is reinforced by the description of 'Male Erectile Disorder' (DSM diagnostic category 302.72), which is described as the '*failure* in a male to attain or maintain an erection until completion of the sexual activity'.

This isn't just about 'sex'. Male sexual identity is so closely tied to the performance of the penis, that a man is not a 'man' if his penis does not work. Hence the vast sums of money spent every year on alleviating male sexual dysfunction – in research, clinical intervention and self-help prosthetic devices to be found in porn shops and the backs of Sunday supplements. In both lay and medical discourse the focus is almost entirely on the material body, with a complete dismissal or denial of the symbolic or discursive issues which are at play here.

Psychologists and sex therapists who continue to position male sexual problems within a biological model, focusing on the physical workings of the penis – with an emphasis on penile tumescence, erections and performance – paradoxically increase male anxiety. Many sex therapists and sexologists *do* adopt multifactorial models of sexuality, acknowledging social and psychological causes of sexual dysfunction, even if few openly question the discursive construction of 'normal' sex. Yet the majority of *men* seeking treatment adopt a biological model of aetiology. This perhaps explains both the fact that it is medicine that men with sexual problems turn to for help, and the popularity of physical interventions such as penile implants

– a common treatment for erectile problems in both Britain and the United States. These consist of a plastic or silicone rod surgically implanted in the penis, with an inbuilt hinge so that the now permanently erect organ can be 'stored' against the body (up or down), or an 'inflatable prosthesis', a device which can pump up the penis on demand, producing an erect penis, from a squeeze bulb device (Melman, 1978). As Leonore Tiefer has asked, is this the perfect penis on demand, with the security that it will never let you down? It is perhaps a shame that minor surgery is the necessary price to be paid. In addition, the failure rate for such devices is high, and there is serious risk of infection. Yet thousands of men undergo such surgery each year, risking anything to get closer to attainment of the elusive phallus (Tiefer, 1986). This is the greatest irony of all: that what is supposed to be at the centre of what it is to be 'man' is actually most likely to let him down.

Male impotence or erectile problems are a serious matter, particularly in a context where the penis, and successful achievement of sexual intercourse, is how 'sex' is defined. But it is a sorry indictment of medicine that the means of addressing such difficulty is increasingly seen as prosthetic aids. Can sex *really* be reduced to the successful achievement of a tumescent penis? It does not take much cynicism to question whose view of sex this is – particularly when very few of the outcome studies examining the effectiveness of these penile implants think even to ask the man's female partner if she is satisfied with the device (Tiefer, 1986, p. 583). Here, woman is implicitly positioned as passive object, penetration of her waiting body the assumed aim of this particular sexual game. If that is achieved, how could she be anything other than satisfied? The irony is that if this were *really* the aim, the man could do worse than use other parts of his body – his fingers perhaps – and provide satisfaction for the woman who enjoys penetration, without having to undergo surgery, as many lesbians (as well as teenagers engaging only in 'foreplay') have long known.

But this is unlikely to occur in a world where 'sex' is defined simply as penetration of the vagina by the penis – which is unfortunate for both women and men. This is not a question of pleasure, or of the most 'natural' means of having sex. It is the conflation of the penis with the phallus – the signifier of sexual difference, of mastery, and of power, and arguably of masculinity itself – which is at issue here. This is a central factor in any understanding of why erectile difficulties or impotence are such psychologically damaging problems for men. Their whole masculinity rests on the performance of that fragile piece of flesh; they cannot demonstrate their status as a 'man' if it fails.

For example, here is Stephen Frosh again, discussing the difficulty of sustaining a masculine identity: 'Much of the excess of masculine sexuality seems to derive from a desperate struggle to retain a conviction of phallic mastery – of potency – when what is being experienced is the impossibility of measuring up to the fantasy of the full phallus' (1994, p. 78). He goes on to say:

> If men claim dominance through the phallus, they are in for a sore surprise. The penis, which men do have, is not the phallus, for the phallus is a symbol rather than a substance; all those bemusing male impotences are linked to this... the real organ cannot match the imaginary one, and the more one tries to make it so, the more incorrigible is the failure likely to be...

The penis is clearly not something to envy – if any woman ever did. So why do many men still hang on to the fantasy, if it puts them at such risk of failure and despair? Perhaps it is because in the realm of the symbolic, the conflation between the penis and the phallus is both maintained and reinforced. Cultural representations are central to the formation of our subjectivity, to the process of our taking up gendered positions. And those cultural representations tell a tale of the *penis* which is almost beyond belief – yet present it as 'true', as 'real'.

PHALLIC MASTERY IN THE PORNOGRAPHIC GAZE

Take pornography: it offers phallic fantasy at its most explicit. There are clearly many complex arguments about pornography, concerning its effects, the reasons for its popularity and whether or not it should be censored (Itzen, 1995; Segal and McIntosh, 1992). However, what I want to focus on in this context is the role of pornography in maintaining the phallic illusion; a role that is most blatant in hardcore heterosexual porn. I am talking here about pornography which shows actual penetrative sex between women and men; non-violent porn, that doesn't depict rape or sexual violence – just literally 'straight sex'.

Hardcore porn officially is illegal in Britain, but is easily obtainable in sex shops (at least in London's Soho) and through mail order

– and advertised widely in daily and Sunday tabloid newspapers. This is not 'specialist' material: researchers estimate that 70 per cent of men have read or viewed hardcore porn at some point in their lives.

In hardcore heterosexual pornography, the penis is at the centre of every scene. It is worshipped. This is a penis that is apparently effortlessly erect, that never fails and can perform repeated acts of penetration without any fear of impotence or premature ejaculation. What is most notable about hardcore porn – at least to someone viewing a broad cross-section of it at once for the first time – is its limited nature. It is the same story again and again, played out with an almost boring regularity. Like the archetypal fantasy, re-enacted again and again in a futile attempt to achieve satisfaction.

The typical scene involves a man having repeated and vigorous penetrative sex with a woman, vaginally, anally or orally. The more lavish film productions will involve some semblance of a story line and a brief interlude of foreplay before the 'real' action begins. In the downmarket films (the majority of the market) the opening shot will be of a penis entering a female orifice. This will continue in every imaginable permutation (and many which defy the imagination) for hours. There are never any problems with the man's performance. The woman is presented as being ecstatically satisfied by this repeated pounding (which looked excruciatingly uncomfortable, if not painful, to me). It is presented as if it is all she ever wanted: the ultimate phallic illusion of the active controlling man and the passive yet responsive woman. Here the penis stands as symbol of his potency and power; literally agent of his mastery and control over woman.

Yet this isn't presented as illusion. In fact, one of the main attractions of hardcore porn is that the sex is supposedly 'real' (Williams, 1992a). This is one reason why the come (or money) shot is found in every film – a shot in which the man visibly ejaculates outside of the body of the woman: often onto her body – on her face or her breasts – but never inside her, because then we wouldn't be able to confirm to ourselves that the man is 'really' doing it, that his arousal and pleasure are authentic, and he is 'really' experiencing a climax. (If hardcore porn is viewed by men attempting to find out what heterosexual sex is really about – which interviews with young men suggest it is – they certainly learn some very strange lessons.)

However, the sex we see in hardcore porn is not simply 'real sex'; it is an illusion. The feats performed in hardcore porn are impossible for all but the most unusual man. To maintain an erection while carrying out vigorous sexual manoeuvres for a protracted period, in front of a camera crew, with all the stops and starts which are normal in filming, takes a particular (one might say peculiar) type of man. Robert Stoller, in his analysis of hardcore pornography, has described how the 'stars' of this genre are a rare breed, who show both exhibitionist tendencies and an apparent defiance of normal rules of physiology, both in terms of their size (most men in porn have an abnormally large penis), their ability to perform penetrative sex for hours without losing an erection, and their ability to resume action with a minimal refractory period after ejaculation (Stoller and Levine, 1993). Are these men bearers of the perfect penis, within the confines of the phallic fantasy?

Hardcore porn serves many functions apart from the obvious – its use as a masturbatory aid. Critics of pornography have seen it as a reflection of misogyny – of man's power over women; of women's subjugation through heterosexual sex; at the very least as what men would *like* to do to women, if they ever got the chance (Dworkin, 1979; Itzen, 1995). Yet in contrast, others have argued that pornography does not simply reflect or reinforce men's power and women's powerlessness: it is a representation of transgressive fantasies (Segal and McIntosh, 1992); that pornography acts to deny or temporarily alleviate men's sexual anxiety through the identification with phallic mastery. It counters an underlying fear of women – a fear well documented in both psychoanalysis, from Karen Horney onwards, and in the social sciences. For in porn the man is always active subject, woman responsive object. Here there is nothing to fear at all. Mainstream heterosexual pornography positions woman not as a person, but as a hole to be penetrated. The symbolic representation of woman in porn arguably acts to denigrate her, to dismiss her and to annihilate her power. She is fetishized in the most obvious manner; split into part object (breast, vagina, mouth) rather than whole object, and the fears she provokes in man are contained: his fears of castration, of not being good enough, big enough – of not being 'man'. A fear of being rejected, or laughed at. In pornography the apparent mystery of 'woman' is thoroughly exposed. There is no question about 'what does woman want' here. No ambiguity about what is inside: as she pulls open her vagina, we can literally see: nothing – only flesh. No danger, or horror; nothing to fear. But pornography also objectifies man – the focus is on his penis, and his position as 'man' is signified by his ability to perform sexually, and ejaculate freely, at will. It is this (mythical) ability which signifies his status and power.

In this view, pornography is as much a representation of what man would like to be in his own private fantasy, but knows he cannot in the material world, as it is about what man really is. This may well be the case for many men.[3] Yet do men simply split off the pornographic representation of the penis as phallus and feel satisfied with the reality of their own material bodies? Undoubtedly, many see and believe. Peter Baker (1992) has described pornography as a 'rite of passage into manhood'. For many, it is certainly an important part of the establishment of a masculine sexual identity, providing essential cues for the establishment 'normal' heterosexuality. Publicly displaying or talking about porn demonstrates that young men are unquestioningly 'man', with unquestioned heterosexual desires and with appropriate masculine feelings towards women (ibid., p. 130). It says: 'I *know* about women, I fancy them, and I can "do" sex.' The sexual bravado or bragging associated with the group sharing of pornography alleviates the dread that any of these points may be untrue (which they so often are). As pornography conflates masculine sexuality with phallic mastery, and porn stars are positioned as 'normal men' having 'real sex', is it then surprising that there are such high rates of sexual anxiety and problems in men? Yet it is important to remember that pornography does not *cause* this conflation. It merely reflects (and reinforces) dominant social constructions of what it means to be 'man', as well as dominant constructions of what is 'normal' heterosexual sex; constructions which do not simply operate at the level of the symbolic, but are irrevocably linked to the workings of the material body.

THE PARODY OF MASCULINITY AS MASQUERADE

Few men (with the exception of hardcore porn stars) own a penis that can always live up to the phallic illusion. But paradoxically, those who acknowledge the phallic illusion and look beyond the corporeal reality of the penis for the enactment of phallic power (or to enact the masquerade that is masculinity) are more likely to be able to enjoy it without anxiety or fear. Which is where we come to the lesbian phallus.

There is now a whole genre of lesbian erotica characterized by magazines such as *Quim* (UK), *On Our Backs* (US) and *Wicked Women* (Australia), in which one of the ubiquitous representations is that of the woman literally taking on the phallus through wearing a prosthetic penis – a strap-on dildo. This often involves the taking on of an archetypal masculine phallic subject position – yet doing so in clear parody, as an obvious masquerade, because these women are still women; there is no attempt to disguise the materiality of the woman's body – that she has breasts, that her 'penis' is not 'real'.[4] In addition, the woman who takes on a masculine or phallic identification, if only temporarily, is deliberately taking up this discursive position while knowing that it is not based on material reality, it is not immutable. She can stop at any time. She can take off the symbolic phallus – literally – in a way a man never can. In this way the masquerade of both masculinity and femininity, of the phallus as a symbol of mastery and power, is played out and exposed. As Linda Williams has argued, 'The point of this play with the phallus to the lesbian viewer ... is neither that the dildo is a penis *manqué*, nor that it is believed in as a substitute for the "real thing", but rather the proof that there is no "real thing" based in biology' (Williams 1992b, p. 256).

Yet this isn't merely about women taking on the phallus at the level of the symbolic, the discursive. These pornographic or erotic representations reflect the sexual practices of an increasing number of lesbian women, particularly those in the younger age groups. The perfect rubber phallus is selling like hot cakes. This might simply be because many women like to fuck, and a strap-on dildo is an interesting alternative to fingers or fists. Or perhaps it is because many women are finding that they can attain pleasure, power or just a sense of amusement through deliberately taking on masculinity as masquerade; and one might say doing it more successfully than the 'real man', because, as Williams notes, 'by possessing a mock penis, this woman accedes to desire without entrapping herself in the masculinity complex of a fantasy masculine identity' (Williams, 1992b, p. 256). For *this* sexualized phallic symbolic never fails – it is always hard. And it is in the complete control of the woman who wears it. There is no anxiety about loss of erections – the perfect performance every time. This doesn't mean that the woman who wears it is under constant pressure to 'do sex' (as defined within phallocentric definitions of sexuality) or that the wearing of this symbolic phallus necessarily ascribes power.

For the woman who takes on this sexual subject position is not inevitably the one who fucks – she and her partner can take turns, both at fucking, and at being fucked. They can take up positions of power and powerlessness – and attain pleasure from each role. This is represented in both lesbian erotica (i.e. Kiss and Tell, 1994) and in lesbian sexual education materials (such as the safer sex video 'Well sexy women'), as well as reported by lesbian women who are interviewed about their sexual practices (Ussher, forthcoming).

The power of the penis at a symbolic as well as at a material level is clearly demonstrated here. Its importance (to men and women), its status, its role as a signifier of sexual difference, is exposed as being not simply an essential pre-given fact, a result of a biological differences between women and men, and the 'natural' role of the penis in 'sex'. The penis has taken on such power and significance, at both an intrapsychic level and at the level of wider cultural discourse, largely because of its symbolic or discursive association with the phallus. This doesn't mean that the material actuality of the penis isn't associated with pleasure, power (or anxiety) for men *or* women – it is certainly not irrelevant in the act of sex (and penetration is certainly pleasurable for many women and men). But this pleasure is not simply *caused* by the biological organ the penis – it is the biological organ (or its symbolic equivalent) in a particular discursive context. Within a different discursive construction of sexuality, the penis might not assume such central importance at all: it is phallocentricism which leads to questions such as 'What do lesbians do in bed?', where 'sex' cannot even be imagined without a penis. 'Sex' *can* exist without a penis, or without penetration, as many lesbians will readily attest. This has also recently become an oft-repeated message in many safer sex campaigns aimed at gay men, which emphasize that penetration is only one part of a sexual script, and that other forms of sexual expression can be equally pleasurable. 'Sex' is therefore reconceptualized and redefined, and the penis as phallus is dethroned.

Lesbian adoption of this potent symbol of masculinity and power is also, as Linda Williams argues, 'a play with an inevitable symbol of normal desire'. As Judith Butler (1990) has argued, this performance radically undermines taken-for-granted assumptions about sex, gender and sexuality, in parodying the heterosexual 'original' and as such threatens to unsettle the whole basis of our understanding of 'normal' gendered positions of 'woman' and 'man'. For this examination of lesbian erotica demonstrates that women can deliberately play out a masquerade – both feminine and masculine – and can switch in and out of gendered positions at will, not being restricted by either role. The fact that women can 'do' masculinity (if that is partly what taking on the symbolic phallus signifies, as is also the case with 'butch' lesbian role play: see Butler, 1990) draws attention to the fact that in other contexts, women are 'doing' femininity: it is not a biological given, but a discursively constructed gendered position.

So to return to my main argument: if we wish to understand sexuality, it is essential that we examine both the material and discursive body; we need to look at both the realm of representation and the realm of corporeality. The issue of the penis/phallus conflation provides one illustration of this. For to understand the role of the penis in 'sex' – for women or men, whether the penis is 'real' or prosthetic – we have to examine it at both a symbolic and material level, without privileging one level of analysis over the other. You can have 'sex' (or even fuck) without a penis; but at the same time, in a phallocentric sphere, the action of the penis has come to stand for 'sex', and its ability to perform, to stand as a signifer of both masculinity and phallic power. Unravelling these connections is a necessary step to developing pluralistic, and positive, theories of sexuality and sex – for both women and for men.

NOTES

1. Based on semiotic theorizing, visual imagery and in particular film, is seen as a system of communication, akin to language, wherein particular meanings are created through the use of 'signs'. This notion is based on the work of Saussure, who argued that the meaning of language is not based in the words or intentions of a speaker, but in the relationships between the elements of the sign system itself (see Hollway, 1989). Saussure argued that within language exists both the *signified* and the *signifier*. The signified is the object in the world, in our case 'woman', the biologically female person. The signifier is the collection of phonemes w-o-m-e-n, making up the word 'woman', which is the sign for a person who is born with breasts, a vagina, etc. The fact that the signifier 'woman' refers to the biological (or social) person that has breasts, etc. is arbitrary – is a construction within language. The fact that the word 'woman' connotes so many different and often contradictory things (beauty, desires, sexuality, emotion, fickleness, weakness, lability) in the twentieth-century developed world is as a result of the sign system which operates in this cultural sphere.

2. Barthes (1975) has claimed that these signs operate as myth – not as a direct reference to the real world Thus the signifier 'woman' either as image, or as

word, does not merely connote female sexuality or gender, but can have a whole new connotative meaning associated with it, which is provided by the particular culture and ideology in which the language or image is situated/ produced. Thus 'woman' can become the sign for weakness, or danger, or sexuality (each a signified) making it a new sign, at a secondary level, what it often called a secondary level of signification.

3. There have been heated debates about the cause and effect relationship between pornography and behaviour – both sexual violence and consensual sex. See Ussher (forthcoming, chapter 3, for a full analysis of these arguments; also Itzen (1995) and Segal and Mackintosh (1992).

4. In contrast, women undergoing sex change operations which include the creation of an artificial 'penis', would claim that their newly acquired organ is 'real'. It is certainly made of flesh, and looks similar (if not equivalent) to a biological penis. However, whether this is the taking on of the phallus, or simply the acquisition of a 'real penis' (which is actually artificial, as the woman was not born with it, and it is constructed out of skin and tissue from other parts of her body), is open to question.

III
SEXUAL SUBJECTIVITIES, SOCIAL CONFLICTS

13 The Context of Women's Power(lessness) in Heterosexual Interactions
Ine Vanwesenbeeck

The topic of this chapter is the context of women's power and powerlessness in heterosexual interactions. Many feminist scholars have stressed the relative powerlessness of women in sexual encounters with men. This asymmetry has been explained in terms of differential economic and social positions (e.g. Worth, 1989; Kippax et al., 1990; Gupta and Weiss, 1993), of differential sexual socialization and prior victimization of women (e.g. Russell, 1984; Allers and Benjack, 1991; Holland et al., 1992) and as a product of the prevailing definitions of (hetero)sexuality (e.g. Burt, 1983; Vance, 1984; Komter, 1985). Dominant discourses of heterosexuality and connected (institutional and social) practices provide an unequal distribution of subject and object positions for women and for men (Hollway, 1984a; Smart, 1995; Tiefer, 1995).

The sexualization and objectification of women, as a core aspect of the main discourse on heterosexuality, has been interpreted by many as the very heart of what renders women powerless in heterosexual encounters. In Dutch we have the expression 'zoals ze verschijnen verdwijnen ze' (Draijer, 1984) ('appearing as a sexual object means disappearing as a sexual subject'). I want to challenge that so-called 'golden rule', and the opposition between subject and object, that is, challenge sexualization and powerlessness being too readily treated as one and the same. If we define the sexualization of women as objectification *per se*, and thereby as degrading and disempowering, we lose touch with an image of strong female (hetero) sexuality, we forget what female sexual (heterosexual) power looks and feels like, and we create difficulties for women about how to promote themselves as heterosexual beings.

I do not share the view of some feminists (e.g. Dworkin, 1981; MacKinnon, 1992; Kitzinger and Wilkinson, 1993) that heterosexuality by definition renders women powerless. I don't believe that heterosexuality is by its nature, necessarily and unchangeably, the foundation for a phallocentric order, in which the phallus is the centre of power and/or in which the phallus, as the symbol of sexual power, can be taken on only by men. Heterosexuality as a phallocentric – and thus male-favourable – order may be an empirical given, but it is not an empirical necessity. Even within a context of sexualization, options and possibilities for subject positions and sexual power still exist for women. Several feminist writers have stressed, that, on closer inspection, heterosexual practices show not only the possibility, but also the reality of female power (e.g. Hollway, 1984b; Segal, 1994; Kitzinger, in press). I want, therefore, to explore the conditions in which young women give accounts of feelings of power in heterosexuality, despite the prevailing definitions of a heterosexuality, where women take subordinate, objectified and less powerful positions. It seems important to explore these so-called 'cracks' in the phallocentric order, because they give us a view of possibilities for change. And I feel it is our task to shape and define a heterosexuality that can provide women with subject positions and that grants them strength and power in actual sexual interactions. Young women's accounts of heterosexual power can help us there.

First, my focus is on prostitution. I shall report on my research findings on the conditions in which prostitutes can be powerful and feel in control in heterosexual interactions with their clients, even within what is in the eyes of many, that utterly objectifying context: prostitution. Building on this research, I want to address the situation of young adult women in non-commercial heterosexual encounters. The situation of young women striving to find sexual pleasure and control over their heterosexuality is different from that of prostitutes, who as a rule want to earn money, not find sexual pleasure – although I was surprised to find how many of them sometimes did. Nevertheless, I want to explore whether my findings on prostitutes also have some equivalent in non-commercial heterosexual interactions. This is really much more tentative, because my research with young women is still in its early stages. While the findings on prostitutes are based on substantial empirical data, those on young heterosexual women are better characterized as preliminary explorations.

PROSTITUTES' WELL-BEING AND RISK

During the course of my years of research as a psychologist working with prostitutes in the Netherlands, I have been mainly interested in the question: 'How do prostitutes fare?' Large differences in the overall well-being of prostitutes quickly become clear to even the most superficial observer. How do these differences come about? Over the years I have spoken to some 200 prostitutes of all ages and in all sorts of prostitution: women working on the street, in windows, in clubs and brothels, as escorts and in their own homes, and also with some 100 of their male clients. Here, of course, I shall present only a small part of my findings, those concerning the matter of control. Consistent condom use with clients can be considered an indicator of control over prostitution contact proceedings. Every prostitute wants to use condoms, and giving in on that points to a lack of control, generally speaking. So what is the context in which prostitutes become risk-takers where condom use is concerned? I found risk-takers (women who relatively often, and unselectively, work without condoms) to differ significantly from other prostitutes on a number of (related) factors. They worked under more stressful conditions, both in terms of financial need and in terms of working routines (i.e. working the more dangerous sites, with more clients, in shorter periods of time, for less money). More of them were drug-users and their level of well-being was lower on a range of different criteria: they reported more dissociative experiences, more psychosomatic complaints, more problems that can be put together under the label 'social insecurity' and, quite importantly, much less job satisfaction. Last, but definitely not least, they had experienced more victimization, both in childhood and in adult life, both off and on the job. They were also younger and more often born outside the Netherlands.

Risk-takers showed a totally different pattern of interacting with clients. They were often engaged in what I have called 'fighting scenarios'. They try to influence their clients in many different ways: by manipulation, negotiation and by high levels of pressure. They used negative emotions as one influence strategy (begging, crying, behaving pitifully) much more often than the other groups. At the same time, risk-taking prostitutes experienced the least control over contact proceedings. They most often attributed the cause of an unwanted course of events with clients to powerlessness and anxious helplessness. Overall, we found that traumatizing

experiences in private life, high financial need, uncomfortable working conditions, violence at the hands of clients and 'unhealthy'
coping responses not only bring about low levels of general well-
being and job satisfaction, but also culminate in an interaction with
clients that characterizes itself by negative emotions, constant struggle and fights, and general feelings of powerlessness on the part of
the prostitute. These interactions are bound to end in unsafe sex
relatively often.

An important factor in these interactions is the clients. There is
insufficient space here to describe them, but one factor is crucial:
because of obvious market mechanisms, it is the risk-taking prostitutes who are most often visited by recalcitrant condom users. Our
evidence shows that clients unwilling to use condoms are notable for
their negative feelings about frequenting prostitutes. They don't
accept the game, and they don't want to play by the rules. Their
objective is more one of confrontation than one of pleasure. The
perceived ambivalence of both parties in this deal sets off a chain-
reaction of reciprocal influence attempts, in which the resort to
violence by clients is more likely. They put a lot of pressure on
prostitutes, and the prostitute who cannot afford to be fastidious is
not able to keep these men in check.

My conclusion is that those women who are the most vulnerable
to begin with, also are put under the greatest pressure. The misery
of women who do not fare well in prostitution, who have least
control and run the highest risk, has often started before they
entered prostitution and piles up while they are on the job. Women
who start from a more positive position manage to achieve more
comfortable conditions and routines once they are working. Victims
of childhood trauma in particular, which more risk-takers are found
to be, often show a reduced ability to protect themselves against
further injuries and less control over contact proceedings. Prostitutes who have been sexually traumatized attach a totally different
meaning to prostitution, and interact differently with clients. They
encounter particular difficulties entering into effective interaction
with their clients. Health considerations hardly play a role here.
Negative well-being and lack of control is embedded in a complex
but consistent way in the histories of certain prostitutes, in which
sexual violence and abuse play a significant part, alongside distres-
sing 'objective' circumstances (such as dire economic need and
stressful working routines) and negative attitudes to their work.
These factors form the context in which powerless, negative inter-

actions with clients and negative outcomes are the more likely (Vanwesenbeeck, 1994; Vanwesenbeeck et al., 1994; 1995).

YOUNG WOMEN'S POWER IN HETEROSEXUAL ENCOUNTERS

Turning from my research on prostitutes, I used my material on heterosexual interactions of young adults[1] to see whether there were any parallels in their encounters. I found that the prostitutes' history of sexual experiences and general conditions affect the meaning of their work, the type of interactions they had and their level of control over them. To date, my group of young women have not been very differentiated when it comes to experiences (with abuse or violence) and conditions. (The girls I shall describe here are all in their early twenties, have gone on to higher education, and have had more than two heterosexual partners in the last year.) At this stage, for a still very limited sample, I can only say something about the meaning sex has for them, and the way these meanings affect the way they interact and their sense of being in control. I shall present some preliminary observations from a first reading of 25 lengthy interview transcripts (out of an proposed total of 80 for the Netherlands and another 80 for the United Kingodm) 17 of which concerned girls.

First, reading these transcripts, it struck me again how difficult it still is for most young women to have enjoyable sex with men of their own age and to be in control of those sexual interactions. I was, for instance, struck by the fact that a considerable number of girls do not expect to have an orgasm when they have sex with a boy. I was also unpleasantly surprised how often sex has an instrumental meaning: sex as a means to establish and maintain a relationship, sex as an instrument to find self-assurance and self-confirmation. Sex for its own sake is still relatively absent in the stories of these young women, whereas it is very present in the accounts of many boys. Another thing that struck me was the extent to which these young women took care of their male partners during their sexual interactions. Statements like 'you cannot expect that of them', 'I don't want to affront him', 'I don't want to push him too far' or 'I don't want to embarrass him' show how strongly the men's sensibilities are taken into consideration. In Holland et al.'s (1990) terms, describing somewhat younger girls, these women have 'the male in the head'. I strongly suspect that, for these young women, especially when they are dealing with inexperienced boys, sexual fulfilment conflicts with their roles as 'mothers' towards boys who 'shouldn't be pushed too much' and 'shouldn't be embarrassed'. This attitude was almost entirely absent among the boys I have studied so far. In fact, in contrast, the only men I have heard talk at great length about what 'one cannot do, with regard to the woman' were a certain category of prostitutes' clients.

In asking what the aspects are that undermine women's pleasure and control in heterosexual encounters, one has first to define the notion of control. In this exploratory phase I define control simply as 'getting what you want', whether in terms of sexual pleasure or in terms of contraception and condom use. Heterosexual power and control to me means 'successfully obtaining sexual pleasure while successfully protecting oneself from risks', whether openly negotiated or not. And the problem seems to be mainly in that last aspect: sex is all too often not negotiated at all. Young women are still to a large extent guided by conceptions of sexuality as utterly romantic and as natural and spontaneous. Their ideas about sexuality are often formulated very vaguely in terms of 'attraction' and 'ecstasy', ideals which do not provide them with concrete operational rules on how to get there. Planning and preparation do not go with romance. Images of romance and spontaneity prevent young women from explicitly formulating personal wishes, and prevent them even more from negotiating them. Negotiation is often perceived as 'being difficult', which is exactly what young women seeking sexual pleasure do not want to be, which means that competent negotiation may only add an extra burden in a situation where sexual pleasure is altogether hard to get and difficult enough as it is. In the romantic image of sex, where it all has to happen spontaneously and 'naturally', the initiative is often left to 'luck', to circumstances, to 'being taken by surprise' or to the other person.

Another observation is that, apart from this overwhelmingly romantic image, young women still express a lot of ambivalence concerning sex. Among many I observed a tension between craving for sexual intimacy on the one hand, and fending it off on the other. This may be to do with the double messages many girls still receive concerning sex: it's positive, but watch out; have it, but don't do it. Among only few women so far have I observed an unequivocally positive image of being sexually active with different partners (which was again very different from the situation among the boys). In the much more prevalent context of ambivalence and contradiction, young women do not develop adequate solutions for the risks that often accompany their ambivalent practices. In a context of confusion and uncertainty girls often convey contradictory messages and signals, and present themselves ambivalently, with all the consequences this has for a successful interaction. If something is negotiated at all it is often 'yes or no', 'whether or not', and only rarely, 'what and how'. Most young women do practise saying yes or no; the women I spoke to often manage to set their limits, but they are much less skilled in actively shaping sexual practice once they decide on it. They are often totally nonplussed if 'nothing happens', or if the boy does not take the initiative. They have learned to say no, but are much less likely to have learned to negotiate the sexual encounter according to their likings once they say yes. Their dependency on his initative is fuelled by their dependence on his approval and confirmation. For many, sex is no fun if he does not like it and if he does not want her, because then it's no sort of self-confirmation. There is, of course, a longstanding tradition of girls being more preoccupied with the boy wanting her, and with what he wants, than with what she herself wants.

The question arises whether these rather general conditions do permit at least some young women to have a hold on or take control of sex. Although it's too early for me to state the percentage of women who do so, it has already become clear that the answer to this question must be yes. Some of the young women whom I interviewed do show evidence of having control over their sexuality and, moreover, do convey attitudes and give meaning to sex in quite a different way from the one discussed above. They do not have an unequivocally romantic image of sex, where pleasure falls from the sky. They are convinced that you have to go for it yourself. They locate control over sex within themselves and therefore they are in control. They are not afraid of sex as a negotiation. They feel free to 'shop around' and only stick to what they like. They do not feel ambivalent about their sexual wishes, but take them very seriously. They are satisfied with having multiple partners, and are not haunted by the idea that they shouldn't have. They are well aware that there are risks involved in sex, and that these need to be addressed in sexual interactions, but they do not feel ambivalent about sexual activity in a normative, moral way. They do not have a vague, all-embracing ideal of sex, but on the contrary acknowledge that sex can be enjoyed in different ways, all with their different qualities, with or without love, in or outside of a steady relationship. They have developed different sexual scripts, matched with different sexual situations, in which they know what they want and know how to get there.

Just as the prostitutes who were in control of contact proceedings had a relatively positive attitude towards their work and did it according to positive behavioural codes, these women who are in control also showed a non-ambivalent, positive attitude towards their sexuality and towards their own desires. They have a positive image of female sexuality and female sexual pleasure, are well aware of their attractiveness to men and do not feel dependent on their approval and confirmation. These positive attitudes, and this independence, give them a much more evident say in sexual inter-action and render them much more in control of both pleasure and protection. Being a sexual object and a sexual subject seems to be hardly in opposition for them. They may very well play at being the object, both in establishing relationships as well as in shaping the sex that turns them on, without having the feeling of losing control.

It is our challenge for the future to find out how this latter group of women can grow. I would say that the dissemination of an image of, and discourse about, sexuality in which object and subject positions are not opposites, but where female sexuality has positive and powerful connotations, is the first precondition of women being in control. Women have to appropriate sexual images of themselves and make them their own. It is a postmodern feminist strategy to appropriate stereotypes of femininity and thereby take control over them. According to this strategy the potential exists for power and subjectivity in annexing our objectification. It is possible to turn something that has always defined women negatively (their objecti-fication) into a positive strength. Of course, this is exactly what prostitutes have always tried to do, which in fact makes them postmodern *avant la lettre*. Prostitutes are *playing* the whore, they are *on the game*, playing with the image of female objectification without losing their subjectivity.

However, we have to acknowledge also that this strategy is easier said than done. It's no use simply shouting that girls should acknowledge their sexual power, and that they should acknowledge that 'they have it and men want it' and enjoy the power that comes with this, as Camille Paglia (1995) does. We do, however, have to rethink feminine 'sexiness' and desirability, and the power it can give, and not simply dismiss it as being 'just objectification'. This can also give way to new concepts of male desirability and sexiness. Still, as women, we also have to acknowledge that being sexual (and playing with it) carries risks. Maybe Madonna can play around with her sexuality with impunity, but for the average girl there certainly are risks involved in doing so. Again, of course, prostitutes above all can testify how high the price of doing so is, both in terms of social acceptance and in terms of vulnerability to sexual violence.

So, a possible strategy exists, but the conditions under which it can be followed, and can be followed successfully in the sense that it leads to interactional control, are still largely unclear. For the girls I have been talking to so far, it seems that differences in the meaning given to sex, and thus differences in control over heterosexuality, can be traced back to the different messages they have received and the images and discourses of heterosexuality made available to them. Without doubt, differences in subjective experiences and differences in objective conditions (among others in relation to men) are of paramount importance. Finding out exactly how and when women can appropriate the sexual images that are prevalent today, and turn them into real power and control, is the great challenge for the future.

NOTE

1. Together with my colleagues Roger Ingham and Emily Jaramazović at the University of Southampton and Gertjan van Zessen at the Netherlands Institute of Mental Health (NcGv), I am in the process of developing and field-testing a protocol for comparative qualitative analyses of young adults' heterosexual conduct and sexual risk behaviour.

14 'Hieroglyphs of the Heterosexual': Learning about Gender in School

Shirley Prendergast and Simon Forrest

This chapter addresses some encounters with and observations of groups of young people during the course of a brief, exploratory fieldwork study in which the authors were looking at boys' experiences of school. The chapter draws on material from three secondary schools, focusing particularly but not exclusively on the boys. The three schools were in many senses a special sample. They had all the indices of deprivation and poverty: a high percentage of pupils having free school dinners, a high rate of absenteeism and teacher turnover, and a very low rating in the previous year's Department of Education and Employment 'league tables' of examination results. Their catchment areas were rundown housing estates with well above average levels of male unemployment and a high proportion of one-parent families. Altogether we spoke to about 100 young people between the ages of 12 and 15, the majority of them boys.[1]

Interviewing, talking, listening to the arguments and discussions that took place in small focus groups, observing interaction in the classroom and playground, our days in school were exhausting but also strangely exhilarating. They were exhausting because, by the time of secondary school, the sexes do not just ignore each other as they do in primary school: what we found in class and elsewhere was an active, radical, articulate atmosphere of confrontation – 'girls versus boys'. Exhilarating because at the same time they were charged with a contagious energy: certainly *something* seemed to be going on. In the early years of adolescence, in these schools at least, the polarities of the sexes were such that girls and boys might just as well have come from different planets.

In one school we emerged each day, shellshocked from this experience, to walk through a kind of no-man's land, a hidden network of narrow alleys cutting behind yards and gardens, connecting the school to the town. Unattended over many years the walls and fences of these alleyways had become covered in graffiti. Flaking, half-erased, written over, superimposed words, names, images, suggestions, accusations, dates, assignations and drawings: wimp, cow, slag, prick, cunt, faces, bodies, hearts and arrows: 'Sarah 4 Mark', 'Andy and Sally', 'Amanda loves Terry' (written over 'Terry is a Wanker').

We discussed how for five years of adolescence, moving between school and home, pupils must pass and repass these signs, many of which no doubt they themselves had made, reminders of the historic struggle for romantic and sexual connection between young women and men. We speculated how long some graffiti had been there, its humour, bravado, crudity, despair and hope reflecting the inherent power, fragility, mystery and contradictions of these connections across time. Half joking, but like all jokes, half in earnest and often unwittingly expressing an element of as yet unperceived truth, we called this writing on the wall the *'hieroglyphs of the heterosexual'*.

BACKGROUND

To date most of the work on emotions and emotional development has been about adult relationships, and much of *that* work is about what happens when adult relationships go wrong. Summarizing, we might say that a large and growing literature suggests that adult women and men come to heterosexual relationships with very different conceptions and expectations of love, communication, intimacy and sharing (Mansfield and Collard, 1988). These differing expectations and the behaviours that they engender often lead to conflict and dissatisfaction with the partnership, and are a major contributing factor in the breakdown of relationships, particularly on the part of women. Women appear to place a greater significance on talking about emotions than do men, and to work harder at monitoring and sustaining emotional ties and doing what Hochschild has called 'emotion work' (Hochschild, 1983; Tannen, 1991). Duncombe and Marsden have pointed out that this imbalance in emotion work is most likely to be experienced negatively by women, and it is an issue which women regularly voice. At the heart of the problem, they note, is the fact that many women express unhappiness primarily with what they perceive as men's unwillingness or incapacity to do the emotional intimacy which appears to them necessary to sustain close heterosexual couple relationships!

(Duncombe and Marsden, 1993, p. 221)

Above all there seems to be a resounding silence from men: what do men think and feel about this issue? Do they experience an imbalance, and if so why do they not raise it themselves? How is it that men's and women's emotional concerns and experiences are so different (Tannen, 1991)? Clearly, heterosexual couplehood does not emerge fully fledged out of the blue: it, and its associated emotional configurations, too universal, numerous and predictable to be dismissed, must be known, rehearsed and learned gradually at other ages across the life-course. Within this debate questions about the development and gendering of emotions have over the years come in for intense scrutiny (Hochschild, 1983; Rubin, 1983; Segal, 1990).

It is useful to look here at some of the changing configurations of heterosexual learning and behaviour, particularly as it aligns with age and peer group behaviour across time. There is evidence to suggest that young children see, describe and act towards each other in polarized, gendered, emotional terms by nursery age, although they may mix and play in mixed-sex groups fairly freely (Walkerdine, 1981; Brown and France, 1993). A little later, by late primary school, while they certainly appear to be rehearsing romantic heterosexual behaviours, 9–11-year-olds actually spend their time playing and working in predominantly single-sex groups, mostly avoiding the opposite sex (Abrams, 1989).

We know, however, that 4–5 years later, by the mid-teens, everything has changed. The WRAP study of gendered sexual attitudes and behaviour around safe sex, done with young adults of 16–19, described the onset of intense heterosexual couple relations (Holland et al., 1991; 1993). Most of these were sexually active and many individuals, significantly young women, were already encountering the same differences, silences and dissatisfactions with their partners that we find in accounts of adult relationships.

Accounts such as these are patchy, and there are even fewer that make any coherent links between and across age groups as processes develop over time. For example, the shift from primary to secondary school has come to mark conceptual boundaries, and researchers rarely cross the transition. The age of 11 then comes as a 'natural' break when somehow childhood ends and adolescence begins, irrespective of maturity (Chisholm et al., 1990). Clearly we need to know much more about forms of normal, ordinary, everyday development around intimacy and emotions, not just when relationships are breaking down, and we need to know about how these everyday expectations are gendered. We need to know too how, when, where and why do girls and boys, young women and men, enter into early emotional and sexual relations, and how the nature of these might develop and change over time.

Using fieldwork and interview material, this chapter reflects upon some aspects of early gender relations, particularly in the connection that might be made between gendered group behaviours and learning about heterosexuality for adolescent girls and boys aged 11–15 in school. We explore three issues:

1. The ways in which formal and informal structures of schooling may operate to shape and perpetuate certain forms of group gender relations and the meanings that group membership may have particularly for boys.
2. The seemingly paradoxical nature of Western constructions of gender in shaping processes that both create heterosexual relationships and that ultimately may also lead to their destruction.
3. The possibility that at a time of intense social and economic change, for some groups gendered heterosexual relations may be becoming more different, more conflictual and more out of step with the supposed new flexibilities of gender.

GENDERED GROUPS: FROM THE BARRICADES?

In our sample girls and boys spent the majority of their time in secondary school in single-sex groups. In the classroom and in the more informal spaces of school single-sex groups are so pervasive, so normal, that they are in many ways invisible and taken for granted by pupils and by teachers. For example, girls clustered in the classroom, discussing what they had done out of school the night before, would drive away boys who tried to eavesdrop with furious insults; boys would creep up on groups of girls sitting in the sun at lunchtime, grab their bags and throw them over the fence; at break the boys headed for and totally occupied the sports fields and

the larger playgrounds while the girls went indoors or sat reading,
doing each other's hair or talking on the margins of the boys
activities.

In lessons our research showed that when pupils were informally
seated, sitting as they wished in class, even if the classroom was
arranged in desks for two in formal lines facing the teacher, pupils
were always in fact in close proximity with a known and selected
single-sex group. If asked to form small groups in class the effect was
rather like holding a magnet over iron filings: with almost no effort
at all, other than the turning of chairs a little this way a little that,
the invisible would become visible and a series of single-sex groups
would draw together and become defined. The prospect of being in
a *mixed* group in class filled both girls and boys alike with horror. We
found very few classrooms where this happened voluntarily, a
situation confirmed by the occasions when mixed groups were
artificially created in class by the teacher.

Three examples spring to mind. First, rarely, a teacher created in
effect a mixed group when she rescued a bullied boy by placing him
in a 'safe' girls group. As we have described elsewhere although the
girls were generally fully aware of the situation of any individual
bullied boy, and may privately have felt indignant about it, that boy
is to all intents and purposes beyond the pale in relation to dominant male groups (Prendergast and Forrest, forthcoming). While not
wishing to hurt him themselves, few girls would want to make
enemies by taking up his cause. The result is a silent, humiliated
and marginalized boy, while the girls continue to work together. It
is worth noting that the reverse, putting a bullied girl into an all-
boys group for safe-keeping, is unthinkable.

A second example, more common but still unusual, happened
where a teacher attempted to break up a disruptive or over-excited
boys' group by dispersing them among the girls. The consequence
was often an increased hilarity and joking between boys across the
groups, or a sense of artificiality and irritation that was hard to
overcome. In such circumstances the girls become resentful, the
boys embarrassed. Nobody will speak and class contributions
dwindle.

Yet a third, perhaps more frequent use of mixed-sex groups
occurs when a teacher wants to promote 'sensitive' or personal
discussion, perhaps in a PHSE (personal, health and sex education)
class. The difficulties the teacher experiences in generating this kind
of discussion in a normal, informally seated class, confirm the

hidden mapping of single-sex groups revealed by our research. In an informally seated classroom the result is likely to be either a kind of theatrical mayhem or an embarrassed silence instigated by the boys, against which the girls attempt a 'serious' conversation. This kind of classroom behaviour was also recalled retrospectively by young people of 16–19 in the WRAP study (Thomson and Scott, 1991). However, unlike the examples described above, girls themselves may approve of teacher intervention in this context. Boys they argue must be 'civilized' if they are ever to become decent future partners and parents, and making them talk about intimate things in mixed groups is one way of bringing this about (Prendergast, 1995).

We can see then that although interaction between and within single-sex groups is the source of much of the disruption and difficulty faced by the teacher, and indeed in the school as a whole, they change this pattern at their peril. The teacher, in solving one crisis, usually a crisis of boys' behaviour, creates another, a gender crisis. By sitting them together, she alienates both the boys *and* the girls. Further, these examples of mixed-sex groups created by the teacher carry intimations of control, or even punishment, and an underlying agenda which suggests that mixed groups in class may be about enrolling girls to control boys. These dilemmas may well contribute to the ways in which some boys increasingly describe teachers as being 'sexist', which will be discussed below.

TEACHERS TODAY ARE SEXIST AGAINST THE BOYS

In the schools we visited, there seemed to be a growing sense of bitter injustice among boys about the processes of schooling. This was not shared by girls in their peer group in the same ways. This bitterness could be heard in the ways in which boys described what they saw as teachers' differential behaviour to girls and to boys.

Boys' accounts

The boys described teachers' treatment of themselves and other boys:

- the teachers' first reaction is to blame *boys* for any disturbance or wrong-doing in school, whoever is to blame;

- boys are more likely to get expelled and suspended;
- teachers do not give boys high marks;
- male teachers in particular can behave in a very aggressive and belittling fashion to boys.

In contrast, boys said teachers treated *girls* very differently:

- teachers favour girls and are nice to them;
- they talk and listen to girls more;
- teachers give girls higher marks than boys;
- they don't punish girls as severely for similar offences;
- they don't blame girls for trouble in class, girls 'got away with murder'.

Girls' accounts

When we compared girls' accounts of teachers behaviour, we found an underlying match with what the boys said. For example, girls said that teachers did blame boys for wrong-doing, they did not give boys high marks and indeed male teachers sometimes were very aggressive to the boys. They said that boys often didn't do their work and talked about sport in lessons. While girls did not use words like favouritism, they described a general sense of girls getting on with teachers, talking to them and of enjoying school more.

There was in fact a kind of shared truth, articulated by boys and girls alike and by what we ourselves saw, which suggested that teachers certainly did seem to behave in many of the ways that boys described. However what was not shared was any explanation as to how and why this state of affairs should have come about. *Girls* said that some boys misbehave in class so much that they are impossible to teach. They are so intent on 'having a laugh' and watching or playing football that they don't bother with homework and fall behind. Girls also note that boys are often so disruptive that nobody else can work in class either. Boys therefore annoy and upset both the teacher and the girls. This, girls say, is the reason that teachers discriminate against boys. *Boys* themselves however have a quite different explanation for their current circumstances: they blame the girls. Girls, boys say, are goody-goodies, teachers' pets, they suck up to teachers. Most powerfully too, boys articulate a discourse of reversed discrimination. Boys say its 'girls, girls, girls', nobody cares about the boys. 'Girls now have everybody on their side, they behave as badly as they want and nobody says anything': indeed it's so bad that 'teachers these days are SEXIST against the boys'.

GIRLS 'WANT IT ALL' THESE DAYS...

Boys' sense of bitterness and frustration can also be gauged from the fatalistic ways in which they spoke about their future lives. While they hoped to get a job locally, these were often described as individual jobs, done by someone known, who with luck might put in a good word, who knew someone's uncle, who might pass this job on to a willing lad. Some mentioned joining the armed services. Alongside ran more fantastical dreams of being 'spotted' by a foot-fall talent scout from a famous team and making a fortune. There was little in between. They spoke of the meaninglessness of school when they saw boredom, unemployment and poverty ahead of them. This echoes the reality of many boys' lives, where indeed in their area a very high proportion of men were unemployed.

In contrast, when asked about their future all girls had plans. They spoke of hairdressing, hospital work, cooking, working with animals or in the supermarket. After school they wanted to leave home, to leave the area, to live with friends. They hoped to have a holiday, perhaps to travel, to have a bit of money to spend and above all to have some fun. While we might question whether the work envisaged by girls would actually support them while they did these things, their plans were not totally unrealistic or unrealizable. Indeed, many of their mothers survived in this way.

Noticeably absent from girls were spontaneous accounts of marriage and children. When we asked they said 'perhaps, maybe, never, later', 'when I'm 35, if I meet someone, if I can afford it, maybe if I do it on my own'. Most decidedly, girls said that if they *did* have children it would not be with those who were at present their male peer group. The boys mucked around, they were wasters. As men they would let you down, they wouldn't work, they didn't contribute, why should any sensible woman have children with *them*?

These are in striking contrast with what girls said about their future lives over a decade ago. In a study done in the late 1970s with girls of the same age as in this current work, marriage and motherhood were actively and centrally present in every girl's description and desires for the future (Prendergast and Prout, 1980). Then, although motherhood may have been viewed with some trepidation and anxiety, as something that might result in 'depression', requiring particular and unique 'ways out' to survive, in no 1970s account was it totally absent. Girls today, compared to boys in their peer group and compared to girls in their situation in the past, speak with a palpable sense of agency, confidence, determination and hope about their future lives, even if their plans may be considered less realistic in a wider context of women's work more generally (Hakim, 1995; Ginn et al., 1996).

GROUP DISCUSSIONS: A THEATRE OF GENDERPLAY...

A final example from the study looks at what young people said and how they spoke about each other and about gender relationships in the small, mixed, focus-group discussions that we convened. Perhaps not surprisingly, given what we have already described regarding mixed group relations in school, the atmosphere in the groups was often highly charged and much energy was expended on what looked like a kind 'theatre of genderplay' between the sexes. This can be seen in the transcribed records of group discussions. For example, the following (group C18:9) summarizes discussion between four girls (Liza, Senda, Kerry and Maggie) and four boys (Robert, Michael, Dave and Andie) in year 9. It covers 14–15 pages of transcript, in response to one question: 'How do girls and boys behave to each other in single-sex groups?'

Girls (G) say boys (B) try to impress people
B say they wouldn't show off to G like *that*
B say G bully them, talk behind B backs, whisper like little whimpers
G say B are dying to know what they are saying
B say *yes*, B do want to know what G say
G say that B want to know because B fancy G
B deny this! B say that G look at B when they are whispering, so
B know it's about them
G say, yes, we are saying 'he's a right pratt'! G won't say that out
loud 'because B would slap them
G say that anyway G are not talking about B, just looking to see if
the B are looking at them

B   say (with considerable vehemence) so that is what G are doing!
    looking at B and *pretending to speak*. G are just trying to wind B
    up. But B are not falling for *that*
G   say that B *are* wound up − they come over and hit the G
B   say that B *really do* talk about the G. But compared to G, B speak
    the truth. B take the mickey, say horrible things about G *because
    they are true* and it's better if girls hear the truth
G   say they beat boys up in year 7 because 'You was littler than us'
B   say that instead B 'mouthed girls off'
B   say Kerry (a very vocal girl) has a reputation for 'slagging people
    down'. G are two-faced
G   say all G are two-faced
B   say B can be too
G   say B *are* two-faced
B   'All right'

The discussion constantly set up 'us and them', *boys v. girls*. It is
noteworthy that in 14–15 pages there are only one or two examples
where one girl and one boy speak individually to, or about each
other, and even these are highly conflictual:

Robert: Ain't I nice sometimes? [unclear, boys agreeing]
Liza: You've hurt my feelings.
Robert: Then why do you go out with me all the time then, if you
            don't like me? [lots of voices, unclear] (p. 10)

As gendered subgroups, boys and girls try to humiliate and
embarrass each other. Swapping insults, teasing, undermining,
mocking revelations, accusations, assertions of different kinds of
power going on. Its amusing, fast and vivid. There is a
rapid exchange of repartee almost like a comic show. Each 'side'
verbally weaves and dodges, pulls devious tricks and outwits the
other.

Michael: See, that's what the girls are doing now, what they're doing
            is looking at you and pretending to speak, so's we'd
            get wound up. But I didn't fall for it. Not yet. [unclear]
            (p. 11)
Dave: No, girls can't even fight.
Kerry: They take the mickey out of everything we do.
Andie: Girls run like gorillas.
Liza: Boys *are* gorillas. (p. 13)

In this engagement each sex draws upon both stereotype and experience to reveal and confront what they see as most difficult and annoying about the opposite sex:

Robert: Yes, if we're going out with someone, you see the girl and she's flirting with someone [unclear, shouted down]

Senda: ... no it's you flirting. You think its different for you ... [unclear, shouted down]

Robert: [persisting] ... so that's why nobody goes out with no one in this year. (p. 6)

Girls object to the insensitive, joking, physicality and power aspects of boys and particularly *boys' groups*, while boys attack the personal, bitchy, two-faced nature of girls' approach and relationships. Just as the girls appear to have established their superiority over the boys, the boys pull the rug from beneath their feet. The boys retaliate by saying that all along they (the boys) were lying, therefore the girls now look foolish for taking them seriously in the first place. Undaunted, the girls pursue their point to the bitter end, and suddenly the boys give up: for the moment the contest is over.

Material from the transcripts can be summarized as follows:

Girls Say about Boys in Groups	*Boys Say about Girls in Groups*
boys bully	girls wind boys up
boys show off	girls are two-faced
boys call girls slags	girls talk all the time
boys are sexist	girls are spiteful
boys use double standards	girls flirt
boys take the mickey	girls lead boys on
boys behave badly in class	girls slag each other off
boys fight	girls are disloyal
boys don't listen	
boys won't talk about things	
boys are only interested in sex	

While these exchanges can be very funny, they have a cost. There is a marked absence of any language of negotiation, communication and intimacy. At their worst there is incomprehension, disconnection and hostility between the sexes. This all sounds depressingly familiar, indeed it rehearses the difficulties and schisms beginning to be found between young people in the WRAP research and most certainly echoes those voiced by adult women and men noted at the start of this chapter: girls talk too much and boys don't talk enough; girls talk and boys don't listen; boys want sex and girls want romance (Holland et al., 1991; 1993). The immediate implications and effects of group interactions of this kind can be heard in the words of Tom, almost 15, in Year 10.

Tom says there are three tutor groups in his year, each with a room off a long corridor. He described how one lunchtime a rumour started in one tutor group that a girl wanted to go out with a boy in another, in a different room. A friend of the girl made the match by shouting down the corridor, asking the boy if he would go out with her friend. After public teasing, insults, negotiation, all shouted up and down the corridor, the boy's friends decided that he would go out with her, and the match was made.

This is an interaction in which the boy and girl are in a sense public currency between the groups. What matters is not so much the individual, but the symbolic act of group connection, in which personal, private feelings are hostage to fortune. Not surprisingly, relationships made in this way do not last long, days or sometimes only hours. Yet must it not be from such encounters that an accumulated knowledge and experience builds, and from which eventually the very stuff of romance, of love, commitment and future lives as couples is supposed to be made?

AN OVERVIEW: DIFFERENCE AND CONFLICT, CONTENT AND PROCESS

We end by trying to summarize some of the connections between difference and conflict in shaping early encounters between young women and men at the present time, and the ways in which these formations contribute to later relationships in adult life. From these few examples from our fieldwork it is possible to get some idea of the power of single-sex groups as they are shaped by and as they shape heterosexual experience of young people in school.

We have suggested that single-sex groups permeate school life and in these groups individuals *retreat* into single-sex friendships, activities and interests. Single-sex groups can be a place of invisibility and, particularly for boys, a place to behave as they wish, safe from the critical regard of the opposite sex. As girls and boys begin to come together in groups, although not yet to engage fully as heterosexual couples, they voice extreme, polarized, although not completely unrealistic gender differences enacted in almost ritualized, joking form. Single-sex groups operate as a solidarity base from which gender identity itself, the gendered characteristics of self and 'other', are actively experienced, defended and attacked.

After a long apprenticeship in single-sex groups, lived out through a history of schooling in the ways we have seen, coming together is of course fraught with difficulty and excitement. In fact it could be said that it is actually the polarities and difficulties that *facilitate* attraction. In group conflict and perhaps only through group conflict can individuals engage with little risk to themselves. The reluctance of boys and girls to mix is in part *because* the only available rationale for mixing is one of romantic and/or sexual attraction. Once in a mixed group this rationale, attraction or denial of attraction dominates almost everything about how girls and boys relate. As we have seen the reactions of teachers, in creating mixed groups to control and even punish, confirm this. A mixed group exposes the mechanisms by which individuals, especially boys, may eventually be 'softened up', teased out of single-sex strongholds, enticed into heterosexual couplehood by the 'civilizing' influence of girls. Perhaps not surprisingly, school, where pedagogy is based almost exclusively on the peer group, may come to be a battleground and site of collective male resistance to such processes.

While as we have seen the content of gendered conflict looks very familiar it is clear that for young people the *content, implications and meaning* of such encounters is secondary to, subsumed by the *process*. While girls and boys name and describe underlying structural features of gendered conflict, with varying degrees of realism, accuracy and detail as we know they are expressed in later relationships, the actuality of these is brushed aside. For example while issues of 'non-communication' are expressed, they are not really heard or addressed: difference of this kind is voiced primarily as a weapon in a kind of 'gender war' between groups. This conflict can be understood as a classic induction into heterosexual relations, in which desire and sexual attraction spring from uniting and bringing together men and women across (some would say socially constructed and polarized) gendered difference (Connell, 1987).

However, evidence suggests that compared to a decade or more ago, these engagements may be more conflictual. First, as we have seen the mostly working-class boys in this study have relatively and absolutely lost ground compared to girls. Older certainties of the job market have gone, and with them other previously taken-for-granted possibilities as husbands, breadwinners, family men and fathers. Second, these girls no longer have quite the same romantic desires and investments in the boys that they know, and have come to articulate more about their own needs and interests. This appears to be true for the girls in our study, who do not discuss their futures, as we have seen, either in terms of 'careers' or professions or inevitable motherhood, but in more modest but possibly achievable expectations. Compared to boys then, girls both seem to get on better day to day in school and to have a more positive sense of the future. At the same time, they are not so ready to accept and be beguiled by the hegemonic behaviour of their male peer group. As a result perhaps, some of the young people discussed here are entering opposite-sex relationships almost as adversaries.

These shifts echo findings in Norwegian studies by Bjerrum Nielsen and Rudberg (1995) of inter-generational change and by Frones (1995) of school achievement and occupational choice. These studies suggest that contemporary Norwegian girls are beginning to be seen as 'having it all' compared to boys. They are different from their mothers in that they expect both equality and the right to be equal *as a girl.* They feel confident enough to play with and take on board their gender. At the same time they expect to lead a life which combines both employment and children (Bjerrum Nielsen and Rudberg, 1995). These expectations appear to be borne out by the ways in which young women are actively succeeding in school and in future work roles (Frones, 1995). The ways in which girls are becoming what Bjerrum Nielsen and Rudberg call 'a project *for themselves*' suggest that increasingly they no longer require relationships with men so much to validate their separateness.

The paradox then, the mystery of the hieroglyphs, may be this: that girls and boys who begin to engage with the reality of romance and sex with each other *as individuals,* do so because of, and with, experiences, models and forms of engagement that spring from *group processes.* These group processes may in fact be counter-productive and even damaging, masking and denying possibilities for addressing those very issues that may lead to so many problems later on. Attraction and desire, the excitement that springs from group-gendered conflict, cannot be sustained by individuals face to face. As Michelle, one of our respondents said, echoing many:

> Like in groups, you are mucking around. There's a lot of muckin' about, kind of like aggro. But you know, it seems like fun and you think you like each other. But then when a girl and one boy go out alone together they start to hate each other. It all ends, and then you are enemies. Worse than before. It's a mystery really. I don't know why

Despite an almost constant flow of interventions to modify young people's knowledge or behaviour, including the most recent suggestions that they should be taught about private pension plans, the workings of the stock exchange and share ownership because 'there is no job security and welfare is no longer free' (*The Guardian*, April 1996) gender is rarely if ever explicitly on the school curriculum. Interestingly, it seemed that our focus groups in school, while they were indeed artificially created mixed groups seemed to have allowed young people to begin to address the deeper underlying issues. These mixed groups were not created, as so often in school, to control (male) group behaviour, but to discuss that very thing that is so central, but usually unspoken in the school context: the nature of gendered groups themselves!

How far the issues raised by this small study are more widely generalizable is a moot point. Certainly some of the underlying structural features we found have been remarked upon in the media and in other studies (Askew and Ross, 1988; Phillips, 1993). In a wider context, research by Kari Vik Kleven on peer groups in school describes how sixth form girls' clubs in Norwegian schools actively initiate gender conflict. These girl gangs collectively battle with boys in a way which brings the content of gendered challenge to the fore. In this situation, she writes: 'open and offensive gender clashes do not hide the existing conflict of interests, but rather bring them to light. The possibilities are therefore greater for developing awareness and working things out.' At the same time 'without distance and differences, there will be less erotic sparks and excitements' (Kleven, 1993, p. 56).

In the schools that we worked in there seemed little to prepare young people for the moment when gender conflict as *group process* turns into gender conflict as *relational reality*. As Jill Lewis writes in this volume, in relation to the knowledge and confidence to have safe sex, at this point, the narrative ends. Just as we find ourselves with the desired but unfamiliar companionship of the 'other', just as a tenuous and fragile heterosexuality/coupledom is achieved, everything that we most want and need to know, about communication, collaboration and negotiation is unspoken and unresolved. We are left to unravel the collective knot alone. How exactly are these 'enemies' described by Michelle to make the kinds of 'equal friendships' that seem to out hold the best hope for future (heterosexual) happiness and stability? The stage is set, it appears, for serious misunderstandings and confrontations of the kind that seem to so characterize relations between women and men in later life.

ACKNOWLEDGMENTS

The authors would like to acknowledge the following:

First, the help of the young people who took part in the study and the teachers and head teachers who made it possible. Second, the financial support of the Health Promotion Research Trust in doing the study. Third, the support of the FPA, the Family Planning Association, in giving us a place to meet in London. Finally they would like to acknowledge the support and assistance of Simon Cavicchia from NACTU, the National Aids Counselling and Training Unit, who contributed to the literature review and in planning the early stages of the work.

NOTE

1. The project took place over two years, between 1993 and 1995. During that time the authors worked with young people between the ages of 12 and 15 and their teachers in four secondary schools, three of which are discussed here. The study used both small-scale qualitative methods, case studies, focus groups, individual interviews or in pairs, observation and classroom activities (about 100 consulted in all) alongside a questionnaire with a larger sample (about 400 questionnaires) Fully informed, advance consent was sought from both young people and their parents. Further details of the research can be found in Prendergast and Forrest, in Bendelow and Williams (1996).

15 Queer Identities and the Ethnicity Model

Alan Sinfield

'It's as if we were an ethnic grouping,' Peter Burton wrote in *Gay Times* (April 1995). Thinking of lesbians and/or gay men as an ethnic group runs counter to the constructed and decentred status of the subject as s/he is apprehended in current theory. None the less, very many lesbians and gay men today feel, intuitively, that they are like an ethnic group. This is partly because, as Steven Epstein (1992, p. 255) suggests, we have constituted ourselves in the period when ethnicity, following the precedent of the Black Civil Rights movement, has offered the dominant paradigm for political advancement. So we too claim our rights: that is what ethnic groups do. The culmination of this tendency is Simon LeVay's belief that he is doing us all a good turn by locating a part of the brain that is different in gay men, because this will enable US gays to claim recognition in the courts as a minority having immutable characteristics (LeVay, 1993; Sinfield, 1994, pp. 177–84). So North American lesbians and gays can get to be as well off as the Indian peoples.

It is not altogether a matter of deciding how far we want to go with ethnicity-and-rights; the dominance of that model is not incidental. For it is not that existing categories of gay men and lesbians have come forward to claim their rights, but that we have become constituted *as gay* in the terms of a discourse of ethnicity-and-rights. This discourse was active, and apparently effective, elsewhere in the political formation, and afforded us opportunity to identify ourselves – to *become ourselves*. This has meant both adding to and subtracting from our potential subjectivities. 'The person who takes up a post-Stonewall gay identity feels compelled to act in a way that will constitute her or himself as a subject appropriate to civil rights discourse,' Cindy Patton (1993, pp. 173–4) observes. Gay men and lesbians *are*: a group, or groups, claiming rights.

However, there are drawbacks with envisaging ourselves through a framework of ethnicity-and-rights. One is that it consolidates our constituency at the expense of limiting it. If you are lower-class, gay lobbying and lifestyle are less convenient and may seem alien. If you are young, the call to declare a sexual identity imposes the anxiety that exploration of your gay potential may close your options for ever. And if you are a person of colour, the prominence of a mainly white model makes it more difficult for you to negotiate ways of thinking about sexualities that will be compatible with your sub-cultures of family and neighbourhood.

Also, fixing our constituency on the ethnicity-and-rights model lets the sex-gender system off the hook. It encourages the inference that an out-group needs concessions, rather than the mainstream needs correction; so lesbians and gay men, Herman observes, may be 'granted legitimacy, not on the basis that there might be something problematic with gender roles and sexual hierarchies, but on the basis that they constitute a fixed group of "others" who need and deserve protection' (Herman, 1993, p. 251). Initially in Gay Liberation, we aspired to open out the scope of sexual expression for everyone, in the process displacing the oppressive ideologies that sexuality is used to police. By inviting us to perceive ourselves as settled in our sexuality, the ethnicity-and-rights model releases others from the invitation to re-envisage theirs.

THE CASTRO AND THE WHITE HOUSE

The ethnicity-and-rights model aspires to two main spheres of political effectivity. One is a claim for space within which the minority may legitimately express itself. For gay men, classically, this was the Castro district of San Francisco. Manuel Castells, in a moment of exuberance in the early 1980s, saw there a recovery of the merchant citizenship of the Italian Renaissance:

> We are almost in the world of the Renaissance city where political freedom, economic exchange, and cultural innovation, as well as open sexuality, developed together in a self-reinforcing process on the basis of a common space won by citizens struggling for their freedom.

Castro gay leaders spoke of a 'liberated zone' (Castells, 1983, pp. 162, 138–9).

However, if it is hard to achieve socialism in one country, as Trotsky insisted against Stalin, it is even less likely that sexual liberation can work in one sector of one capitalist city. Castells observes how inter-communal hostility developed in and around the Castro, as gentrification (also known as 'gay sensibility') raised property values and squeezed out other, mainly Black and Latino, minorities. In fact, the clashing of competing interests is endemic to the ethnicity-and-rights model. Castells observes: 'each player defines him/herself as having to pursue his/her own interests in a remarkable mirror image of the ideal model of the free market' (Castells, 1983, p. 171). However, the free market, we should know, does not generally present itself in 'ideal' form. Generally, it sets us all at each other's throats.

The second sphere where the ethnicity-and-rights model aspires to political effectivity is through the organs of the state. In *Close to the Knives* David Wojnarowitz (1992) propounds an urgent critique of US political, religious and judicial systems (that aspect of his book is left out of Steve McLean's 1994 film, *Postcards from America*). However, alongside that, Wojnarowitz manifests an underlying vein of surprise that gay rights have not been acknowledged; he is shocked to read of a Supreme Court ruling (presumably *Bowers* v. *Hardwick*), that it is 'only people who are heterosexual or married or who have families that expect these constitutional rights' (Wojnarowitz, 1992, p. 81). Lamenting the suicide of his friend Dakota, Wojnarowitz asks: 'Man, why did you do it? Why didn't you wait for the possibilities to reveal themselves in this shit country, on this planet?' (ibid., p. 241). Despite his indictment, Wojnarowitz still expects Uncle Sam to come up trumps eventually. A persistent leitmotif in *Close to the Knives* is that if only President Reagan would pay attention to AIDS, we would begin to get somewhere with it. Wojnarowitz writes:

> I imagine what it would be like if, each time a lover, friend or stranger died of this disease, their friends, lovers or neighbors would take the dead body and drive with it in a car a hundred miles an hour to washington d.c. and blast through the gates of the white house and come to a screeching halt before the entrance and dump their lifeless form on the front steps.
>
> (ibid., p. 122)

It is as if recognition in official quarters would not only help resource a campaign to alert gay men to HIV and AIDS; not only legitimate the campaign; but somehow magic away the epidemic.

Is homosexuality intolerable? That is the ultimate question. One answer is that actually lesbians and gay men are pretty much like other people but we got off on the wrong foot somewhere around St Paul; it just needs a few more of us to come out, so that the nervous among our compatriots can see we really aren't so dreadful, and then everyone will live and let live; sexuality will become unimportant. The other answer is that homophobia contributes crucially to structures of capital and patriarchy, and that lesbian and gay people constitute, willy-nilly, a profound challenge to prevailing values in our kinds of society. We cannot expect to settle this question. However, it would be rash to suppose that the criminalizing and stigmatizing of same-sex practices and lifestyles is an incidental kink in an otherwise reasonable structure; that the present system could, without cost, relinquish its legitimations and interdictions. Consider: parents will repudiate their offspring because of gayness. Something very powerful is operating there.

In my view, the pluralist myth which legitimates the ethnicity-and-rights model affords useful tactical opportunities, but it is optimistic to suppose that it will get us very far. Nevertheless, I shall argue that we cannot afford entirely to abandon a minoritizing model because we cannot afford to abandon subculture.

DIASPORA AND HYBRIDITY

Meanwhile, in another part of the wood, theorists of 'race' and 'ethnicity' have been questioning how far those constructs offer a secure base for self-understanding and political action. ' "Black" is essentially a politically and culturally *constructed* category,' Stuart Hall writes, 'one which cannot be grounded in a set of fixed transcultural or transcendental or transcendental racial categories and which therefore has no guarantees in Nature' (Hall, 1992, p. 254). In similar vein, Henry Louis Gates, Jr calls for a 'thorough critique of blackness as a presence, which is merely another transcendent signified' (Gates, 1988, p. 237).

In respect of European and American – *diasporic* – Black peoples, this may seem merely a necessary move: after forced migration, forced miscegenation and all kinds of economic and cultural oppression it must be hard to isolate an uncontaminated Africanness. 'Because of the experience of diaspora,' says Gates, 'the fragments that contain the traces of a coherent system of order must be reassembled' (Gates, 1988, p. xxiv). 'Diaspora' is a Greek, biblical term, denoting the captivity of the Hebrews in Babylon and, latterly, the worldwide dispersal of Jewry; usually it invokes a true point of origin, and an authentic line – hereditary and/or historical – back to that. However, diasporic Black culture, Hall says, is defined 'not by essence or purity, but by the recognition of a necessary heterogeneity and diversity; by a conception of "identity" which lives with and through, not despite, difference; by *hybridity*' (Hall, 1990, p. 235). Paul Gilroy, in his book *The Black Atlantic*, offers the image of a ship, situated in mid-Atlantic, in continuous negotiation between Africa, the Americas and Western Europe (Gilroy, 1993, p. 4).

Recognition that race and ethnicity might be constructed, hybrid and insecure, but yet necessary, has obvious resonances for lesbian and gay cultural politics, and may help us to think about ourselves. For gay subculture, certainly, is hybrid; to the point where it is difficult to locate anything that is crucially gay – either at the core of gayness, or having gayness at its core. What about drag, then? Mostly – from pantomime and music hall to working men's clubs and film and television comedy – it is consumed by straight audiences. Drag plays with gender boundaries, and all sorts of people are interested in that. The disco scene, perhaps? Well yes, except that a standard feature is the latest diva calling down God's punishment on people with AIDS. The ancient Greeks, maybe? Well, the organizing principle of their sexual regime seems to have been that a citizen (male) may fuck any inferior – women, slaves, boys. That is the stuff heroes are made of, but hardly sexual liberation. Camp then? Since Susan Sontag's defining essay of 1964, it has appeared to be anybody's, and now it is co-opted into 'the postmodern'. There is art and literature: surely gay men are justly famed for our achievement there? Yes, but we have been allowed to produce quality culture on condition that we are discreet, thereby confirming our unspeakableness. Decoding the work of closeted homosexual artists, I have argued elsewhere, discovers not a ground for congratulation but a record of oppression and humiliation (Sinfield, 1992, pp. 294–9). Opera even – since The Three Tenors were offered as a curtain-raiser for the World Cup Final in 1994 – now correlates with football rather than, in Wayne Koestenbaum's title, *The Queen's Throat*.

When Frank Mort writes of 'a well-established homosexual diaspora, crossing nation states and linking individuals and social constituencies', we know what he means (Mort, 1994, p. 202). However, as Michael Warner remarks, there is no remote place or time, not even in myth and fantasy, from which lesbians and gay men have dispersed (Warner, 1993, p. xvii). Our hybridity is constituted differently. Indeed, while ethnicity is transmitted usually through family and lineage, most of us are born and/or socialized into (presumptively) heterosexual families. We have to move away from them, at least to some degree; and *into*, if we are lucky, the culture of a minority community. In fact, for lesbians and gay men the diasporic sense of separation and loss, so far from affording a principle of coherence for our subcultures, may actually attach to aspects of the (heterosexual) culture of our childhood, where we are no longer 'at home'. Instead of dispersing, we assemble.

The hybridity of our subcultures derives not from the loss of even a mythical unity, but from the difficulty we experience in envisaging ourselves beyond the framework of normative heterosexism – the *straightgeist* – as Nicholson Baker (1994) calls it, on the model of *Zeitgeist*. If diasporic Africans are poised between alternative homelands – in mid-Atlantic, Gilroy suggests – then lesbians and gay men are stuck at the moment of emergence. For coming out is not once-and-for-all; like the Africans, we never quite arrive. Now, I am not proposing any equivalence between the oppressions of race and sexuality – anyway, there is not one oppression of either race or sexuality, there are many. But, while in some instances race and ethnicity are not manifest, for lesbians and gay men inadvertent passing is almost unavoidable. It rehearses continually our moment of enforced but imperfect separation from the straightgeist. You can try to be up-front all the time – wearing a queer badge or T-shirt, perhaps – but you still get the telephone salesperson who wants to speak to the man of the house or to his lady wife. Or the doorstep Christian who catches you in only your bathtowel, bereft of signifiers. The phrase 'coming out', even, is not special to us. It is a hybrid appropriation, alluding parodically to what debutantes do; the joke is that they emerge, through balls, garden parties and the court pages of *The Times*, into centrality, whereas we come out into the marginal spaces of discos, cruising grounds and Lesbian and Gay Studies.

This implication in the heterosexism that others us has advantages. It allows us to know what people say when they think we aren't around. And at least we can't be told to go back to where we came from, as happens to racial minorities in Britain. Conversely though, it makes us the perfect subversive implants, the quintessential enemy within. We instance what Jonathan Dollimore calls a 'perverse dynamic': we emanate from within the dominant, exciting a particular insecurity – 'that fearful interconnectedness whereby the antithetical inheres within, and is partly produced by, what it opposes' (Dollimore, 1991, p. 33). The lesbian or gay person is poised at the brink of a perpetual emergence, troubling the straight-geist with a separation that cannot be completed, a distinction that cannot be confirmed. It makes it hard for us to know, even to recognize, ourselves. It is a kind of reverse diaspora that makes our subcultures hybrid.

Because the prime strategy of ideology is to naturalize itself, it has been tempting to suppose that virtually any disruption of symbolic categories or levels is dissident. This can lead to the inference that hybridity is, in its general nature and effects, progressive. Thus Homi Bhabha:

> hybridity to me is the 'third space' which enables other positions to emerge. This third space displaces the histories that constitute it, and sets up new structures of authority, new political initiatives, which are inadequately understood through received wisdom.... The process of cultural hybridity gives rise to something different, something new and unrecognisable, a new area of meaning and representation.
>
> (Bhabha, 1990, p. 211)

Now, symbolic disjunction may indeed disturb settled categories and demand new alignments. However, we have supposed too readily that to demonstrate indeterminacy in a dominant construct is to demonstrate its weakness and its vulnerability to subversion. That is optimistic. To be sure, the ideologies of the British and US states exhort us to credit the stabilizing virtues of our political institutions and cultural heritage. But in actuality, as Marx tells us, capitalism thrives on instability:

> Constant revolutionizing of production, uninterrupted disturbance of all social conditions, everlasting uncertainty and agitation distinguish the bourgeois epoch from all earlier ones. All fixed, fast-frozen relations, with their train of ancient and venerable prejudices and opinions, are swept away, all new-formed ones become antiquated before they can ossify.
>
> (Marx, 1973, p. 70)

Capital ruthlessly transforms the conditions of life: industries are introduced and abandoned; people are trained for skills that become useless, employed and made redundant, shifted from town to town, from country to country.

It is easier than we once imagined to dislocate language and ideology; and harder to get such dislocations to make a practical difference. Hybridity has to be addressed not in the abstract, but as social practice; it is both an imposition and an opportunity. Which of these will win depends on the forces, in that context, against us, and on our resourcefulness. 'Once "camp" is commodified by the culture industry, how do we continue to camp it up?' Danae Clark asks. 'The only assurance we have in the shadow of colonization is that lesbians *as lesbians* have developed strategies of selection, (re)appropriation, resistance, and subversion' (Clark, 1993, p. 199).

SUBCULTURE

Hybridity may or may not disconcert the system. My case is that being always-already tangled up with it makes it hard for lesbians and gay men to clear a space where we may talk among ourselves. We used to say that we were silenced, invisible, secret. Now, though our subcultures are still censored, there is intense mainstream investment in everything that we do, or are imagined as doing. We are spoken of, written of and filmed everywhere, but rarely in terms that we can entirely welcome.

In the face of such pressures and opportunities, my case is that we need various but purposeful subcultural work – with a view neither to disturbing nor pleasing the straightgeist, but to meeting our own, diverse needs. Lesbian and gay subcultures are where we may address, in terms that make sense to us, the problems that confront us. We may work on our confusions, conflicts and griefs – matters of class, racial and inter-generational exploitation; of misogyny, bisexuality and sado-masochism; of HIV and AIDS. For it is dangerous to leave the handling of these matters within the control of people who, we know, do not like us. Wojnarowitz and Kramer wanted to catch the attention of the president and the mayor, but it is gay subculture that has taught us about safer sex.

Am I proposing a 'gay ghetto', then, in which we must all think the same? There is no question, in practice, of this. Subculture in our countries today is not a matter of side-stepping hybridity, but of maintaining any space at all that is not entirely incorporated, in which we may pursue our own conversations.

The problem, rather, is this: I have been writing 'we'. In so far as 'we' address 'our' problems today and work through 'our' history and 'our' culture, in the face of inevitable hybridizing pressures, 'we' suppose a minority awareness. Despite all the arguments I assembled initially about the damaging consequences of the ethnicity-and-rights model, a project of subcultural work leads us back towards a version of that model. It is to protect my argument from the disadvantages of the ethnicity model that I have been insisting on 'subculture', as opposed to 'identity' or 'community': I envisage it as retaining a strong sense of diversity, of provisionality, of constructedness.

For if we cannot afford to abandon minority awareness, our subcultural task will have to include a reappraisal of its nature and scope. We have to develop a theory and a politics that will help us to tolerate permeable boundaries. We need to draw upon the experience of elderly gays. We have to maximize opportunities for lesbian and gay alliances, and to explore sexualities that the gay movement has treated as marginal – bisexuality, transvestism, transsexuality. We need to speak with gay people who proclaim themselves to be 'straight-acting' and who demand and promise discretion in contact ads. We must be ready to learn from the different kinds of 'gayness' that are occurring in other parts of the world, and among ethnic and racial minorities in Western societies. For it would be arrogant to suppose that the ways we have 'developed' in parts of North America and Northern Europe of being lesbian and gay constitute the necessary, proper or ultimate potential for our sexualities.

It is because we believe that culture constructs the scope for our identities that we may believe those identities to be contingent and provisional, and therefore may strive to revise our own self-understanding and representation. Subcultural work is our opportunity to support each other in our present conditions, and to work towards transforming those conditions.

NOTE

This chapter is an abbreviated version of parts of an article that was first published in *Textual Practice*, 10: 2 (1996).

16 Seeing the World from a Lesbian and Gay Standpoint
Mary McIntosh

In the growing field of lesbian and gay studies one of the issues under discussion is whether lesbian and gay studies should be concerned with studying the lives of lesbians and gay men or whether it should take on the potentially more radical task of studying the world from a lesbian and gay standpoint. To express it more politically: some of us see one of the contributions that lesbian and gay studies can make to the movement as being to reveal to the straight world how bizarre it seems from our perspective.

Of course, most of the time we do not see the straight world as bizarre and, indeed, an aspect of our self-oppression (nowadays often psychologized as 'internalized homophobia') is that we do share a straight view of the world, placing ourselves at the margin rather than the centre. One of the things that is meant by the term 'standpoint', as in feminist standpoint theory (Hartsock, 1987), is not necessarily the way you experience the world every day, but the way you can perceive it if you consciously adopt a particular perspective. Marx, a bourgeois, could adopt a proletarian stand-point – which might be miles away from how most proletarians see the world – a man may take a feminist standpoint; anyone, indeed, may take a lesbian and gay standpoint. I don't want to dignify this by calling it an epistemology, or even a different form of knowledge. It must be judged, simply, by whether it comes up with anything interesting.

A first step would be to problematize the taken-for-granted nature of heterosexuality. This was done in an amusing way in an article called 'The Twilight World of the Heterosexual' in an early issue of the Gay Liberation magazine *Come Together*:

What then is heterosexuality? Simply put, it is the inability to love your own sex and the consequent turning for sexual release to the opposite sex. Many hardened heterosexuals will attempt to turn it round and insist that heterosexuality is the ability to love the *opposite* sex. But if this were true it would have to be an ability that grew out of a complete homosexual fulfilment – for it stands to reason that you can't love something different from your self unless you can first love people the same as you.

(Pollack, 1980, p. 170)

More seriously, a lesbian and gay standpoint enables us to question concepts that may be taken for granted in the straight world. An example is the 'age of consent' – the age at which a young woman is deemed capable of consenting to intercourse. For pragmatic reasons, the gay movement has adopted the same terminology in fighting for a reduction in the age at which gay male sex becomes legal. It demands an equal age of consent. But actually, the current law, and any future law, is not about consent at all; it is about the age at which sexual *activity* is legal, and both parties including the one below that age are guilty of a crime. The model of *consent* is a bit like the model of rape: intercourse is seen as something that a man does to a woman, her part in it being to consent or not consent. Current ideas of heterosexuality find the idea of a woman raping a man unthinkable – though this has not been true in all societies. We have become accustomed to the idea that a woman may 'take the initiative' in heterosex, but even then, we do not think of the man as 'consenting'.

Pragmatically, again, feminists have retained the language of consent in campaigning around social responses to rape. Some theorists may say, like Catharine MacKinnon (1990, p. 4), that 'consent is not a meaningful concept' in a patriarchal society; others may admit that the notions of free will contained in the idea of consent are rather dubious. Nevertheless, in the condition of sexual scarcity and patriarchal structuring that Bob Connell has pointed out in this volume, women have very much wanted the right to refuse consent to heterosex.

To say that the asymmetry of consent is characteristic of heterosex in our society, is not to say that there is no non-consensual homosex or that lesbians and gays are superior beings who are above sexual violence and coercion. It is simply to say that there is no rigid understanding of who will be coercive to whom. Given two young men of 17 and 18, there is no knowing who will take the initiative, who – if either – will be 'active' and who 'passive', who insertive and who receptive (not necessarily the same as active/

passive), or who might turn coercive. Given a young man of 16 and a woman of 15, the law thinks it knows and most of the time we all share that presumption.

Then there is the question of what 'it' is to which one might consent. In heterosex it is clearly the procreative act: except where minors are involved, everything else is considered less significant – less harmful, less pleasurable. In homosex, for the long centuries before the cultural invention of the homosexual, 'it' was buggery. Since then it has spread out into what the law calls 'gross indecency', a wide spectrum of activities, many of them often called 'foreplay' in the heterosexual world. But buggery remains the act that straight people seem to find easiest to understand. The anus and the vagina are seen as homologous and the passivity of the receptive role is deeply despised – with all that implies about women's receptive role in heterosex. An old limerick reflects the way in which lesbians appear in the straight imagination: they

> Argue all night
> Over who has the right
> To do what, and with which, and to whom.

This confusion extends to the scientific community. The categories of lesbian sexual activity reported in the National Survey of Sexual Attitudes and Lifestyles (Wellings et al., 1994) are rather baffling. In the questionnaire, the women were asked to report on 'oral sex, by a partner to you', 'oral sex, by you to a partner' and 'any other form of sex with a woman involving genital contact but not also oral sex' (pp. 428–9). One thing that is interesting is the way in which this privileges oral sex, which if present becomes the defining characteristic of the sexual encounter – how different from its role as foreplay in heterosex. In the analysis, things become even more mysterious. The categories 'oral sex' and 'non-penetrative sex' are reported as if they exhaust the possibilities and 'non-penetrative sex' is once given with 'mutual masturbation' in brackets after it (p. 226).

What is apparently obvious and pre-given in heterosexuality, is more fluid and negotiable in the lesbian and gay world. The SIGMA project, which used sexual diaries to chart the sequencing of activities in sexual encounters between men, found an enormous variety of patterns, though the 'end marker', as they put it, may always be ejaculation, oral sex may precede or follow anal sex, and anal penetration itself occurs in only about 30 per cent of encounters (Davies et al., 1993; Coxon and Coxon, 1995; Coxon, 1996). But this is not to suggest that lesbians and gays can or should abandon penetration, in the voluntaristic way recommended by some radical feminists, let alone that heterosexuals should. Nor is it to suggest that because sexual meanings are social, all sexual acts can be equivalent in terms of meanings. This was shown vividly in the Netherlands when, in an early response to AIDS, gay leaders tried to persuade gay men to give up anal sex. They were unsuccessful, even though most gay men do not have anal intercourse all the time and many do not have it at all. In the same way, radical feminists have not succeeded in convincing women to give up what they see as the 'colonization' of heterosexual penetration. It is interesting to observe how central is the place occupied by the procreative act in a sexuality that is now only marginally constrained by the imperatives of reproduction.

THE PROLIFERATION OF SEXUAL IDENTITIES

A central focus of lesbian and gay studies has been on the slow historical emergence of the gay and the lesbian sexual identities that are recognized today in the Western world – and increasingly globally. A lesbian or gay is someone for whom important aspects of their social life and identity are organized around their sexuality. We are usually not married, often live with a partner at some period of our lives. (It is worth noting that lesbians and gays took up serial monogamy soon after Hollywood invented it. As straights have followed suit, lesbians and gays have come to seem less strange to them.) We are recognized and recognizable as gay in many situations, though the question of how 'out' we are is a burning one for many of us. We live in the context of a subculture[1] – formerly known as the gay ghetto – and the possibility of a social life, which we may or may not take part in for various reasons. This is a way of life that is dominated by white middle-class people.

The lesbian or gay way of life is one that is simply not possible in many societies. For one thing, it depends upon being able to live outside a family. Individuals may have found ways to do this in the past – two spinsters running a school together, or two bachelors sharing lodgings – but this did not give them an identity, as there was no one to identify with. There is a world of difference, too, between a cultural pattern in which some married men have sexual relations with younger or effeminate men and the modern Western idea of the gay man. In Turkey at present, and probably in other countries as well, both patterns exist side by side (Tapinc, 1992), each very threatening to the other.

Many writers have pointed to the proliferation of new socially and politically identified erotic minorities (Weeks, 1986, p. 80). It is interesting that most of these have arisen within the lesbian and gay – or more broadly, the queer – world. The straight world has produced swinging couples, paedophiles, possibly satanists, and not much else outside its mainstream. But it is important to distinguish between those identities that correspond to a way of life and those that arise primarily out of a need to make a political case, a need to contact others for erotic purposes and a common style. Many of these minority identities – like SM dykes or gays who are into piercing – are transient, both in terms of history and in terms of individuals' biographies. The 'structures of social relations' surrounding them – to use Bob Connell's phrase – are less elaborated and less permanent.

The putative bisexual identity is an interesting case, and one that is currently much discussed. Undoubtedly many people experience themselves as bisexual in varying degrees. Some bisexuals have a pattern of serial relationships, sometimes with a man, sometimes with a woman. They may feel that they do not belong among either lesbians and gays, or straights; they may feel excluded by both of them. Others have a main partner of one sex (usually the opposite) and subsidiary sex or love relations with people of another sex. These may feel they belong in both groups and may claim heterosexual privilege when it suits them and enjoy gay fun as well. So far there is no sign of a bisexual way of life emerging, but people seem to live out bisexual inclinations in very varied ways, usually inserting themselves more or less comfortably into existing heterosexual or homosexual institutions.

What I am suggesting is that although the homosexuality that emerged in Europe in the nineteenth century was indeed a form of sexuality, it was also a way of life. Indeed, one of the 'histories' of the lesbian is that she started as someone with a way of life – romantic friendship or domestic partnership – and became sexualized only by a controlling patriarchal discourse. Of the male homosexual, Foucault said: 'Nothing that went into his total composition was unaffected by his sexuality' (1979, p. 43).

That 'total composition' unfitted him to be a husband or father, a soldier or a civil servant and eventually any man who approximated to this new figure was forced to carve out a different life. But just as his total composition was sexualized, so his sexuality was acculturated: camp culture, gay sensibility, the gay scene, the pink pound, gay fashion, gay relationships, gay 'families', gay politics, AIDS support. This process of acculturation has gone so far that in the Netherlands they use the language of multiculturalism to articulate an ideal of live-and-let-live tolerance for diversity.[2]

This potential resolution of multiculturalism suggests a new understanding of the straight world that can be gained from the lesbian and gay standpoint. If lesbian and gay culture is both sexuality and way of life, so too is contemporary Western heterosexual culture. It is no accident, as we used to say, that the homosexual emerged as a type of person at the same time that romantic love and marriage were being hitched together 'like a horse and carriage'. Marriage and family have become sexualized during the same transformation and many of the current explosion of 'social problems' around the family are a result of a disappointed assumption of a neat fit between sexual desire and family life: a high divorce rate, a failure to support or care for children after divorce, children's failure to provide grandchildren.

The adoption of the idea of multiculturalism has a certain absurdity, since lesbians and gays do not reproduce their culture from generation to generation; they are mostly brought up by heterosexuals and if they have children themselves they mostly do not grow up gay. This highlights the assumption that all other cultures – ethnic, racial, religious, class, regional, national – reproduce themselves through the heterosexual family, and that people belong to the same culture as their parents and as their children. This assumption downplays other kinds of culture, those of occupation, education or other kinds of affinity – the sects rather than the churches – which do not recruit through inheritance. This assumption also allows a very limited kind of liberalism, that straight parents should bring up their children in their own straight culture, but if they once struggle through to identify as gay then good luck to them

Multiculturalism as a progressive policy for a racist society has rightly been criticized for ossifying and homogenizing cultures and leaving dissident individuals within a culture to the tender mercies of their community leaders. A girl from a Plymouth Brethren family who wants sex education or a campaign against Harley Street clitorodectomy operations cannot be supported because each culture must be valued and not judged by any external criteria. Turn that around to supposed sexual cultures and you get a situation where, in return for not being attacked for promiscuity or other despised habits, gays relinquish the right to criticize the patriarchal assumptions of the culture they were reared in. In addition, multi-culturalism pretends that all cultures are equal to start with. It does not recognize, and does not challenge, the fact that one culture is hegemonic − in this case, the culture of marital heterosexuality. Jeffrey Weeks's claim, in this volume, that 'there is no longer a hegemonic discourse telling us how we ought to behave' is a piece of wishful thinking. We live in a society where 'outing' someone as gay is a threat and confirming them as heterosexual is not, where even the most popular of entertainers, like Michael Barrymore, will deny his gay sexuality until it is forced out by the media (who have 'outed' more public figures than queer activists ever did). We live in a society where a primary school head teacher[3] can be hounded and vilified by the press and by her own Council and Director of Education for deciding not to take a party of nine-year-olds to the ballet 'Romeo and Juliet', partly on the grounds that it is heterosexist. Even the 'live-in lover' beloved of the tabloid press has an air of prurience and salaciousness. The primacy of marital heterosexuality and the deviancy of all other forms is everywhere so taken for granted that we are scarcely aware of it.

LESBIAN VERSUS GAY

Another issue much discussed in lesbian and gay studies is what, if anything, lesbians and gays have in common, in terms of identity, way of life, community, politics. Twenty-five years ago, 'gay' covered women as well as men; but as tensions developed between women and men in the gay movement, women insisted on mentioning lesbians specifically so as not to get submerged. Many lesbians preferred to identify with feminism and not work alongside men at all. Those who stayed tried to redefine the movement as 'lesbian-and-gay', but all the time they were fighting against the tendency for this to be just another way for men to talk about lesbians as if they were the same as gay men. 'Queer', too, has become an identity rather than a politics and it is one that is not sex-specific.

Some strands of feminism have developed radically different ways of defining the lesbian, in terms of independence from men and being 'woman-identified', rather than in terms of same-sex erotic desire (for instance, Kitzinger, 1987). But the history of the current lesbian identity has usually been traced back to romantic friendships between bourgeois women in the nineteenth century, which became sexualized and stigmatized in the early decades of this century. Some of this lesbian history espouses an essentialist position, like Lillian Faderman (1985), some a thoroughly social constructionist one, like Carroll Smith-Rosenberg (1975) whose account gives a historical specificity to the feelings between women as well as to the identities around them. But all of it places gender and its asymmetries at centre stage. In contrast, in gay male histories gender has not usually been very significant, apart from a concern with the manliness or effeminacy of individuals. Where lesbian history usually starts with romantic friendships (apart from another subordinate strand that refers to 'female husbands' in the seventeenth and eighteenth centuries), male gay history starts with sodomy and traces the shift from a sexual act to a type of person. Women's history has tended to downplay the sexual and the transgressive, men's to downplay love relationships and the gender inequalities of heterosexual institutions. So we academic lesbians and gay men re-enact our gender roles!

The same kind of gender stereotypes can be seen time and again in lesbian and gay life. Gay male culture features impersonal sex, cottaging, cruising, back rooms – a world of sexual plenitude is the way Bob Connell puts it, in his chapter in this volume – but is it just the realization of the dream of hegemonic masculinity? Lesbian culture features couples, children sometimes, networks of friends, camaraderie rather than sex. Gay men typically come to gay sex young and stick to it. Lesbians often start with heterosexual relationships and discover women later, which could be seen as taking a long time to become sexually autonomous. As Gagnon and Simon (1974) long ago argued, lesbians have more in common with other women than with gay men. Evidently sexual orientation is not as deeply embedded in gender as is often supposed.

Yet Monique Wittig was able to state, 'Lesbians are not women', on the grounds that ' "woman" has meaning only in heterosexual systems of thought and heterosexual economic systems' (1992, p.

32). At an empirical level, this is both true and not true. But, when she says, 'If we as lesbians and gay men continue to speak of ourselves and think of ourselves as women and men we are instrumental in maintaining heterosexuality', she is issuing a warning to any feminism that takes heterosexuality for granted.

NOTES

1. Though Alan Sinfield, in his chapter in this volume, has questioned its coherence.
2. In his chapter in this volume, Alan Sinfield discusses in much more detail a similar idea of Dennis Altman's of 'gay men as something like an ethnic group'.
3. Jane Brown, of Kingsmead School in the London Borough of Hackney.

17 The Good Homosexual and the Dangerous Queer: Resisting the 'New Homophobia'

Anna Marie Smith

In 1995 I went to the Lesbian Avengers' annual dyke march in New York on Lesbian and Gay Pride weekend. I joined the thousand-strong crowd of lesbians in the north-west corner of Bryant Park. The park lies behind the wonderful New York Public Library, a few blocks east of the boarded-up theatres of Times Square – an area that was once known as a decrepit haven for pornography outlets, but will soon become the site of massive redevelopment by the likes of the Disney Corporation. A jazz band was playing in the park, white-collar thirty-somethings were drinking designer beers and cruising each other, and homeless street people were lounging on the folding chairs. It was just another day in New York City, just another moment in the complex history of American public space.

True to their anarchist style, the Avengers had not asked for a permit for their women-only march, but they had not encountered any serious police harassment in the past. This year, however, the Avengers had to contend with unprecedented official hostility. The new Republican mayor, Rudolph Giuliani, had told the press that he was going to take a firm line with disorderly lesbians and gays during the Lesbian and Gay Pride weekend. Giuliani's political strategy is basically designed to maintain the support of his core constituency, the wealthy and the morally conservative. He has introduced large reductions in personal income taxes and property taxes for the wealthy while imposing massive cuts in services for the poor. He has even stated that it would be a 'good thing' if the poor decided to leave the city because of the public hospital closures and the drastic cutbacks in welfare and Medicaid (Conason, 1995, p. 782). He has also taken a law and order position against public drunkenness and begging, pornography shops, prostitution and gay bathouses. At the same time, he has sought support from moderate

minority and community groups and has marked his independence
from the state Republican leadership by giving his endorsement to
the former Democratic Governor, Mario Cuomo.

A few days before Pride weekend, Giuliani held a special breakfast meeting with a handpicked group of Republican lesbian and
gay leaders at which he professed his deep concern about lesbian
and gay rights. The conservative lesbians and gays who were in
attendance gave Giuliani high marks in their glowing reports about
the meeting to the press. When Giuliani himself marched in the
Lesbian and Gay Pride parade, he deliberately joined in well south
of St Patrick's Cathedral so as not to offend his Catholic constituents who constitute a powerful voting bloc in local politics. Giuliani's contingent was carefully stage-managed: he was surrounded at
all times by the Log Cabin group of Republican gay men and
lesbians. Whenever someone standing in the crowd recognized him
and started up a chorus of boos, his conservative lesbian and gay
entourage would burst into applause.

While Giuliani did seek the support of right-wing lesbian and
gays, he also sent reassuring signals to his morally conservative
constituents. The Mayor's Office told the press that the New York
police would aggressively respond to any lesbian and gay marches
that did not have a permit. The spokesperson specifically mentioned that any women who went topless during the weekend would
be charged on the spot for engaging in indecent behaviour. Need-
less to say, both of these statements were directed precisely at the
Lesbian Avengers. Giuliani used the Log Cabin Republicans to
position himself as a supporter of 'lesbian and gay rights', and
constructed the Lesbian Avengers as a symbol of public disorder
and indecent behaviour. As a result, he was able to curry favour
among conservative lesbians and gays while simultaneously reinforcing his law and order reputation.

In retrospect, it is no surprise that the Lesbian Avengers' women-
only march was met with a belligerent police reaction. As we moved
into the street, police officers swarmed menacingly all around us.
Without any warning or negotiation, they fanned out down the
street and unrolled an orange plastic fabric fence along the traffic
side of our march. They came for us *en masse*, pushing, shoving and
punching through the plastic fabric, effectively corralling us on the
west side of the street. Each officer sported a half-dozen plastic
handcuffs and numerous police vans were parked nearby; they were
obviously quite prepared to allow the situation to deteriorate into a

riot. It was only after we sat down on the street that an uneasy truce between the march and the police was struck, and we were allowed to walk down Fifth Avenue to Washington Square Park.

This small confrontation symbolizes some of the tremendous transitions in the politics of public space that are central to contemporary American politics. The area that we were in is being transformed by the Bryant Park, Times Square, Grand Central Partnership and 34th Street Business Improvement Districts (BIDs). There are about 1000 BIDs in American cities. Each BID taxes property owners in the area to pay for services such as private security, street repairs and street cleaning. The BID decisions, however, are made not by local residents but by the property owners themselves, with the majority of decision-making power typically reserved exclusively for those owners with the most valuable property. BIDs are becoming privatized worlds unto themselves. In April 1995, it was revealed that the Grand Central Partnership had hired thugs to drive homeless people from the area through intimidation and assault, and had paid untrained 'security guards' $10 a day to protect the individuals who used the 80 neighbourhood automatic teller machines (Gallagher, 1995, p. 788).

Central Park lies a few blocks uptown. There, a hallowed public space has become a tool for private corporations' marketing schemes. The mayor rented out Central Park to Disney for $1 million for an open-air screening of the children's animated film, *Pocohontas* during the summer of 1995. When challenged about this use of precious common land to further a private corporate good, the Mayor's Office replied that the park rental was justified since the animated film was set outdoors and therefore had an environmental theme.

There is nothing accidental about these different incidents of the privatization of public space. According to Susan Buck-Morss (1995), we Westerners no longer collectively imagine urban Utopias as we once did in the nineteenth and early twentieth centuries. The disappearance of urban Utopias is a reflection of large-scale structural transformations. Mass consumption has given way to atomized and isolated forms of consumption in late capitalism. Consumption is increasingly located in suburban shopping malls where the land is owned by private corporations and the open mall space is policed by private security firms.

Where urban spaces once offered important sites for disseminating political information and organizing public protests, the private malls are completely different. Social and political dissenters' rights to free expression and assembly are routinely violated in these corporate spaces. Even the gathering together of consumers in the private malls may become increasingly obsolete as shopping by phone, cable television and even the Internet is becoming more popular. As large corporations bid for oligarchical control of these media, we shall probably see more anti-democratic closure in these new sites of consumption. Add to this the deindustrialization and restructuring of America's urban centres – as industrial capital seeks lower wages by relocating factories to the underdeveloped countries, or seeks lower rents by moving factories from urban centres to America's rural south. Cities like New York and Los Angeles are becoming increasingly dominated by the financial, insurance, information technology and real estate sectors. This is a massive transformation of urban space.

These transitions do not mean that urban centres as we knew them in the 1960s and 1970s – the period in which our contemporary lesbian and gay communities became consolidated – will disappear altogether. But it does mean that as urban spaces become more and more privatized, urban politics will be transformed in turn. Gay historians have documented the tremendous impact that migration to urban spaces has had on our communities and movements (Garber, 1990; Bérubé, 1990; Davis and Kennedy, 1990; D'Emilio, 1990). It is true that urban spaces may be less important for some lesbians. Many of the American lesbians whom I have met in up-state New York would consider rural land – such as the location of the Michigan Women's Music Festival – and small towns – such as Provincetown, Massachusetts with its women-only beach and thriving lesbian subculture – as more important sites of lesbian pilgrimage than San Francisco and New York. Other lesbians, myself included, would argue that urban areas such as the Castro in San Francisco, Toronto's Church Street and Queen Street areas, the London club scene, and the Village in New York have been just as important as these rural places and small towns in making our coming out process possible, in fostering our political activism and in giving our cultural projects a geopolitical home.

What, we should now ask, is going to happen to our communities as the urban spaces that have been so important to us as lesbians, gays, bisexuals and transgendered queers are being more and more defined by private corporate interests that only care about us in so far as we constitute an upmarket fashion trend ('lesbian chic') or a marketing target group with a sizeable disposable income (the 'pink dollar/pound')? (I should note in passing that Sarah Schulman's writing (1984; 1986; 1988; 1991; 1992; 1994; 1995) is exceptional in its attention to the impact of the contemporary transitions in urban spatial politics on the lesbian and gay communities.) It is beyond the scope of this chapter to give a full answer to this question. We can nevertheless note that race theorists have already begun to address similar questions.

In her analysis of the Los Angeles uprisings that followed the acquittal of the police officers who brutally assaulted the unarmed Rodney King, Rhonda M. Williams notes the extraordinary pressures on young black males in an urban area that is undergoing dramatic deindustrialization. This particular structural transition leads directly to a shrinkage in the number of skilled and unionized industrial jobs that were often the only road out of America's racial ghetto for many working-class people of colour (Williams, 1993). Mike Davis documents the intersection of property development and transnational finance capital interests, policing strategies and racial politics in the development of Los Angeles' urban planning. According to Davis, specific geographical areas in the city have been designated as spaces that must be secured against unrest and criminality, while others have been deliberately neglected and allowed to become centres of criminal activity. It is no coincidence that the protected areas are overwhelmingly defined by the interests of white middle-class businessmen and home-owners. It is also no coincidence that the Los Angeles uprisings spread easily from African-American neighbourhoods into surrounding Asian areas while the financial district and the white-dominated suburban gated communities were left untouched (Davis, 1991; 1992).

Patricia J. Williams has described the ways in which racism is advancing in the New York area through the privatization of public space. In one particularly striking case, defence lawyers justified the actions of their clients – a group of young white men who had brutally assaulted three black men – on the grounds that they were provoked because their black victims had merely walked into their white neighbourhood (Williams, 1991, pp. 58, 67–9). Clearly, the shifts in the structures of urban spaces are ushering in a new and particularly violent era of governmentality for minorities. We need not indulge in the fantasy that there ever was a public space that was equally open to people of colour, immigrants, women, the working class, the poor or sexual minorities to assert that we are the ones who will have the most to lose as the privatization of public space continues unabated.

The interests of minorities as a whole – women, people of colour, lesbians and gays, workers and the poor – will be increasingly ignored as corporate interests define more and more of what used to be public space such as park lands, urban centres, housing developments, streets and roads, public broadcasting and telecommunications. The effects of privatization, however, will be distributed in a post-colonial manner in the sense that they will reproduce the divide-and-rule structures of colonialism. In other words, it is specifically the unassimilable fraction of minorities that will bear the brunt of the privatization of public space. Colonialism did not take the form of a singular assault on Asians and Africans. It isolated the assimilable 'natives', turned them against their own people, and offered them substantial material and symbolic rewards in so far as they attended European schools and adopted European values. Ultimately, the racist character of colonialism was partially concealed as the assimilated natives were put to work in the administrative disciplining of their own people (Fanon, 1968; 1986).

The European colonial forces, then, made an important distinction between the assimilable and unassimilable 'natives'. Since the mid-1960s, contemporary racism has increasingly borrowed its structures from this aspect of Europe's colonial heritage. This 'new racism' is specific to Europe after the shock of decolonization; a Europe that wants to forget its racist imperial past, and therefore erects taboos against explicit racism. The new racism is also specific to America after the rise of the civil rights movement. Most white Americans now fantasize that racism basically ended with the passage of the Civil Rights Act 1964 and the Voting Rights Act 1965, and that racism lives on only on the extreme fringes of society, in the form of white fascism and black separatism (Howell and Warren, 1992).

The widespread white blindness to the perpetuation of institutional racism against people of colour at virtually every power centre in European and American society is made possible by the new racism's shift from explicit discourse about white superiority to a whole set of racial cultural codings. The new racism masquerades as an anti-racism as it distances itself from explicit racism. Instead of making blatant claims about the inferiority of racial others, it argues instead against an 'unnatural' mixing of 'incompatible' groups, the crossing of 'thresholds of tolerance', the illegitimate denigration of

Western traditions through multiculturalism, and so forth. The new racism reconstructs its bigotry as 'tolerance' by finding the equivalent of an assimilable 'native'. It conjures up an imaginary racial otherness that pretends to include the assimilable immigrant, the south Asian British entrepreneur with conservative family values, the East Asian American student from the 'model minority' who, unlike the African American, does not need affirmative action to get ahead in American schools and universities, the John Taylors and Clarence Thomases who 'mainstream' themselves for the white Right by virtually denouncing the anti-racist and civil rights struggles.

Then the new racism can unleash its attack on actual minority communities through devastating public policy 'reforms': racist immigration policies, the elimination of affirmative action, cutbacks to the welfare state, the destruction of the public education system, the promotion of corporate interests and the demonization of the very notion of responsible government. At the same time, however, it can position itself as 'fair', 'tolerant' and 'democratic'. It can even represent itself as the defender of democratic pluralism in so far as it successfully demonizes virtually every form of radical anti-racist resistance as irrational, separatist 'balkanization', and even fascist totalitarianism.

In my book on the British New Right (Smith, 1994), I took up this analysis of the new racism that can be found in the writings of Barker (1981), Balibar and Wallerstein (1991), Hall (1978; 1980; 1988), Hall et al. (1978) and Gilroy (1987). I attempted to develop various aspects of the concept of the new racism through a poststructuralist interpretation of the anti-immigrant racism of Enoch Powell. Then I applied this concept of the new racism to an analysis of contemporary homophobia. It seems to me that the divide-and-rule tactics that we find in colonialism and the new racism can also be found in anti-lesbian and anti-gay bigotry as well. Contemporary homophobic politicians and activists – even some of the most extremist right-wing religious bigots in the United States – practice what we could call the 'new homophobia'. Like the new racism, the new homophobia feigns tolerance of homosexuality, but promises to include homosexual otherness only in so far as we become thoroughly assimilated into an unchanged heterosexist society.

The MPs and members of the House of Lords who spoke in favour of clause 28 of the Local Government Bill which prohibited the promotion of homosexuality often claimed that they were not opposed to homosexuals who knew their 'proper' place in society; they stated that they were only opposed to those leftist extremists who flaunted their homosexuality, spread disease and corrupted children. The US military policy on homosexuality – 'don't ask, don't tell, don't pursue' – allows lesbians and gays to remain in the services only if we refrain from engaging in 'homosexual conduct'. The American neo-conservatives now have various prominent gay male intellectuals in their camp. Even the religious Right extremists claim that they 'hate the sin' of homosexuality but 'love the sinner'.

The new homophobia in a sense promises inclusion in return for our transformation from the 'dangerous queer' into the figure of the 'good homosexual' who is closeted, disease-free and monogamous, white, middle-class and right-wing. The 'good homosexuals' ask only for limited inclusion, distance themselves from the sexual liberation movement and feminism, abandon the critique of hetero-sexism, remain content with the so-called democratic system as it now stands, avoid all forms of solidarity with progressive struggles, and promise to express homosexual difference only within state-approved private spaces. Of course, like the new racism, the new homophobia's pretence of 'tolerance' only conceals its actual vicious bigotry which has manifested itself in clause 28, attacks on AIDS education and funding, and the attempts in the United States to reverse local by-laws that protect lesbians and gays against discrimination.

These sorts of divide-and-rule tactics have always had a spatial dimension. While the dangerous native was quarantined in the colonial shanty-town, migrant workers' barracks, slaves' and servants' quarters, casbah, or 'homelands', the assimilated native elite was actually encouraged to travel abroad to the capitals of Europe. It is true, of course, that slavery, imperialism, colonialism and nineteenth-century scientific racism never achieved a perfect spatial management of racial difference. Some slaves successfully escaped or gained their freedom through special arrangements and then migrated northwards or travelled by sea to Africa or Europe. For Gilroy (1993), the forced and voluntary transnational migrations by sea of the African diaspora are so crucial to its identity that he chooses the 'ship' as its central metaphor, rather than a geographical space of containment such as the slave quarters or the colonial ghetto.

The spatial distribution of disciplined bodies that marked the most intense moments of slavery and colonialism finds its analogy today in the extraordinary incarceration of massive populations of young black males in the American penitentiary system and the deployment of intensive racially defined 'community' policing. In the current law and order environment in American politics, much of the burden of new criminal legislation is falling primarily on the black community. The penalties for the possession of crack – a relatively inexpensive drug that is routinely sold in small quantities and is therefore readily available in America's poorest neighbourhoods where people of colour are over-represented – are much more severe than those for cocaine. As a result, sentencing has been racially skewed. The US Sentencing Commission estimates that although blacks make up only 13 per cent of the national population, 88 per cent of federal crack cocaine defendants are black. With respect to those who are convicted of selling cocaine, by contrast, 32 per cent are white and 27 per cent are black (Gordon, 1995, p. 705). A recent study has found that only 13 per cent of African-Americans are regular drug users, but make up 35 per cent of those arrested for drug possession, 55 per cent convicted for possession and 74 per cent of the total serving sentences for possession (Wideman, 1995). The mobility of even the most privileged racial 'others' always remains somewhat constrained as racist police officers detain the wealthiest black men or immigration officers subject the documents of professional non-whites to intensive scrutiny. Nevertheless, the new racist institutions grant the more assimilable racial 'others' much more spatial mobility than their demonized counterparts – the young poor black male (suspect criminal), the young poor black and Latina female (suspect unwed mother), the young poor Latino male (suspect gang member), the poor Mexican or Chinese worker (suspect illegal immigrant), and so on.

As for homophobia, I would add this observation to the findings in my book: part of the qualification for achieving inclusion under the category of the 'good homosexual' is the abandonment of any claim to a collective right to occupy public space. This was, of course, the most significant difference between the Lesbian Avengers and the Log Cabin gay Republicans – the latter only marched on public streets on Giuliani's narrow terms. It is interesting to note that in the British context, the decriminalization of homosexuality in 1967 was twinned with a dramatic escalation in the policing of 'public decency' offences. The Sexual Offences Act 1967 decriminalized only the private sexual acts between adults over the age of 21. It also introduced strengthened restrictions concerning offences involving 'minors', male soliciting ('cruising') and sexual practices in 'public' places. It defines 'public place' quite broadly as any place where a third person is likely to be present (Weeks, 1981, pp. 239–44, 274–5). The 'tolerance' that was promised to gay men in 1967 already differentiated between the 'good homosexual' and the 'dangerous queer': the former could be included in the social order only in so far as he did not contaminate public space.

Bowers v. *Hardwick* complicates matters somewhat. In this 1986 decision, the US Supreme Court ruled that there is no right to privacy for consenting adult gay males who engage in sexual practices in their own homes. In this sense, even the highly inadequate British Sexual Offences Act 1967 would be an advance over the sodomy laws as they currently stand in America. In any event, the American Right is currently focusing its homophobic campaign on attempts to cleanse all traces of homosexuality from public spaces – by eliminating multicultural education and sex education curricula with pro-gay imagery, by censoring lesbian and gay art, by blocking local by-laws that prohibit discrimination on the basis of sexual orientation on the grounds that they 'promote homosexuality' and 'homosexual affirmative action', and by banning homosexuals from serving in the military. These initiatives are not only aimed at lesbian and gay rights, they are aimed specifically at eliminating our presence from public spaces, both material (the banning of lesbian and gay contingents from public parades, the attack on gay teachers in schools or the censoring of gay artists who exhibit in public venues) and metaphorical (the Right's loathing for the queer in US military uniform and its smear tactics against Clinton when he voiced moderate support for lesbian and gay rights).

The debates on the rights of lesbians and gays to join in public parades under a banner that declares our sexual orientation have been particularly fierce. In New York, the Irish Lesbian and Gay Organization has attempted to join the St Patrick's Day Parade but right-wing Catholics who now dominate the Parade's organizing committee have successfully used various legal and political tactics to stop them from doing so. The South Boston Allied War Veterans Council, a Catholic-dominated group that sponsors Boston's St Patrick's Day Parade, has also tried to stop lesbians and gays from marching in the parade. The Supreme Judicial Court of Massachusetts originally decided in 1994 that the sponsors had to allow lesbians and gays to join the parade. It ruled that the event constituted a 'public accommodation', and that discrimination in access to public accommodation on the basis of sexual orientation is prohibited by state civil rights legislation. The Supreme Court, however, overturned this decision. In a unanimous ruling, the Supreme Court found that the parade constituted a form of expression, and that the government could not interfere with the content of that expression. The ruling nevertheless represents a step forward for lesbian and gay rights: it deplores the homophobia of the parade sponsors and it implies that wherever lesbians and gays attempt to identify ourselves as homosexuals by carrying signs in a parade, we are exercising our right to free speech just as much as the sponsors of a homophobic parade are also doing in their discourse. This precedent will undoubtedly play an important role in legal challenges to the Clinton administration's 'don't ask, don't tell' policy on homosexuals in the military (US Supreme Court 1995) (Greenhouse, 1995).

At its most extreme, the Right's assault on our collective right to be included in public space takes the form of physical assault and even murder. In the months leading up to the vote in Oregon on the 1992 Ballot Measure 9 – a state-level measure that would have overturned local by-laws protecting lesbians and gay men from discrimination, and would have required that all state agencies and schools recognize homosexuality as 'abnormal, wrong, unnatural and perverse' – there were more incidents of assaults suffered by lesbians and gays in Portland than in Chicago, New York or San Francisco. This fact is all the more remarkable given the small size of Portland's population – 437 000 – as compared to those of the other cities – 6 177 000, 17 931 000 and 3 484 000 respectively. An Oregon lesbian, Hattie Mae Cohen, and her gay male friend, Brian Mock, were murdered by homophobic bigots when their house was attacked by arsonists. One especially disturbing aspect of this violence is that the homophobic assailants concentrated specifically on attacking lesbian and gay activists and their heterosexual supporters (Ballot Measure 9 1995). In extreme moments such as these, the assault on our right to be included in the public space becomes a direct attempt to stop us from participating in the political process by any means necessary – a strategy that is always deployed against the 'anti-social' minorities in fascist regimes.

While many of these developments are quite serious setbacks for the sexual liberation movement, we should also remember that the

Right's mobilization of racism and homophobia can become quite complicated and even counter-productive. In Gramsci's terms, to win power a political force must win not only the economic struggle but also the struggle to establish new moral and cultural norms. To accomplish this, a political force cannot impose its will, it must instead 'organize consent', and achieve 'hegemony' (Gramsci, 1971). In other words, a political force wins a political battle decisively only if it manages to make its particular project appear to be compatible with popular traditions, and then gradually introduces its new ideas so that they appear to be legitimate and normal. No political force can survive in a context that remains in some nominal way defined by the liberal democratic tradition if it appears to violate democratic norms at every turn.

How can the American Right convince people that there is no alternative to its agenda – especially when that agenda includes a devastating attack on what is left of the welfare state and huge cuts in education spending to finance tax giveaways for the rich, and all this at a time when massive lay-offs are affecting entire sections of the middle class, as well as the working class? It is of course true that the rich vote in much greater numbers than the poor and the working class; but the Right still needs to gain support from some of the people who are going to suffer economically under its policies. How does it win their support?

For the populist right-wing, part of the answer lies in mounting vicious reactionary campaigns against the cultural demons of the day who may or may not have anything to do with specific economic issues. We should note, of course, that cultural demonizations are but one part of the answer. Populist right-wing blocs also attempt to realign class differences – think of Thatcher's programme for selling council housing to the working-class tenants, thereby symbolically inviting them into the middle class – and to disenfranchise the working class and the poor either directly – such as the poll tax – or indirectly – by moving the political centre so far to the right that centre-left forces move rightwards as well, giving disenfranchised constituencies no reason to vote.

There are, nevertheless, many risks attached to the Right's demonization strategies. We are, after all, supposed to be working in a liberal democratic framework, not a fascist one. As such, the populist Right has to engage in a complex balancing act. It mobilizes bigotry and yet conceals its bigotry through its superficial appropriation of liberal democratic values – an appropriation that will ultimately subvert the entire meaning of liberal democracy. The hegemonic status of the populist Right would be jeopardized if it began to appear extremist to the majority of voters: it must always occupy an imaginary 'middle ground'. Even the most opportunistic right-wing leaders must always be concerned about their 'prime ministerial' or 'presidential' appearance. For example, the political career of Newt Gingrich, the Speaker of the House of Representatives, will always be hampered by his 'unpresidential' radical right-wing image. By contrast, Bob Dole, the Republican Presidential candidate in 1996, has been much more successful in articulating extreme right-wing positions while maintaining an imaginary 'centrist' appearance.

From a progressive perspective, the 'middle ground' occupied by authoritarian hegemonies and leaders is, of course, quite far to the right. The (false) 'middle ground' appearance must nevertheless be constantly reconstructed, for the majority of the intolerant misidentify it as 'tolerant'. They want to be reassured, especially in the midst of national crises and popular panics, that they are supporting moderate leaders who are cautiously but firmly leading the country towards a sound recovery. The aims of the intolerant are contradictory: they want official permission to unleash their bigotry and, at the same time, they want to congratulate themselves on their 'moderate', 'liberal democratic' values.

A hegemonic authoritarian project must provide the necessary structures for these contradictory identifications. A total exclusion of a demonized figure may weaken the authoritarian project's claim to universality. It has to pretend to accommodate virtually every legitimate social element; it has to appear to be utterly unaffected by the multiplication of new social differences. At the same time, it has to pursue populist strategies. It must mobilize and reproduce the reactionary forces that provide its political momentum. It must also drag the political centre so far to the right that the conservative elements within the centrist and centre-left parties become more prominent and move their parties to the right. This is turn contributes to the increasing alienation among the voters who traditionally support the centre-left and leftist parties, such as progressive lesbians and gays, workers, blacks and feminists. Ultimately, the authoritarian populism of the new right and the neo-conservatives is itself contradictory since it depends simultaneously on the permanent mobilization of a small cadre of right-wing voters and the virtual disenfranchisement of the majority of the electorate.

In the United States, for example, evidence of the advance of authoritarian populism should be sought not only in the electoral victories of Reagan, Bush and the Republicans in the 1994 Congressional elections but also in low voter turn-outs and the increasing sense of political alienation. In the 1994 election, for example, there was a sharp decline in the turn-out of low-income voters. Sixty per cent of American voters with incomes of $50 000 went to the polls, an increase of almost one full percentage point from the turn-out in 1990. For voters with incomes under $5000, the turn-out was only 19.9 per cent, down from 32.2 per cent. The decrease in turn-out for the voters with incomes between $5000 and $10 000 was from 30.9 percent in 1990 to 23.3 percent in 1994. The proportion of voters from the highest income groups as compared to the total voting population rose from 18 per cent in 1990 to 23.4 per cent in 1994. Turn-out rates for the eligible electorate as a whole in congressional elections that do not include a Presidential race are relatively stable – 46 per cent in 1986, 45 per cent in 1990 and 44.6 per cent in 1994. It is only in the distribution of voters according to income that sharp transitions in turn-out are taking place. According to Curtis Gans of the Committee for the Study of the American Electorate, the data suggest that upper-income voters 'saw an opportunity for the Republicans to get in' and responded (*New York Times*, 1995).

The deployment of the imaginary assimilable 'other' allows authoritarian populism to resolve some of these contradictions in at least a partial manner. By constructing the imaginary figure of the assimilable homosexual – the 'good' gay man or lesbian who knows his or her proper place: the closet – and by pretending to include this figure within their authoritarian vision of the social order, the populist Right is able to transform its homophobic extremism into a tolerant, moderate and inclusionary discourse. Why is the inclusion promised by the populist Right an illusion, a cruel joke? We, the lesbians, gay men, dykes, fags, queers and fairies can only return to the closet through self-annihilation. It need hardly be said that the 'good homosexual' does not and cannot exist, for she is a contradiction in terms. Totally isolated from a lesbian and gay community, bereft of political solidarity, alienated from sexual relationships and purified of every last fragment of 'abnormal' sexual desires, the 'good homosexual' would be the last homosexual. If we ever did manage to squeeze ourselves into the total confines of this final position, we would, in effect, commit collective suicide, for we would destroy the conditions necessary to our survival as a viable alternative community and political movement. Thatcherism already knew this: it already knew that every social group's collective survival depends on the 'promotion' of its specific socio-cultural imaginary, for it had already seized on the idea that only the vigorous 'promotion' of a 'proper' (read: a heterosexist and racist) education would save the 'authentic' (heterosexual, white, Christian English) British people from cultural extinction. The populist Right in the United States also already knows this; hence the vicious culture wars in arts funding and educational policies.

This contradiction – the fact that no one can actually occupy the position of the 'good homosexual' – does not block the invocation of this ·figure in homophobic discourses that want to re-code themselves as 'tolerant'. Where the British measure, section 28, prohibits the promotion of homosexuality, the US military policy bans the manifestation of homosexual conduct. The US military also promises inclusion only to the extent that we conform to the rules of the 'good homosexual'. The policy states that 'sexual orientation will not be a bar to [military] service unless manifested by homosexual conduct'. In both cases, the utterly chaste, socially isolated and politically inactive homosexual is supposedly tolerated as a legitimate member of 'normal' society. This so-called 'tolerance', therefore, effectively takes the form of cultural genocide: if lesbians and gays could actually conform to the rules of inclusion and thereby pass as legitimate members of 'normal' society, we would have to pay the price of self-destruction.

There are, however, many lesbians and gay men who are all too willing to disown those of us who are committed to radical social change in order to get their little moment of inclusion: their ticket to a breakfast with a Republican mayor; or their right to marry in a country that has declared war against single mothers on welfare (Kirk and Madsen, 1989; Bawer, 1993; Sullivan, 1995). Here, as always, we must remember that the imaginary can have material effects. In this case, the imaginary inclusion of the 'good homosexual' adds to the power of right-wing lesbians and gays and consequently to the foreclosure of a lesbian and gay movement that solidly allies itself to socialist, feminist and anti-racist struggles.

If we submit the contradictory discourse of the new racism and the new homophobia to the test for instrumental rationality, it might appear that these gestures of imaginary inclusion of the assimilated other do not make sense. If racism and homophobia really are so pervasive in Britain and the United States – and I for one believe that they are – then the Right's exclusion of people of colour and lesbians and gays should be a relatively cost-free strategy. Likewise, there should be little benefit to be gained from the construction of these imaginary inclusions of the 'model minority' and the 'good homosexual'.

The contradictory juxtaposition of exclusions and the imaginary inclusion of assimilated racial and sexual otherness is nevertheless coherent. First, even the extremist neo-conservatives and religious Right must appeal to racists and homophobes who want to imagine that they are centrist defenders of the democratic tradition. Without the pretence of inclusion and the fiction of a right-wing 'multicultural diversity', these bigots who phantasmatically identify as 'centrists' would find their bigotry unbearable (Balibar, 1991, p. 19).

Second, the populist Right wants to occupy and subvert the entire liberal democratic tradition. It deliberately borrows the terms of the great democratic movements, such as liberal egalitarianism, secular humanism, cultural relativism, feminism, the civil rights movement and even anti-imperialism. Then it hollows out these terms and re-infuses them with utterly reactionary meanings. In this manner, it aims to advance a truly hegemonic project. The populist Right does not want to remain one movement among many; it wants to redefine the political agenda such that its peculiar definitions of 'tolerance', 'diversity', 'equality' and 'democracy' become the only acceptable definitions. It aims to eviscerate the liberal democratic tradition and to demonize any leftist or even centrist political discourse that falls outside its framework as 'unpatriotic', 'Stalinist', 'communist', 'fascist' or 'totalitarian'.

In this sense, the populist Right is deploying what I call the 'logic of exhaustion': it wants to redefine liberal democracy so that its discourse exhausts democratic discourse itself, such that no alternative definitions are allowed and democratic dissent itself is ruled out of order. Authoritarian populist pseudo-inclusions are performed such that the new racism, the British New Right and the American neo-conservative and religious Right can position themselves as liberal democratic discourses. Thus gender and racial equality is redefined as 'gender neutrality' and 'colour-blindness', such that white men can construct themselves as victims of affirmative action; 'self-determination' becomes a legitimation for racist immigration policies; 'parent choice' and 'local autonomy' become the basis for the defence of segregated schools; and the demand for the protection of democracy against a tyrannical minority is used to dismiss lesbian and gay rights as an authoritarian imposition of 'special rights' onto an otherwise 'egalitarian' society.

Thus Ralph Reed, the spokesperson for the Christian Coalition, has attempted to 'mainstream' Pat Robertson's extremist and anti-Semitic discourse. Reed has represented the Coalition as a liberal democratic movement by calling for new coalitions between the religious Right and African-Americans and right-wing Jews, and by denouncing the Ku Klux Klan, George Wallace and anti-Semitism. Thus New York's Republican mayor has breakfast with Republican lesbians and gays, so that the Lesbian Avengers appear to be positioned even further outside the mainstream. As leftist forms of resistance were increasingly excluded as illegitimate, the message that came from Giuliani's office effectively took the following form: 'The reasonable homosexuals have already done a deal with City Hall, what are all these crude topless hairy lesbians doing sitting down on 5th Ave?'

In these conditions, those of us who are situated in the American context and remain committed to a radical democratic pluralist vision of social change are obviously going to have to dig in for even more tough battles ahead. It is nothing less than fatal for the Left that the Centre-Right – here I am referring to Clinton's leadership and the majority of the Democratic Party – is attempting to accommodate the Right's agenda, such as its devastating cuts to the welfare state, its pro-corporate policies, its elimination of pollution controls and its efforts to balance the budget while cutting the taxes of the wealthy. Every time that Clinton and the centre-right Democrats make the apparently democratic move of addressing the concerns of the Right's imaginary figures, such as the 'concerned' homophobic parent who wants to save his/her child by stopping the mythical promotion of the homosexuality or the 'angry white male' who wants to stop the mythical 'reverse racism' by eliminating affirmative action programmes, they only contribute to the normalization of the Right's agenda. Structural analysis of the real reasons for the anxieties of parents and white males – the drastic cutbacks in education funding, corporate downsizing, de-industrialization, international relocation of American industry, the displacement of well-paid skilled industrial jobs with poorly-paid service sector work, declining incomes for everyone except the very wealthy, massive cuts in the health care system and the attack on organized labour – is thereby foreclosed. This sort of accommodationism is disastrous: the political centre has been dragged so far to the right that no political movement can even position itself as 'centrist' without contributing to the evisceration of the struggles for real freedom, equality and democracy.

As many feminists, anti-racists, queer activists and militant labour organizers already know, the radical democratic pluralist Left in America has to defend the positive aspects of the liberal democratic tradition. This means demanding universal access to education and health care; fighting the censorship of the arts and the formation of powerful oligopolies in the entertainment, broadcasting, publishing and communications sector; defending the separation of the church and state; mobilizing against the anti-immigration and anti-affirmative action movements and in support of a progressive multiculturalism; struggling for improved AIDS funding and basic civil rights for lesbians and gays; and organizing service sector workers, especially the women and people of colour who are struggling to survive in the least secure and worst-paid jobs. From a progressive minority perspective, the liberal democratic tradition has always failed to deliver on its promise of 'freedom', 'equality' and 'self-determination' (Macpherson, 1962; 1965; 1977; Eisenstein, 1981), but the activists working in these struggles know that we cannot advance towards radical democracy without securing the basic liberal democratic reforms that are now under attack in America.

We are also learning from other struggles that have faced the twin forces of assimilationism and coercion. Our lesbian and gay movement is not the only one that has been split into two camps, with the officially sanctioned camp breakfasting with the mayor, while the outlaw camp faces a hostile police force on the public street. We already know that there are many valuable lessons to be learned about resisting assimilationism and coercion from the anti-imperialist, anti-racist, civil rights, black power and women of colour feminist movements. Hence the contradictory cultural situation in the United States: the right is everywhere on the advance, but, at the grassroots level, many of us in America remain profoundly committed to the struggle to keep the radical democratic pluralist tradition alive.

18 Death Camp: Feminism vs Queer Theory
Mandy Merck

'There is feminism and there is fucking.' With this provocative parallelism, Lynne Segal moves to the conclusion of her study of *Straight Sex*, a practice which she has spent no less than 318 pages defending (Segal, 1994). Why, I catch myself wearily wondering, should this still be necessary, eleven years after Vance's *Pleasure and Danger* (1984), twelve since Cora Kaplan's ruminations on 'pleasure/sexuality/feminism' in her influential essay 'Wild Nights' (1986), and how long since every feminist text not titled *Breaking the Silence* seemed to be called *Female Desire*? This is yet to mention the even more venerable works of those who now describe themselves as our senior feminists, including the declarations of at least one – circa 1970 – in favour of group sex, cunt power and the elimination of the patriarchal state via 'the reconquest by women of their own sexuality'.

Historians of political thought will reply that the 'pro-sex' polemicists of the contemporary women's movement have been up against a long, and in many ways foundational, feminist legacy ascribing women's social inferiority to their sexuality. Where radical feminists like Sheila Jeffreys find precedents for their critique of heterosexuality in the social purity campaigns of the late nineteenth century, which combined support for women's suffrage with opposition to intercourse even within marriage, Kaplan confronts Wollstonecraft's *Vindication of the Rights of Women* and its insistence on 'the depravity of the appetite that brings the sexes together'. In turn, Wollstonecraft's argument – that femininity, in its vanity, coquettishness and cultivated ignorance, is tailored to the requirements of male sexuality – uncannily anticipates Dworkin and MacKinnon's arguments for the engendered eroticization of subordination. And so the loop closes, with 'feminism' and 'fucking', the two 'f' words of our time, apparently still at odds (MacKinnon, 1987).

In 1987, the prospects for their reconciliation were dealt a further blow from an unlikely quarter – a discussion of the AIDS epidemic and its representations by the gay literary theorist, Leo Bersani. Bersani's essay, 'Is the Rectum a Grave?' (1987), was first published in the AIDS issue of *October* and is, in part, a review of the work of another gay theorist, Simon Watney's *Policing Desire* (1987). But where Watney's book denounces the popular equation of male homosexuality with death, specifically the impassioned annihilation of the self, Bersani endorses it: '[I]f the rectum is the grave in which the masculine ideal . . . of proud subjectivity is buried, then it should be celebrated for its very potential for death.' 'Male homosexuality', his essay concludes, 'advertises the risk of the sexual itself as the risk of self-dismissal, of *losing sight* of the self' (Bersani, 1987, pp. 218–19). For fucking, in Bersani's description, is the agency by which the ego's phallic, power-seeking pretensions can be mercifully destroyed.

The argument here derives from a more extended meditation on masochism, *The Freudian Body*, which Bersani published the previous year (Bersani, 1986). In an ingenious account of Freud's metapsychology filtered through Laplanche and Foucault, Bersani reads Freud's *Beyond the Pleasure Principle* to produce a sexuality defined as pleasurable unpleasure. Rejecting the various hierarchies of libidinal and death instincts which Freud erected and inverted across his writing, Bersani discerns 'a collapse of Freud's dualisms and a reconsideration of sex as death, or, more exactly, the hypothesis of an identity between a sexualized consciousness and a destabilized, potentially shattered consciousness' (ibid., p. 40). *The Freudian Body* assigns this masochism to human sexuality in general, forced from birth to find pleasure in sensations which overwhelm its infantile capacities for psychic organization. Indeed, Bersani describes masochism as an inherited survival mechanism for a species whose lengthy sexual maturation would otherwise ill-adapt it to reproduction.

One year – and a sexually transmitted epidemic – separate this hypothesis from Bersani's *October* article. Although the latter recapitulates his general observations on 'sex as self-abolition', the subject of 'Is the Rectum a Grave?' is not human sexuality *tout court* but that of gays and women. Taking his cue from Watney's comparison of Victorian representations of female prostitutes as 'contaminated vessels' of syphilitic contagion with AIDS-related discourses on gay men, Bersani extrapolates from the promiscuity attributed to both groups to their popularly imagined lust for annihilation. In the significations of veneral disease, Bersani argues, 'Women and gay men spread their legs with an unquenchable appetite for destruction' (Bersani, 1987, p. 212). A footnote to this rather extravagant description underscores the homology it proposes between the vagina and the rectum as 'privileged loci' of HIV infection as well as widely fantasized counterparts. Note too the homology of sexual position which secures the comparison. It recurs on the next page in Bersani's evocation of the 'seductive and intolerable image of a grown man, legs high in the air, unable to refuse the suicidal ecstasy of being a woman' (Bersani, 1987, p. 212).

If this is what Bersani thinks people think about women and gay men, it also proves to be what he himself will argue, supported by Foucault's description of the classical Greek strictures against anal receptivity in intercourse between men. But if penile penetration undermined civic authority in ancient Athens, must it do so today? Enter Andrea Dworkin and Catharine MacKinnon, admittedly unlikely bedfellows for a gay sadomasochist like Foucault, but as convinced as any ancient Greek of what Bersani describes as 'the distribution of power both signified and constituted by men's insistence on being on top'. And like Bersani (who describes pornography in this essay as 'legalized violence'), MacKinnon's *Feminism Unmodified* deploys the language of *The Freudian Body* to describe the 'male supremacist definitions of female sexuality as lust for self-annihilation' (MacKinnon, 1987).

I have to admit to a certain degree of pleasure in observing this encounter between radical feminism and a conservative modernist like Bersani, who will go on in this article to reject Dworkin and MacKinnon's attempts to reinvent sex to celebrate instead its value as 'anticommunal, antiegalitarian, antinurturing, antiloving'. At the very least there is the fascination of watching two of feminism's greatest mistresses of hyperbole finally meet their match (in more than one sense, as I shall argue below). But if Leo's *pas de troix* with Andrea and Catharine enthralls as well as worries me, the consequences of his argument for the current theorization of male homosexuality are less seductive. Some of these consequences are displayed at great length in Bersani's new, and valiantly scandalous, polemic against queer theory's anti-identitarian politics, entitled *Homos*. Here I'd list his assertion – *contra* Foucault – for the complicity of gay SM with political authoritarianism, on the basis that both deal in dominance and submission, an argument which he then characteristically qualifies to accept that sadomasochism does usefully 'expose', 'make explicit', 'lay bare' the erotic appeal of structures of social dominance – 'but' (a further qualification), 'in its open embrace of the structures themselves and its [SM's] undisguised appetite for the ecstasy they promise, it is fully complicit with a culture of death' (Bersani, 1995).

What culture of death? The 'little death' that every human purportedly suffers in enduring the ego-shattering effects of erotic intensities? Or the representations of AIDS deaths which led Bersani to refocus his general theory of human masochism into a particular account of the annihilation of gay men through their feminine receptivity to penetration? Despite the dismissals of the popular associations of AIDS and anality seeded throughout the *October* essay, I suspect that the epidemic's relation to the new gay interest in the death drive is more constitutive than conditional.

Witness Jonathan Dollimore's recent thoughts on the relation between the homophobic representations of the epidemic as collective gay suicide and the historical associations of homosexuality and morbidity in works by homosexual authors from Oscar Wilde to Oscar Moore. Although Dollimore (1995) argues that in Moore's novel about a randy youth who dies of AIDS, *A Matter of Life and Death*, the epidemic is simply ' "used" as just another brutal material proof of how the interests of death inhabit [all] desire', his reliance on such contemporary examples – Randy Shilts' denunciation of gay promiscuity's contribution to the epidemic in *And the Band Played On*; James Miller's fantasy biography of Foucault deliberately infecting others in sadomasochistic orgies; the poet Thom Gunn's AIDS collection, *The Man with Night Sweats* – suggest that it is the epidemic which homosexualizes the death drive in current thinking, both straight and gay (Dollimore, 1995, p. 28). This is not to deny the poignancy in Dollimore's account of lovers whose dying renders 'desire itself as a kind of grieving', but it is to question the association of homoeroticism with any exceptionally destructive impulse, even if – in Dollimore's amusingly vanguardist argument – 'the sexually dissident have always tended to know more about it, confronting and exploring what the sexually conventional typically disavow, the strange dynamic which, in western culture, binds death into desire' (Dollimore, 1995, p. 33).

In my meaner moments, I call this style of argument Death Camp, in acknowledgement of an actual AIDS publication by an American group called Gays Against Genocide, but also in recognition of the wild exaggeration with which, as Dollimore himself observes, it is often performed. If we turn his rhetorical analysis back to Bersani, we may discover something of relevance both to gay men and to feminists. I'm thinking of the homology which the *October* article proposes between the rectum and the vagina, a homology supported by those Athenian protocols forbidding sexual bottoms to become political tops. Bersani compares this ancient disparagement of the supine position with Dworkin and MacKinnon's opposition to 'the distribution of power both signified and constituted by men's insistence on being on top', a gender hierarchy which they argue is eroticized by pornography (Dworkin, 1981; Mackinnon, 1987). But other feminists have read this topography more critically, protesting, for example, that they 'don't see an image of a woman being penetrated in the missionary position as symbolic of a woman as a *victim*'. And commenting on MacKinnon's identification of sexual penetration with personal violation, Drucilla Cornell has noted how exquisitely *masculine* this terror is: 'What is the worst imaginable disaster to the masculine self? To be fucked' (Cornell, 1991). In a similar vein, Wendy Brown has remarked on the 'insistent and pounding' rhetoric which characterizes MacKinnon's almost pornographic prose, the most phallic example of which must be her hilarious opening of a paragraph criticizing another feminist: 'I am getting hard on this and am about to get harder on it' (Brown, 1995, p. 78). No wonder that Cornell identifies in her analysis the equation of masculinity with selfhood and her consequent aspiration ' "to be" like a man' (ibid., p. 90).

In comparison, Bersani's investments in the very phallic identification – 'the masculine ideal . . . of proud subjectivity' whose demise he celebrates – are both more overt and more oblique than MacKinnon's. As he is at pains to point out in *Homos*, a gay man may both desire and identify with 'culturally dominant images of misogynist maleness'. That possibility, and the related reversibility of the supine position, suggests another reading of 'Is the Rectum a Grave?', not as the funeral of the phallus, but rather as its resurrection. The penis, like the prostrate male to which it is attached, will rise again. For what is all this talk of its 'shattering' and 'ego-annihilating' powers but phallic narcissism by other means? (And isn't this why both Bersani and MacKinnon, for all their ostensible interest in female sexuality, can never address those women who fuck without the penis, us lesbians?)

Still, read my way, Bersani's account of the drive to death, as he says of Freud's own, is impossible to separate from its opposite and commensurate impulse, the drive to life. For gay men attempting to survive the second decade of a devastating epidemic, for feminists attempting to fuck, I hope it affords some consolation.

19 'So How Did Your Condom Use Go Last Night, Daddy?' Sex Talk and Daily Life

Jill Lewis

He said: 'I know I should have, but ah . . . it just felt so, so good at the time . . . . I mean, you know how it is . . .'[1]

It is surprising, really, in this AIDS era, how little everyday discussion there is about safer sex. 'Safer sex' has settled as a rather abstract term, still more often associated with information leaflets, various images of condoms or with that old, problematic notion of 'target groups' than with you or me or the man next door. It often surfaces in talk about 'gay men' generally and their assumed, generalized response to the epidemic or about education strategies for that amorphously invoked category 'young people'. In one way or another safer sex seems usually to end up related to some group 'out there' – a way of thinking that has plagued the HIV/AIDS epidemic and anxious responses to it everywhere. Ways of thinking about prevention strategies concerning the spread of HIV always seem to locate the issue more easily with someone else. The categories and behaviour risks named often seem to have the curious effect of placing the everydayness of 'you and me' somewhere off the map, however old you and I may be, whatever our sexual identities or realities, whoever our relatives, friends, lovers. As if the discourse about safer sex has come to spin its own cocoon within the AIDS field world, the media hype and an endless array of government authority funded leaflets, but lingers impotent outside the thresholds of this house or that apartment, outside the door of that kitchen where people are talking round a table, or this bedroom where the sheets are being drawn back.

Condom sales have increased in most European countries to some degree in the last six years since preventive education campaigns began. But most studies on sexual behaviour patterns, STD and teenage pregnancy statistics reveal relatively limited changes in safer sex practices. Condom users are still in the minority. Condom use is frequently irregular and usually not sustained within 'long-term' relationships (Abrams, 1992; Berer and Ray, 1993; Wellings, 1994; Friedrich and Heckman, 1995). But condoms are, of course, only part of the answer to the problem societies are facing in attempts to stop the sexual behaviours that nurture the conditions for HIV transmission. Gender differences, questions of power and agency, very fixed notions of what 'real sex' is and the persistent workings of very little contested homo phobia all complicate the picture. Condoms appear as a 'practical', easily identifiable, technical, 'sellable' solution to a more complicated problem. And we are not engaging well, yet, with this problem. It concerns how sexuality, its practices and relationships are represented in our cultures. How behaviours occur within reference to these scripts. How these cultural 'imaginings' of sex affect the landscape within which young people, or any of us, are able to envisage sexual safety and well-being.

In popular novels, classics and magazines which parents and schools filter onto the bookshelves of young people, there is very little that maps out any agenda of sexual safety. The 'cut- off' point of appropriateness of the sexualized body for 'young people' usually comes very quickly in family and education circles (Patton, 1991). Fiction of the Western heritage (from *Jane Eyre* to *Ronia the Robber's Daughter*, Nancy Drew's sagas to *Four Weddings and a Funeral*, *Beauty and the Beast* to *Golden Eye*) stage dramas of emotions, sentimental adventures, traumas or triumphs of passion, explicit or latent romantic or erotic hopes – but present limited visualizations of sexual negotiation of the body itself, virtually nothing at all on variables of physically 'well' sexual practices. As if sex itself is so within the veiled boundaries of the natural and universal, that not actually tracing its processes with the body itself is part of the very rituals of desire.

'I'm very much in love,' he said, as we left the pub. 'The sex is extraordinary. He is utterly beautiful.' 'And you're keeping safe, aren't you?' I asked. His eyes widened slightly, he hesitated, drew in his breath then said, 'Yes. Yes. Of course we are.' But there was something unfinished in the air as we parted. 'Be well,' I said as he kissed my cheek. 'You too,' he replied as I kissed his.

The irony of this is that the 'love story' (the 'getting to know you', 'can they, can't they?', 'will they, won't they?' scenarios, etc.) always has written into it the titillating subtext of doing '*it*'. Most fiction provides places where the innocent or experienced mind leans into the 'desirability' of what's at the end of the love tunnel, the suggestive things, partially named, but somehow 'known' beyond the coded signs of the sentence: the penetrative sex. Anticipation of this final intimacy is the addictive bait of contemporary soap operas and romance novels, the pivot of much humour and innuendo, a central media selling point. Sex is a central, obsessive lure in our cultures. Yet the 'full' or 'real' experience is always somehow just round the corner, just beyond the images, where, if time and place and possibility are right, you or I might... The details of the body's actual enactments, towards which the bait lures us, either occur in sexual activities beyond the page, where some kind of 'we all know what happens' prevails, and meanwhile we all have our own little fill-in scenarios of arousal or suspended anticipation. There is, in fact, quite a sparse staging of actual sensual possibilities in mainstream Western cultures. Sexual activities are repetitively stylized and scripted within particular codes of beauty and pleasure (Coward, 1983; Patton, 1991; Modleski, 1984). And the problem is that irresistible *unsafe* practices are always in the wings, awaiting their cue, clothed in cultural allurements of the erotic.

Even today, some 15 years into the AIDS era, the kind of literature and films which emphasize the body – the erotic genres, classic and popular (the kind you would never think to give your mother for Christmas) – pay strikingly limited or very erratic attention to strategies or preventative measures to keep the body safe (except now in some gay literature). A 1993 study of articles on anticipation of or advice on holiday romance and sex in a wide cross-section of British popular magazines (teenage and adult, heterosexual and gay, men's and women's) found all the hallmarks of sentimental and sexual appetite-whetting along with a virtual total absence of references to managing the desiring/desired body safely (Clift, 1994).

The English actress Imogen Stubbs wrote in the *Guardian* a few years ago of her training in Britain's top drama colleges and with the Royal Shakespeare Company. She described how she had been trained into the spectrum of tragedy and comedy, learned how to fence, how to faint or die, how to act older or younger – but never how to act the 'love' or 'sex' scenes, which she had often since been cast to play on stage and screen. She said these scenes were the hardest in her whole career – the point where the director would sort of 'let go', with a 'you know how this bit goes' wink. But it was the very moment when she felt she in fact most wanted guidance, the most unscripted moment, the blank full of only clichés – the actual staging of sexual desire and connection. She had an image of generations of actors all imitating how they had seen sex/love represented in *other* plays or films or books, conjuring up stereotypical postures, expected gestures. And then audiences watching the scenes and taking into their lives these limited, endlessly repeated scenarios.

> *'Ah,' the boy said as the TV screen showed them sliding their clothes off smoothly and melting into each other on the bed of the luxurious hotel room. 'Another pre-AIDS era movie. Still no condoms around.' 'And all they do is hump,' his sister added. 'The interesting stuff is always left out.'*

Perhaps we need to pay attention more to the absence of a current language in which people talk together or think about sexual realities rather than fictions. We need ways to visualize (beyond our own private agendas) the body and its foibles, its awkwardnesses, idiosyncrasies, fumblings and tentative possibilities. We need to address the silences around the real body – not that the 'real body' can be fully narrated, but there are certain absences and gaps in everyday discourse about the real body which now carry enormous consequences. We need new efforts to generate critical discussions of the overabundant presence of the actual culturally constructed body – the idealized body, the smooth merging of heart and flesh, or the ecstatic climaxing of erotic flesh, where it all happens inevitably. Because those taut, sheer-line bodies, the bodies 'not like' yours or mine *really* are' (in flesh or in our minds), these bodies that do not age or sag or swell, not quite feminine or masculine enough somehow in this way or that, are not very good mental equipment to take into the bedroom really (Coward, 1983; Butler, 1990; 1993; Singer, 1993). And rather barren, impermeable ground for the well-intentioned seeds of education about sexual safety education. These are complicated but important questions, which need to emerge creatively from the confines of important feminist research, in an age where sex/AIDS education (when looked at financially from the top down, not measuring its actual reception or effectiveness) is an international, hugely funded, but not very effective project of the 1990s.

> *She sat opposite me in the café. 'There was this man last year, visiting Liverpool for the conference. An American. He was rather attractive, and we got involved. It was all very nice. Though for a while I feared I was pregnant.' She looked at me. 'But then I was at risk for other things too, wasn't I?' she said. 'I know about AIDS and all that, but, somehow, when it comes to the very point... it doesn't seem to matter. Neither of us had said anything about any kind of protection. I'm 33, an adult woman, and I didn't feel I could. It somehow wasn't appropriate. It was as if we assumed...'*[2]

When you learn to drive a car, you have to understand how the basic mechanisms work – the clutch, the steering wheel, the brake system. You need to be able to visualize and enact what co-ordinations are possible and necessary, how to link vision (I need to brake, to put on lights, to add oil) and strategies (I put my foot effectively onto the brake pedal, I turn on the lights not on full beam, I get the oil and put it in myself or with help), and what system of rules prevails (what consequences there are if I do not do these things: I crash, I lose control, I risk destroying the engine, doing damage with huge cost, I am injured, I die). You have to learn how to gauge well timing and distance and internalize all the regulations of highway codes. *That* means there are now steep bends, *this* that there is a school and children around, *here* there must be fog ahead, *there* it is one way only. You have to be familiar with and accept the agreed social conventions about car driving – what side of the road you drive on, when you have to stop or give way, what the speed limit is, how you dip lights not to dazzle an on-coming car driver. You need to know that drinking and driving runs a risk of very inconvenient loss of your right to drive, as well as physical damage or death. In order to drive, you don't just look through lots of car magazines, read *On the Road*, watch *Thelma and Louise*, check out some James Bond movies, glance once over a highway code leaflet, or a one-page menu of 'safer driving possibilities' – if by chance some official educator brings it to your attention – and then glide off into the sunset and drive happily ever after.

> *At the London FPA conference on sex education, the group was discussing condom use and HIV. Should everyone use condoms all the time, except for conception now? Yes, the majority felt. 'But how do you get everyone to do that?' someone asked. The facilitator moved things on. 'Talk about your own safer sex practices,' he suggested. The woman, a sex educator about 45 years old, was very definite. 'We don't need condoms,' she said. 'I have a coil. We've been married 26 years, you know. A very solid marriage. I trust him, he trusts me.'*

In fact, we train our populations well for driving – not that society can eliminate accidents or risky behaviour, but we do have a national system for initiating everyone into the rules, the realities and acquisition of skills and techniques. And we do have an uncontested, established (though it has had to be invented, constructed over the century of car presence) consensus of social conventions which shapes the approach to driving itself. We can name gearsticks and oil, do not hesitate to comment on conservation issues and petrol quality. By law, we go through a process which checks we have really absorbed and internalized safety behaviours and skills, that we can apply our knowledge. We demand regular checks on the mechanisms of the body involved and drivers enter into a social agreement about the driving strategies society expects of them. It's not just a matter of assuming you and everyone else know the ropes instinctively, of imagining the road system will function well 'naturally', or of just 'doing your own thing'. After these processes of initiation, of course, everyone is off on their own, with different vehicles, driving styles, different destinations and different high-tech car equipment – or not. There are, of course, no guarantees that individual behaviours sustain safety and comply with the consensus. There are always human errors and technical fallibilities, always some macho boys, some distracted parent, some argument on the road, some mechanical breakdown which risks causing accidents. The road is a risky place to be. But at least there is common reference to certain codes of behaviour: to drive on *that* side of the road, to stop there, not to overtake here, to slow down when risk factors heighten, not to keep motorway driving with a flat tyre … Society requires and provides processes for acquiring detailed knowledge, standardized training in skills, obligatory rehearsal/practice and experience and a clear understanding of the rules and safety codes. It has established a social consensus around appropriate and necessary practices of driving, because driving is both an individual and highly social activity.

To shape a consensus regarding codes, rules, skills and practices there has to be strategic vision, social commitment to the practicalities of enactments necessary and processes which enable and require widespread personal involvement. For significant behaviour change to occur within any community, a major shift in the consensus of that community is crucial (Carr, 1992). This has not begun to happen yet in Western societies regarding sexual safety and health, and the HIV epidemic makes this inability to prioritise a new consensus about the necessary discussion of details of sexual practices highly dangerous. And the cost will be paid in lives.

Some groups have been identified as 'risk groups' (as if people 'in there' exist in some kind of cloned, insulated, disconnected way), and information is deployed in their direction (King, 1994; Patton, 1994). The problem appears, from the language of this strategy, to be contained and able to be solved within these 'exceptional', marginal places. Mainstream, 'general public' culture, the 'regular' families (from which, of course, young people, gay men, drug users, sex workers, sexually active circulating adults actually emerge) hold course as 'non-risk groups', with prevailing taken-for-granted attitudes to sexual mores and normative 'givens' of everyday thought about... love, desire, passion, marriage, the respectably 'normal' world, where everyone is meant to imagine all the people they know circulate. And there is always embedded in these 'mainstream' assumptions a subtext of endless exceptions, that each of us can activate at will – and do activate, quite regularly. Knowledge of our own experiences and partial information about lives of others connect many people directly to the marginal behaviours targeted. Except we are not 'there', where extra care and information is needed, but 'here', where really we do not need to pay attention except in casual chat. And all of us are highly invested in maintaining the expected behaviours of our communities, families and

> *'It's all very well for you to criticize us.' The teenage boy stood up defiantly and responded to the British MP. 'But what about you? Do you use condoms every single time?' 'Listen young man,' Edwina Currie replied authoritatively, 'I've been happily married for 18 years and have three children.'*

even subgroups. The contradictions, the deviances from the expected norms and healthy 'propernesses' rarely have voice – except only to be categorized into the marginal, the exception, with readjustment of status and value. The norm strengthened and proved by the exception. The acknowledgement of the variables of sexuality is rarely present with any ease within the family in Western cultures.

It is worth pausing on this point a moment. How many children, for example, grow up saying to parents or friends, at say age 7 or 12 or even 16: 'When I grow up, the man or the woman I end up involved with, living with…'? Is there an ordinary emotional space within which those children (yours? mine? theirs?) who *will* live lesbian or gay or bisexual lives can feel the rooted acceptance, the social viability of their experience? And where those who grow up to live heterosexual lives, can grow up in an environment, at home and school, which enables them to have less problematic feelings about their friends, family and workmates who are in gay relationships or shift sense of sexual identities across their life span, in the context of relationships they form? How many of us speak about the range or our sexual experiences, even *within* one long relationship – let alone in different ones over time? Where are the cross-generational discussions (not 'personal confessions', which could be stifling), the round-the-table discussions of friends and family of all

---

They were all about 17 years old, fine young pupils, talking enthusiastically about their peer AIDS education project. 'So what do you talk about with the others, concerning homosexuality, or what did the teachers say?' was the question. 'Nothing really', they said. 'It isn't necessary except for infection figures…'

… 'In the school yard lessie or queer are the worst put-downs really,' I hear her say. 'Kids use them all the time, even in class, specially the boys.' 'If you say nigger,' this twelve year old is telling me, 'the teacher probably says something. They say it's wrong. But with gay mocking, they never say a word.'

---

ages of various experiences about condom use, advantages or disadvantages of oral sex, the pleasures and dangers of anal sex, the pleasures and comforts of masturbation? The acknowledgement of difference, preferences and difficult navigations? Where do people hear talk of the individual right to likings and dislikings of any one sexual practice, that penetrative sex is not the 'be all and end all' of sexual fulfilment, and how no sexual practices have intrinsic values in themselves? That sex feels different every time you do it (whatever it is), even with the same person? How sex involves desires and tiredness, clumsiness and attentiveness, synchronized and discordant connections and is infused with all the other agendas of relationship and non-relationship? Where are the active conversations about how intimacy is not 'property', even in marriage, how right of bodily access is always up for renegotiation and its terms involve, at some level, respect for the different reality of the other person involved? How sex is something invented in relationship and is a place of possible delicate as well as possible dangerous risk, as well as a place for possible (but not inevitable) pleasure? Where *do* our children become knowing about the terms they will be dealing with in future relationships? We are implicated in that process, both actively and by default. Our attitudes, silences, prejudices, judgements set the tone, prolong or contest the notions of reality, reinforce or question what appears to be possible or probable. We are of the process *whether we like it or not*. And now, in this era of a new epidemic advancing hour by hour, where globally, of the 40 million HIV infections anticipated by the year 2000 by the World Health Programme, some 90 per cent or more will have been transmitted sexually, and in a context where estimates of some 25 per cent of new HIV infections are being identified in young people under the age of 25, surely there is some new process we need to become committed to, to be part of the daily elaboration of preventive strategies (Panos Institute, 1994; WHO, 1995)?

The contingencies of human existence, and in particular of our mobile societies and their sex-focused, sex-commercialized cultures, mean that people (the people we know – granny, uncle, mummy, daddy, family best friend, son, daughter, colleague, neighbour, mate, I myself) often have different, various experiences of intimacy with *other* people – not just people in the 'family scenario' which remains centred in the 'appearances', not just in the ways public narratives of various societies assume (Coontz, 1992). How do we prepare children for the world of these real diversities, real options, real bodies, real contexts? Where, to whom and how are we talking about these processes? It is one of the tragic ironies of the AIDS context, that those who, in all kinds of communities and cultures, are most invested in 'traditional moralities' concerning sexual practices and the social organization of sexual relationships risk preparing worst those in their communities who go on to lives which do not quite adhere to those mores and values, or whose lives encounter unexpected, unanticipated contradictions between beliefs and real, lived situations. And by our silences and inertia, are most of us not part of that same inadequate preparation process, passively carrying those unhelpful categories of social appearances within the networks of people we link with, of the young people whose lives overlap with ours?

> *This is what he told me on the phone. He was an educated Englishman, with an upper-class accent. 'We have been together 11 years,' he said, 'are a very stable couple. I do want counselling before the test...but I don't think he will. The situation is that he has a weakness now and then, wants to sleep with women. And last year he was lover of a woman', he paused, 'whose husband', he paused, 'used to cruise and pick up men for sex along the sea front, so we learned...So we realised there was perhaps a risk that...'*

One of the problems is that we adults, most often, have minimally begun to talk openly together about the vagaries of sexual experience. Sex is still generally seen as both 'instinctive'/biological and also as private and individual. Yet the way each of us leads our sexual life is powerfully infused with socially constructed sexual standards and scenarios, endlessly silhouetted against the terms of social sexual cultures which imbue us with some images and edit out others. Within such a public deployment of sexual scenarios, the 'personal', secret nature of sexual intimacy – especially in long-term relationships – has led to enormous silencing of talk about the practicalities, dilemmas, humour, fears, mistakes, possibilities, lonelinesses, illusions, changes, experiences and dreams. Yet these are realities, to some degree or other, of the sexual dimension of everyone's life. And, ironically again, most women now infected with HIV globally have been infected within a stable, long-term relationship or marriage (Berer, 1993; WHO, 1994). Public, social conventions have not found ways yet of deploying personal practices of sexual safety into the behaviours of real private experiences. So what can we do to change that?

What is the new knowing, the new to-be-for-taken granted code of sexual behaviours which all relationships, all territories of physical intimacy need to incorporate? When it comes to sexual health and safety the mechanics are the same for everyone at a basic level. *All forms of penetrative sex carry risk of potential infection*, for everyone, whatever their sexual preferences, whether in long or short, dating or married, love or fling contexts. Though rates of new infections vary, dipping here, plateauing there, rising there, more men, especially young, are still becoming HIV+ from sex with another man, some of the steepest infection graphs now mark women's infections, young people under 25 are showing up positive in frightening numbers in many different cultures, from Europe to Asia or the Americas. HIV infection is increasing in every country where it has been identified (it doesn't matter what speed that rate of infection is moving: nowhere is it decreasing, and the channels of potential infection proliferate) (Panos Institute, 1994: WHO, 1994a; UNAIDS, 1996). Chlamydia and herpes are on the rise too, as are other sexual infections needing important medical interventions. The vast majority of people who are HIV+ or have AIDS acquired the HIV virus through sexual transmission: this means (let us spell it out slowly and clearly) through unprotected or failed-protected penetrative sex, sex involving one man's penis having contact with the body fluids of his partner, and/or delivering sperm into someone else's body. It is thought so 'natural' that a man delivers sperm into another's body, that nobody is being really very inventive about creating a new conscious, social consensus about the importance of 'sperm management', let alone opening up new scripts of sexual behaviour which sustain intimacy and pleasure, but maybe minimize or marginalize the sperm delivery risk practices. Unprotected or inadequately or unsystematically protected vaginal penetration, not irrelevant to unwanted pregnancies, is an issue in whatever kind

> *In the classroom, the trained teenagers all geared up to give peer education about HIV/AIDS and sexual safety describe their training and how they are running the courses for other pupils. 'And what about each of you?' I ask. 'How do you practise or plan to practise safer sex?' Grins, glances. The girl seems utterly confident and assured. 'I don't need to,' she says. 'I'm in a long-term relationship. We've been together 11 months. My boyfriend's in Italy now. We'll probably get engaged next year.' She is very certain. 'We're very much in love,' she says, 'and I am on the pill.'*

of relationship it occurs (Berer, 1993; Hamblin and Reid, 1992; WHO, 1994). Anal penetration, in marriage beds or saunas, whenever it is performed without proper knowledge and protective care, does carry higher risk of infection. Important to mention here that while many studies suggest that fewer gay men have anal sex than popular imagination would have (and have often reduced this practice or rendered it maximally 'safer' in gay communities), studies also suggest that more heterosexual encounters include anal sex than mum or the biology teacher ever believe – or mention. Only socially consensual, meticulous attention to the safety practices for all penetrative or fluid exchange activities, all the time – as the norm involving us all – or shifting 'doing it' away from its penetrative obsession, can affect the safety of penetrative practices in any radical way. How can we move to bring into circulation and day-to-day currency of sex talk culture a prioritizing of intimate, sentimental, erotic, pleasureable imaginings of 'sex' which do not carry the illness and death risk possibilities that the old standard ritual of penetrative intercourse now is shadowed by – whether we like it or not?

> *He is about 26, very vivid and attractive in his presence, his eyes moving over the group with kindness and focus. 'How did you get infected then?' the sixteen-year-old boy suddenly asks. He laughs, and looks the boy straight in the eyes for a minute. 'Love,' he replies. There is a silence. They watch his face. 'We'd been together for months. A really, really good relationship. I was just very much in love. And one night... we just didn't bother...' There is still silence in the crowded room. 'Do you understand?' he asks. 'I was very much in love and I didn't care enough about the risks. And then it was too late.' 'I was only 18,' he is saying. 'I didn't really see that if... later I found out that in fact...'*

But most of us adults, the ones wanting to promote the safety of future generations, are not practising safer sex. The young people know it and breathe in our 'I don't need to' air, because we never talk to them about how *we do* it. The adult world we inhabit is permeated with attitudes where 'I am the exception', where 'the naturalness of the moment sweeps those concerns away', where 'we trust each other – it is other people who need to take care'. 'We've been together for so long, it doesn't affect us.' 'We are not/I am not in the *real* risk area.' 'He/she isn't like that, he's/she's not a risk.' Ah, the old 'it couldn't happen to me... it only happens to them' syndrome. 'I love you, therefore I trust you. Let us have no barriers between us. I will love you for ever.'

In Britain now virtually half of all marriages end in divorce, many people are single, many sexual lives are in erratic circulation- and transition. The adult world is riddled with repressions of our own sexual history, hidden, forgotten secrets, stories which do not gel with how we are 'known', how we circulate publicly in the world. We 'know' that you never 'know' someone else's sexual history, that you never own someone else's sexual experience.

> *She has been working in research on young people's sexual behaviours for many years now, on national survey data. 'There is a blank,' she is saying. 'A kind of silence within the culture. It claims to have strong codes within which young people should learn to be responsible in relationships. But at the same time, apart from biological details, no one actually talks with them about sex itself. There is a kind of coded discretion about realities of the body, the feelings that emerge in the actual process of...' 'Yes, a kind of blank, or silence,' she picks up again. 'And that doesn't help anyone practically, when it comes to the crunch of being safe, does it?' she asked.*

We 'know' that sexual trajectories are never completely within rational control, but depend on chance, influences and encounters we had never imagined, decisions which are reformulated in differ- ent contexts in different places, at different stages of life. But that is not the convention by which we live, nor is it the terms of discussion within which we talk with younger people, nor with each other. We all ride wildly on the appearances of the social conventions. And we pass that on to younger people. We give them the abstract theory of safety within one or another brand of 'morality', but edit out the skills, silence experience, demonstrate suggestively our own bad practice of silence and inertia, and train them meticulously, all the while, by our silences and unthinking behaviours, in the problema- tically gendered, homophobic, erotophobic, conventionally pene- trative terms of our highly sexed cultures.

What I have wanted to raise here is the concern that we begin, individually – not to mention culturally, educationally, politically – to shift the terms of the discourse, to contest these conventions. The safer sex terrain is still not being adequately prepared, in this internationally mobile world, these cosmopolitan, mass-media cul- tures we – and the children and the teenagers and young adults –

inhabit. Formal efforts by Authorities – sporadic media campaigns, erratic sex/AIDS education sessions in schools and youth clubs, Health Authority leaflets – to inform about safety can only go so far in their delivery of information. Safer forms of sexuality can only evolve if there is a will to reassess, dare to shift and reformulate the way we talk together, question and acknowledge the very terms in which sex functions in our lives and culture. Even realizing how powerfully the discourses we invoke, even as we speak, risk reinforcing the terms of the problem. I recently heard an HIV educator comment: 'The drag is – we've got to go on about sex, even if, when you come down to it, real sex isn't *really* as important always as its made out to be in our actual lives.' And in one way, that of course, is true. But then, in this era of AIDS, maybe a new kind of sex talk is more important than ever.

> *She is 16, about to go to New York for four weeks, on her own, to a summer school. She sips late-night chocolate, and launches into the speculative artificiality of our 'AIDS talk'. 'We had really, really good sex education sessions at school, you know,' she tells me. 'The teacher was ever so nice, not embarrassed, really open about EVERYTHING. You know... even AIDS.' But within minutes she is turning to me suddenly, in mid-sentence, saying. 'What do you mean in the sperm? The virus isn't actually right in the sperm, is it? But the... what do you do... I mean, that means that... that means I...'*

The World Health Organization reckoned that 16.9 million people globally were HIV+ by the end of 1995 'allowing for under-diagnosis, incomplete reporting and reporting delays' (UNAIDS, 1996). The anticipated figure for the year 2000 is 40 million. The European situation (which I single out, along with the US, since this publication will circulate most in European and US bookshops, and in our imaginations the real problems are always elsewhere) is that by 1995 154 103 people had been diagnosed with AIDS, some half a million people in Europe were already known to be HIV+ and there is increase of infection, to varying degrees, year by year in all European countries (European Centre for Epidemiological Monitoring, 1995; UNAIDS, 1996). In the United States alone, it is believed that well over 1 million people are HIV+, 501 301 are known to have developed AIDS (UNAIDS, 1996), and statistics from the Centre for Disease Control suggest that on average every 13 minutes someone is infected with HIV (AIDS ACTION, Boston assembled data). In Britain, as of September 1995 25 316 are HIV+ (National Aids Trust Annual Report, 1996), 11,494 have developed AIDS (UNAIDS, 1996), and, averaging out new HIV infections over the previous 21 months, some 4 people a day become HIV+. These are all low infection levels, not meriting daily attention in national media or daily conversations. It is known and envisaged that infections in parts of Africa and Asia way outpace these 'low infection' levels, though registered diagnosis UNAIDS statistics register lower cases of AIDS in Africa than in the US. International movement is more accessible or obligatory than it has ever been. Millions of people live displaced from their homes for reasons of social strife, war, economic need, international work and leisure. Migrant work, from Britons in Berlin, Mexicans in California, Turks in Switzerland, multinational corporations, business and academic connections, military deployments, is higher than ever.

From marriage bed to brothel, economic need to leisure, singles clubs to religious orders, military regiments to syndromes of domestic sexual abuse, from holiday resorts to refugee camps, homes to rented rooms:

the virus is moving...

and its context needs, somehow,

to be talked about much, much more

NOTES

1. The quotes in this chapter are transcribed from situations or conversations the author has personally encountered.
2. As I edit this article today, in Spring 1996, I rethink this quote in the light of data published last November in the *New York Times*: that 1 out of every 92 men in the US are currently estimated to be HIV+. The statistics are on the increase everywhere, but we go on as if our world is not implicated, with imaginary thresholds of reality checks. 'When people start knowing people with HIV/ AIDS, when it comes closer to home, they will take more notice' I hear, over and over again. A fine urban myth. Nowhere, it seems, has that proved true, except in the most extreme epidemic conditions.

Bibliography

Abrahams, D. (1992) *AIDS: What Young People Believe and What They Do* (Institute of Social and Applied Psychology, University of Kent).

Abrahms, D. (1989) 'Differential Associations: Social Developments in Gender Identity and Intergroup Relations during Adolescence', in S. Skevington and D. Barker (eds), *The Social Identity of Women* (London: Sage).

Aggleton, P. (1989) 'Evaluating Health Education about AIDS', in P. Aggleton, G. Hart and P. Davies (eds) *AIDS: Social Representations, Social Practices* (Lewes: Falmer Press).

Aggleton, P., P. Davies and G. Hart (1993) *AIDS: Facing the Second Decade* (London: Falmer Press).

AIDS Strategic Monitor (1991) *Report on the Survey Period November 1987–December 1988* (London: BMRB/HEA).

AIDS Strategic Monitor – Gay Bars (1991) *Report on a Quantitative Survey in Gay Bars, January–February 1990* (London: BMRB/HEA).

Alexander, S. (1994) *On Becoming a Woman* (London: Verso).

Allers, C.T. and K.J. Benjack (1991) 'Connections Between Childhood Abuse and HIV Infection', *Journal of Counseling and Development*, Vol. 70, pp. 309–13.

Altman, D. (1972) *Homosexual: Oppression and Liberation* (Sydney: Angus and Robertson).

Altman, D. (1995) *Rupture or Continuity? The Internationalisation of Gay Identities*, unpublished paper (Latrobe University).

Ardill, S. and S. O'Sullivan (1989) 'Sex in the Summer of "88"', in *Feminist Review*, Vol. 31, Spring.

Arguëlles, M. and J. Arguëlles (1977) *The Feminine: Spacious as the Sky* (Boulder, CO: Shambhala).

Askew, S. and C. Ross (1988) *Boys Don't Cry: Boys and Sexism in Education* (Milton Keynes: Open University Press).

Baker, N. (1994) 'Lost Youth', *London Review of Books*, 9 June, p. 6.

Baker, P. (1992) 'Maintaining Male Power: Why Heterosexual Men Use Pornography', in C. Itzen, *Pornography* (Oxford: Oxford University Press, 1995).

Balibar, E. and I. Wallerstein (1991) *Race, Nation Class* (London: Verso).

Ballot Measure 9 (1995) documentary film, director and producer Heather MacDonald (New York: Zeitgeist Films).

Banner, L.W. (1984) *American Beauty* (Chicago: University of Chicago Press).

Barker, M. (1981) *The New Racism: Conservatives and the Ideology of the Tribe* (London: Junction Books).

Barthes, R. (1975) *Mythologies* (New York: Hill & Wang).

Bauman, Z. (1992) *Mortality, Immortality and Other Life Strategies* (Cambridge: Polity Press).

Bawer, B. (1993) *A Place at the Table* (New York: Poseidon Press).

Baxandall, R. (1995) 'Marxism and Sexuality: The Body as Battleground', in S. Callari *et al.* (eds), *Marxism in the Postmodern Age* (New York: Guilford Press).

de Beauvoir, S. (1988) *The Second Sex* (first published 1949) (London: Picador).

Bech, H. (forthcoming) *When Men Meet: Homosexuality and Modernity* (Cambridge: Polity Press).

Benjamin, J. (1990) *The Bonds of Love: Psychoanalysis, Feminism and the Problem of Domination* (London: Virago).

Benjamin, J. (1995) 'Sameness and Difference: Toward an "Over-inclusive" Theory of Gender Development', in A. Elliott and S. Frosh (eds), *Psychoanalysis in Contexts* (London: Routledge).

Berer, M. and S. Ray (1993) *Women and HIV/AIDS: An International Resource Book* (London: Pandora).

Bersani, L. (1986) *The Freudian Body: Psychoanalysis and Art* (New York: Columbia University Press).

Bersani, L. (1987) 'Is the Rectum a Grave?' *October*, No. 43, Winter, pp. 197–222.

Bersani, L. (1995) *Homos* (London: Routledge).

Bérubé, A. (1990) 'Marching to a Different Drummer: Lesbian and Gay GIs in World War II', in M. Duberman, M. Vicinus and G. Chauncey Jr (eds), *Hidden from History: Reclaiming the Gay and Lesbian Past* (New York: Penguin Books).

Bhabha, H. (1990) 'The Third Space', in J. Rutherford (ed.), *Identity: Community, Culture, Difference* (London: Lawrence & Wishart).

Bjerrum Nielsen, H. and M. Rudberg (1995) 'Gender Recipes among Young Girls', *Nordic Journal of Youth Research*, Vol. 3, No. 2, May, pp. 71–88.

Bland L. (1995) *Banishing the Beast: English Feminism and Sexual Morality, 1885–1914* (London: Penguin Books).

Blee, K.M. (1991) *Women and the Klan: Racism and Gender in the 1920s* (Berkeley: University of California Press).

Bluham, R.C. (1921) Letter to Edward Carpenter, Sheffield City Archives Mss 384/34.

Blumm, M. (1984) in Teresa de Lauretis, *Alice Doesn't Live Here Any More: Feminism, Semiotics, Cinema* (London: Macmillan).

Bock, G. (1984) 'Racism and Sexism in Nazi Germany: Motherhood, Compulsory Sterilization, and the State', in R. Bridenthal et al. (eds), *When Biology Became Destiny: Women in Weimar and Nazi Germany* (New York: Monthly Review Press).

Bonacci, M.A. (1992) *Senseless Casualties: The AIDS Crisis in Asia* (Washington, DC: International Voluntary Services).

Brennan, T. (ed.) (1989) *Between Feminism and Psychoanalysis* (London: Routledge).

Bridenthal, R., A. Grossman and M. Kaplan (eds) (1984) *When Biology Became Destiny: Women in Weimar and Nazi Germany* (New York: Monthly Review Books).

Bristow. J. (ed.) (1992) *Sexual Sameness: Textual Differences in Lesbian and Gay Writing* (London: Routledge).

British Medical Journal (1898) 'Medico-Legal: Charge of Publishing and Selling Obscene Literature', ii, p. 1466.

British Medical Journal (1902) 'Reviews: Sexual Psychology and Pathology', i, pp. 339–40.

British Medical Journal (1909) 'Reviews: The Uranian', i, pp.1546–7.

British Society for the Study of Sex Psychology (1913) Minutes of the Preliminary Meeting of the British Society for the Study of Sex Psychology, 12 August 1913,

British Sexology Society archives, Harry Ransom Humanities Research Center, University of Texas at Austin.

British Society for the Study of Sex Psychology (1914), Publication No. 1, *Policy and Principles: General Aims* (London: for the Society).

Brown, N. and P. France (1993) ' "Only Cissies Wear Dresses": A Look at Sexist Talk in the Nursery', in G. Weiner (ed.), *Just a Bunch of Girls* (Milton Keynes: Open University Press).

Brown, W. (1995) 'The Mirror of Pornography', in *States of Injury: Power and Freedom in Late Modernity* (Princeton, NJ: Princeton University Press).

Browne, F.W.S. (1918) 'A New Psychological Society', *International Journal of Ethics*, Vol. 28, pp. 266–9.

Browne, S. (1912) Correspondence, *The Freewoman*, 21 March.

ten Brummelhuis, H.A.N. and G. Herdt (eds) (1995) *Culture and Sexual Risk: Anthropological Perspectives on AIDS* (New York: Gordon and Breach).

Buck-Morss, S. (1995) 'The City as Dream and Ruin'. Paper presented at Cornell University, 3 March (unpublished).

Bullough, V.L. (1994) *Science in the Bedroom: A History of Sex Research* (New York: Basic Books).

Burleigh, M. and W. Wipperman (1991) *The Racial State. Germany, 1933–1945* (Cambridge: Cambridge University Press).

Burstyn, V. (ed.) (1985) *Women against Censorship* (Vancouver: Douglas & McIntyre).

Burt, M.R. (1983) 'Justifying Personal Violence: A Comparison of Rapists and the General Public', *Victimology: An International Journal*, Vol. 8, pp. 131–50.

Butler, J. (1990) *Gender Trouble: Feminism and the Subversion of Identity* (London: Routledge).

Canning, K. (1994) 'Feminist Theory after the Linguistic Turn', *Signs*, Vol. 19, No. 2.

Caplan, P. (ed.) (1987) *The Cultural Construction of Sexuality* (London: Tavistock).

Carpenter, E. (1930) *Love's Coming of Age* (first published 1896) (London: T. Fisher Unwin).

Carr, A. (1992) *Behaviour Change: Some Analogies and Lessons from the Experience of Gay Communities*. Issue Paper 7 (New York: UNDP).

Castells, M. (1983) *The City and the Grassroots* (London: Edward Arnold).

Charney, M. (1981) *Sexual Fiction* (London: Methuen).

Chauncey, G. (1994) *Gay New York: Gender, Urban Culture and the Making of the Gay Male World, 1890–1940* (New York: Basic Books).

Chisolm, L., P. Buchner, H. Kruger and P. Brown (eds) (1990) *Childhood, Youth and Social Change: A Comparative Perspective* (London: Falmer Press).

Clark, D. (1993) 'Commodity Lesbianism', in H. Abelove et al. (eds), *The Lesbian and Gay Studies Reader* (New York: Routledge).

Cliff, D. (1979) 'Religion, Morality and the Middle Class', in R. King and N. Nugent, *Respectable Rebels: Middle-class Campaigns in Britain in the 1970s* (London: Hodder & Stoughton).

Clifford, J. and G. Marcus (eds) (1986) *Writing Culture: The Poetics and Politics of Ethnography* (Berkeley: University of California Press).

Clift, S. (1994) *Romance and Sex Holidays Abroad: A Study of Magazine Representations*. Travel Lifestyles and Health Working Paper No. 4 (Centre for Health Education and Research, Christchurch College, Canterbury).

Clift, S. and Page, S. (1996) *Health and the International Tourist* (London: Routledge).

Clift, S. and D. Stears (1990) *The HIV/AIDS Education and Young People Project (Phases I and II)* (Horsham: Avert).

Coates, T. (1993) *Prevention in Developed Countries*, Abstract RT–08, IXth International Conference on AIDS, Berlin, June 1993.

Communicable Diseases Report (1993) *The Incidence and Prevalence of AIDS and Other Severe HIV Disease in England and Wales for 1992–1997: Projections Using Data to the End of June 1992*. Report of a Working Group (Chairman: Professor N.E. Day), 3, (Supp. 1): S1–S117.

Conason, J. (1995) 'Police Mayor in FIRE City', *The Nation*, 18 December, pp. 781–3.

Connell, R.W. (1987) *Gender and Power* (Oxford: Polity Press).

Connell, R.W. (1995) 'Democracies of Pleasure: On the Goals of Radical Sexual Politics', in L. Nicholson and S. Seidman (eds), *Social Postmodernism: Identity Politics and Beyond* (Cambridge: Cambridge University Press).

Connell, R.W. and G.W. Dowsett (eds) (1992) *Rethinking Sex: Social Theory and Sexuality Research* (Melbourne: Melbourne University Press).

Coontz, S. (1992) *The Way We Never Were: American Families and the Nostalgia Trap* (New York: HarperCollins).

Cornell, D. (1991) 'Feminism always Modified: The Affirmation of Feminine Difference Rethought', in *Beyond Accommodation: Ethical Feminism, Deconstruction and the Law* (London: Routledge).

Coward, R. (1983) *Patriarchal Precedents: Sexuality and Social Relations* (London: Routledge).

Coward, R. (1992) *Our Treacherous Hearts: Why Women Let Men Get Their Way* (London and Boston, MA: Faber and Faber).

Coxon, A.P.M. (1996) *Between the Sheets: Sexual Diaries and Gay Men's Sex in the Era of AIDS* (London: Cassell).

Coxon, A.P.M. and N.H. Coxon (1995) 'Risk in Context: The Use of Sexual Diary Data to Analyze Sequencing in Homosexual Risk Behavior', in H.A.N. Brummelhuis and G. Herdt (eds) *Culture and Sexual Risk* (New York: Gordon and Breach).

Crosland, C.A. (1956) *The Future of Socialism* (London: Jonathan Cape).

Csincsak, M. et al. (1990) 'School-based Sex Education in Flanders: Problems, Barriers and Perceived Needs for Future Practice', *Health Education Research*, Vol. 9, No. 4, p. 473–83.

Davidoff, L. (1995) 'Class and Gender in Victorian England: The Case of Hannah Cullwick and A.J. Munby', in *Worlds Between* (Cambridge: Polity Press).

Davies, P., F.C.I. Hickson, P. Weatherburn and A.J. Hunt (1993) *Sex, Gay Men and AIDS* (London: Falmer Press).

Davis, M. (1991) *City of Quartz: Excavating the Future in Los Angeles* (New York: Verso).

Davis, M. (1992) *Urban Control: The Ecology of Fear* (Westfield, NJ: Open Magazine pamphlet series).

Davis, M. and E. Kennedy (1990) 'Oral History and the Study of Sexuality in the Lesbian Community: Buffalo, New York, 1940–60', in M. Duberman, M. Vicinis and G. Chauncey Jr (eds) *Hidden from History: Reclaiming the Gay and Lesbian Past* (New York: Penguin Books).

Dawkins, R. (1982) *The Extended Phenotype* (Oxford: Oxford University Press).

Dawson, G. (1994) *Soldier Heroes, British Adventure, Empire and the Imagining of Masculinities* (London: Routledge).

De Cecco, J.P. (1990) 'Sex and More Sex: A Critique of the Kinsey Conception of Human Sexuality', in D.P. McWhirter et al., *Homosexuality/Heterosexuality: Concepts of Sexual Orientation* (New York: Oxford University Press).

D'Emilio, J. (1983) *Sexual Politics, Sexual Communities: The Making of a Homosexual Minority in the United States, 1940–70* (Chicago: University of Chicago Press).

D'Emilio, J. (1990) 'Gay Politics and Community in San Francisco since World War II', in M. Duberman, and M. Vicinus and G. Chauncey Jr (eds) *Hidden from History: Reclaiming the Gay and Lesbian Past* (New York: Penguin Books).

Dennis, N. (1993) *Rising Crime and the Dismembered Family. How Conformist Intellectuals Have Campaigned against Common Sense* (London: IEA Health and Welfare Unit).

Dennis, N. and G. Erdos (1992) *Families without Fatherhood* (London: IEA Health and Welfare Unit).

Des Jarlais, D.C., N.S. Padian and W. Winklestein (1994) 'Targeted HIV-Prevention Programs', *New England Journal of Medicine*, Vol. 331, pp. 1451–3.

Diepold, J. Jr and R.D. Young (1979) 'Empirical Studies of Adolescent Sexual Behavior: A Critical Review', *Adolescence*, Vol. 14, pp. 45–64.

Dollimore, J. (1991) *Sexual Dissidence: Augustine to Wilde, Freud to Foucault* (Oxford: Oxford University Press).

Dollimore, J. (1995) 'Sex and Death', *Textual Practice*, Vol. 9, Issue 1, Spring.

Draijer, N. (1984) 'Seksueel Geweld en Heteroseksualiteit' (Den Haag: Ministerie SoZaWe).

Duncombe, J. and D. Marsden, (1993) 'Love and Intimacy: The Gender Division of Emotion and "Emotion Work" ': A Neglected Aspect of Sociological Discussion of Heterosexual Relationships', *Sociology*, Vol. 27, No. 2, May.

Durham, M. (1991) *Sex and Politics: The Family and Morality in the Thatcher Years* (Basingstoke: Macmillan).

Durham, M. (1994a) 'Major and Morals: Back to Basics and the Crisis of Conservatism', *Talking Politics*, Autumn.

Durham, M. (1994b) 'The Road to Victory? The American Right and the Clinton Administration', *Parliamentary Affairs*, April.

Dworkin, A. (1979/1981) *Pornography: Men Possessing Women* (Chicago: University of Chicago Press/London: Women's Press).

Ehrenreich, B. (1983) *The Hearts of Men: American Dreams and the Flight from Commitment* (London: Pluto Press).

Einhorn, B. (1991) 'Where Have All the Women Gone? Women and the Women's Movement in East Central Europe', *Feminist Review*, No. 39.

Eisenstein, Z. (1981) *The Radical Future of Liberal Feminism* (New York: Longman).

Ellis, H. H. (1915) *Studies in the Psychology of Sex: Volume II: Sexual Inversion*, third edition (Philadelphia: F. A. Davis Co.).

Ellis, H.H. (1918) Letter to Edward Carpenter, Sheffield City Archives Mss 257/32.

English, D., A. Hollibaugh and G. Rubin (1982) 'Talking Sex: A Conversation on Sexuality and Feminism', *Feminist Review*, Summer, No. 11.

Epstein, S. (1992) 'Gay Politics, Ethnic Identity', in E. Stein (ed.), *Forms of Desire* (New York: Routledge).

Etzioni, A. (1995) *The Spirit of Community: Rights, Responsibilities, and the Communitarian Agenda* (London: Fontana).

Euromonitor (1989) *Young Britain: Stage II Report* (London: Euromonitor).

European Centre for Epidemiological Monitoring of AIDS (1995) *AIDS Surveillance in Europe* (St Maurice, France).

Evans, B.G. et al. (1993) 'Sexually Transmitted Diseases and HIV-1 Infection Among Homosexual Men in England and Wales', *British Medical Journal*, Vol. 306, pp. 426–8.

Evans, J. et al. (1986) *Feminism and Political Theory* (London: Sage).

Faderman, L. (1985) *Surpassing the Love of Men: Romantic Friendship and Love between Women from the Renaissance to the Present Day* (London: Junction Books).

Faderman, L. (1992) *Odd Girls and Twilight Lovers* (London: Penguin Books).

Fanon, F. (1968) *The Wretched of the Earth* (New York: Grove Press).

Fanon, F. (1986) *Black Skin, White Masks* (London: Pluto Press).

Fast, I. (1984) *Gender Identity* (Hillsdale, NJ: Analytic Press).

Finch, J. (1989) *Family Obligations and Social Change* (Cambridge: Polity Press).

Fitzsimmons, D. et al. (eds) (1995) *The Economic and Social Impact of AIDS in Europe* (London: Cassell).

Foucault, M. (1979) *The History of Sexuality: Volume I: An Introduction* (London: Allen Lane).

Friedrich, D. and W. Heckman (eds) (1995) *AIDS in Europe: The Behavioural Aspect*, 1994 Berlin Conference Papers: WHO/EC Commission/Kohn Institute, AIDS-Zentrum (Berlin: Sigma).

Fromm, E. (1971) *The Art of Loving* (London: Allen & Unwin).

Frones, I. (1995) 'Gender Revolution: Gender, Generation and Social Change in Norway'. Paper given to ESRC Seminar series: *Childhood and Society*, December, Institute of Education.

Frosh, S. (1991) *Identity Crisis: Modernity, Psychoanalysis and the Self* (London: Macmillan).

Frosh, S. (1994) *Sexual Difference: Masculinity and Psychoanalysis* (London: Routledge).

Gagnon, J.H. and W. Simon (1974) *Sexual Conduct: The Social Sources of Human Sexuality* (London: Hutchinson).

Gallagher, T. (1995) 'Trespasser on Main St. (You!)', *The Nation*, 18 December, pp. 786–9.

Gallop, J. (1985) *Reading Lacan* (Ithaca, NY: Cornell University Press).

Garber, E. (1990) 'A Spectacle in Color: The Lesbian and Gay Subculture', in M. Duberman, M. Vicinus and G. Chauncey Jr (eds), *Hidden from History: Reclaiming the Gay and Lesbian Past* (New York: Penguin Books).

Garske, J.P. (1975) 'Interpersonal Trust and Construct Complexity for Positively and Negatively Evaluated Persons', *Personality and Social Psychology Bulletin*, Vol. 1, No. 4, pp. 616–19.

Gates, H.L. Jr (1988) *The Signifying Monkey* (New York: Oxford University Press).

Giddens, A. (1991) *Modernity and Self-identity: Self and Society in the Late Modern Age* (Cambridge: Polity Press).

Giddens, A. (1992) *The Transformation of Intimacy: Sexuality, Love and Eroticism in Modern Societies* (Cambridge Polity Press).

Gilbert, H. ed. (1993) *The Sexual Imagination: From Acker to Zola* (London: Jonathan Cape).

Gilder, E. (1989) 'The Process of Political Praxis: Efforts of the Gay Community to Transform the Social Signification of AIDS', *Communication Quarterly*, Vol. 37, No. 1, pp. 27–38.

Gill, A. (1995) *Ruling Passions: Sex, Race and Empire* (London: Roger Bolton).

Gillick, V. (1989) *A Mother's Tale* (London: Hodder & Stoughton).

Gilligan, C, (1982) *In a Different Voice: Psychological Theory and Women's Development* (Cambridge, MA and London: Harvard University Press).

Gilroy, P. (1987) 'There Ain't no Black in the Union Jack', *The Cultural Politics of Race and Nation* (London: Hutchinson).

Gilroy, P. (1993) *The Black Atlantic: Modernity and Double Consciousness* (London: Verso).

Ginn, J. et al. (1996) 'Feminist Fallacies: A Reply to Hakim on Women's Employment', *British Journal of Sociology*, Vol. 47, No. 1, pp. 167–74.

Glassner, B. (1988) *Bodies: Why We Look the Way We Do (and how we feel about it)* (New York: Putnam).

Godelier, M. (1981) 'The Origins of Male Domination', *New Left Review*, no.127, May/June.

Goodey, T. (1912) Letter to Edward Carpenter, Sheffield City Archives Mss 271/130.

Gordon, D. (1995) 'Crack in the Penal System', *The Nation*, 9 December, pp. 704–6.

Gramsci, A. (1971) *Selections from the Prison Notebooks of Antonio Gramsci*, ed. and trans. Q. Hoare and G. Nowell Smith (London: Lawrence & Wishart).

Greenberg, D.F. (1988) *The Construction of Homosexuality* (Chicago: University of Chicago Press).

Greenhouse, L. (1995) 'High Court Lets Parade in Boston Bar Homosexuals', *The New York Times*, 20 June.

Grossberg, L. (1988) 'Wandering Audiences, Nomadic Critics', *Cultural Studies*, Vol. 2, No. 3.

Grosskurth, P. (1980) *Havelock Ellis: A Biography* (London: Allen Lane).

Grosz, E. (1990) 'The Body of Signification' in J. Fletcher and A. Benjamin (eds), *Abjection, Melancholia and Love: The Work of Julia Kristeva* (London: Routledge).

Gruneau, R. and D. Whitson (1993) *Hockey Night in Canada: Sport, Identities and Cultural Politics* (Toronto: Garamond).

Guardian (1996) 'Children "to Learn Finance". City-led Group Will Urge Lessons on Responsibility', 13 April, p. 1.

Gupta, G.R. and E. Weiss (1993) 'Women's Lives and Sex: Implications for AIDS-prevention', *Culture, Medicine and Psychiatry*, Vol. 17, pp. 399–412.

Haas, D.F. and F.A. Deseran (1981) 'Trust and Symbolic Exchange', *Social Psychology Quarterly*, Vol. 44, No. 1, pp. 3–13.

Haire, N. (1920) Letter to Havelock Ellis, 31 May, British Library Department of Manuscripts, Additional Manuscripts 70540.

Hakim, C. (1995) 'Five Feminist Myths about Women's Employment', *British Journal of Sociology*, Vol. 46, No. 3, pp. 429–55.

Halcrow, M. (1989) *Keith Joseph: A Simple Mind* (London: Macmillan).

Hall Carpenter Archives, Lesbian and Oral History Group (1989) *Inventing Ourselves* (London: Routledge).

Hall, L.A. (1985) '"Somehow Very Distasteful": Doctors, Men, and Sexual Problems between the Wars', *Journal of Contemporary History*, Vol. 20, pp. 553–74.

Hall, L.A. (1991) *Hidden Anxieties: Male Sexuality 1900–1950* (Oxford: Polity Press).

Hall, L.A. (1994) '"The English have Hot-water Bottles": The Morganatic Marriage between the British Medical Profession and Sexology since William Acton', in R. Porter and M. Teich (eds), *Sexual Knowledge, Sexual Science: The History of Attitudes to Sexuality* (Cambridge: Cambridge University Press).

Hall, L.A. (1995) ' "Disinterested Enthusiasm for Sexual Misconduct": The British Society for the Study of Sex Psychology, 1913–1947', *Journal of Contemporary History*, 30, pp. 665–86.

Hall, S. (1974) 'Deviance, Politics and the Media', reprinted in H. Abelove, M. Barale and D. Halperin (eds) *The Lesbian and Gay Studies Reader* (London and New York: Routledge, 1993).

Hall, S. (1978) 'Racism and Reaction', in J. Rex et al., *Five Views of Multi-racial Britain* (London: Commission for Racial Equality).

Hall, S. (1980) 'Race Articulation and Societies Structured in Dominance', in UNESCO (ed.), *Sociological Theories: Race and Colonialism* (Paris: UNESCO).

Hall, S. (1988) *The Hard Road to Renewal: Thatcherism and the Crisis of the Left* (London: Verso in association with *Marxism Today*).

Hall, S. (1992) 'New Ethnicities', in J. Donald and A. Rattansi (eds), *'Race', Culture and Dissidence* (London: Sage).

Hall, S. et al. (1978) *Policing the Crisis: Mugging, the State and Law and Order* (London: Macmillan).

Hamblin, J. and E. Reid (1992) *Women, the HIV Epidemic and Human Rights*, Issues Paper 8 (New York: UNDP).

Hamer, D. et al. (1993) 'A Linkage between DNA Markers on the X Chromosome and Male Sexual Orientation', *Science*, Vol. 261.

Harding, S. (ed.) (1987) *Feminism and Methodology: Social Sciences Issues* (Milton Keynes: Open University Press).

Hart, G. (1989) 'AIDS, Homosexual Men and Behavioural Change', in C.J. Martin and D.V. McQueen (eds), *Readings for a New Public Health* (Edinburgh: Edinburgh University Press).

Hart, G., J. Dawson, R. Fitzpatrick, M. Boulton, J. McLean, M. Brookes and J.V. Parry (1993) 'Risk Behaviour and anti-HIV and anti-HBc Prevalence in Clinic and Non-clinic Samples of Gay Men in England, 1991–1992', *AIDS*, Vol. 7, pp. 863–9.

Hartsock, N. (1987) 'The Feminist Standpoint: Developing the Ground for a Specifically Feminist Historical Materialism', in S. Harding (ed.), *Feminism and Methodology* (Milton Keynes: Open University Press).

Hearn, J. and W. Parkin (1987) *'Sex' at 'Work': The Power and Paradox of Organization Sexuality* (Brighton: Wheatsheaf Books).

Heller, A (1987) *Everyday Life* (London: Routledge & Kegan Paul).

Heller, A. and F. Fehrer (1988) *The Postmodern Political Condition* (Cambridge: Polity Press).

Herdt, G. (1981) *Guardians of the Flutes: Idioms of Masculinity* (New York: McGraw Hill).

Herdt, G. et al. (1992) *Gay Culture in America: Essays from the Field* (Boston: Beacon).

Herman, D. (1993) 'The Politics of Law Reform: Lesbian and Gay Rights Struggles in the 1990s', in J. Bristow and A.R. Wilson (eds), *Activating Theory* (London: Lawrence & Wishart).

Herman, D. (1994) *Rites of Passage: Struggles for Lesbian and Gay Equality* (Toronto: University of Toronto Press).

Hewitt, J.P. and R. Stokes (1975) 'Disclaimers', *American Sociological Review*, Vol. 40, pp. 1–11.

Higgins, D.L. et al. (1991) 'Evidence for the Effects of HIV Antibody Counselling and Testing on Risk Behaviours', *Journal of the American Medical Association*, Vol. 266, pp. 2419–29.

Hillman, J. (1973) 'The Great Mother, her Son, her Hero, and the Puer', in P. Berry (ed.), *Fathers and Mothers* (Zurich: Spring Publications).

Hite, S. (1976) *The Hite Report: A Nationwide Survey of Female Sexuality* (New York: Dell).

Hochschild, A. (1983) *The Managed Heart: The Commercialisation of Human Feeling* (Berkeley: University of California Press).

Holland, J., C. Ramazanoglu, S. Scott, S. Sharpe and R. Thomson (1990) 'Sex, Gender and Power: Young Women's Sexuality in the Shadow of AIDS', *Sociology of Health and Illness*, Vol. 12, pp. 335–50.

Holland, J., C. Ramazanoglu, S. Scott, S. Sharpe and R. Thomson (1991) 'Between Embarrassment and Trust: Young Women and the Diversity of Condom Use', in P. Aggleton, G. Hart and P. Davies (eds), *AIDS, Responses, Interventions and Care* (London: Falmer Press).

Holland, J., C. Ramazanoglu, S. Scott, S. Sharpe and R. Thomson (1992) 'Pleasure, Pressure and Power: Some Contradictions of Gendered Sexuality', *Sociological Review*, Vol. 40, No. 4, pp. 645–74.

Holland, J., C. Ramazanoglu and S. Sharpe (1993) *Wimp or Gladiator: Contradictions in Acquiring Masculine Sexuality* (London: Tufnell Press).

Holland, J., S. Arnold, D. Fullerton, A. Oakley and G. Hart (1994) *Review of Effectiveness of Health Promotion Interventions for Men who have Sex with Men* (London: Social Science Research Unit/Institute of Education).

Holloway, W. (1984a) 'Gender Difference and the Production of Subjectivity' in J. Henriques et al., *Changing the Subject: Psychology, Social Regulation and Subjectivity* (London: Methuen), pp. 227–63.

Holloway, W. (1984b) 'Women's Power in Heterosexual Sex', *Women's International Forum*, Vol. 7, No. 1, pp. 63–8.

Hollway, W. (1989) *Subjectivity and Method in Psychology* (London: Sage).

Horney, K. (1967) *Feminine Psychology* (London: Norton).

Housman, L. (1931) Letter to George Ives, 26 November, Harry Ransom Humanities Center, University of Texas at Austin.

Howell, S. and S. Warren (1992) 'Public Opinion and David Duke', in D. Rose (ed.), *The Emergence of David Duke and the Politics of Race* (Chapel Hill, NC: The University of North Carolina Press).

Humphries, S. (1988) *A Secret World of Sex* (London: Sidgwick and Jackson).

Itzen, C. (1995) *Pornography* (Oxford: Oxford University Press).

Jacoby, R. (1975) *Social Amnesia* (Hassocks: Harvester Press).

Jeffreys, S. (1985) *The Spinster and Her Enemies* (London: Pandora Press).

Jeffreys, S. (1990) *Anti-climax: A Feminist Perspective on the Sexual Revolution* (London: Women's Press).

Jenkins, R. (1959) *The Labour Case* (Harmondsworth: Penguin Books).

Johnson-George, C. and W. C. Swap (1982) 'Measurement of Specific Interpersonal Trust: Construction and Validation of a Scale to Assess Trust in a Specific Other', *Journal of Personality and Social Psychology*, Vol. 43, No. 6, pp. 1306–17.

Jordanova, L. (1989) *Sexual Visions. Images of Gender in Science and Medicine between the Eighteenth and Twentieth Centuries* (London: Harvester Wheatsheaf).

Joseph, Lord (1990) *Rewards of Parenthood? Towards More Equitable Tax Treatment* (London: Centre for Policy Studies).

Jung, C. (1911–12/1952) *Symbols of Transformation*, in *Collected Works*, Vol. 5 (London: Routledge & Kegan Paul/Princeton, NJ: Princeton University Press).

Jung, C. (1946/1952) *The Psychology of the Transference*, in *Collected Works*, Vol. 3 (London: Routledge & Kegan Paul/Princeton, NJ: Princeton University Press).

Kaplan, C. (1986) 'Wild Nights: Pleasure/Sexuality/Feminism', in *Sea Changes: Culture and Feminism* (London: Verso).

Katz, J. (1995) *The Invention of Heterosexuality* (New York: NAL/Dutton).

Kegeles, S., R. Hays and T. Coates (1992) 'A Community-level Risk Reduction Intervention for Young Gay and Bisexual Men'. Abstract PoD 5749, VIII International Conference on AIDS/III STD World Congress (Amsterdam, July).

Keller, E. (1983) *A Feeling for the Organism: The Life and Work of Barbara McClintock* (New York: Freeman).

Kelly, J.A. et al. (1991) 'HIV Risk Behaviour Reduction Following Intervention with Key Opinion Leaders of Population: An Experimental Analysis', *American Journal of Public Health*, Vol. 81, pp. 168–71.

Kelly, J.A. et al. (1992) 'Outcomes of a 16-city Randomized Field Trial of a Community-level HIV Risk Reduction Intervention'. Abstract ToD 0543, VIII International Conference on AIDS/III STD World Congress (Amsterdam, July).

Kelly, J.A. et al. (1993) 'Social Diffusion Models Can Produce Population-level HIV Risk Behaviour Reduction: Field Trial Results and Mechanisms Underlying Change'. Abstract PO-C23-3167, IX International Conference on AIDS/IV STD World Congress (Berlin, June).

Kennedy, E. and M. Davis (1993) *Boots of Leather, Slippers of Gold: The History of a Lesbian Community* (New York and London: Routledge).

Kennedy, J. (1995) cited in J. Illman, 'Mother Courage', *The Guardian* (tabloid section), p. 5.

King, D. (1981) 'Gender Confusions: Psychological and Psychiatric Conceptions of Transvestism and Transsexualism', in K. Plummer (ed.), *The Making of the Modern Homosexual* (London: Hutchinson).

King, E. (1994) *Safety in Numbers: The Degaying of AIDS* (London).

King, E., M. Rooney and P. Scott (1992) *HIV Prevention for Gay Men: A Survey of Initiatives in the UK* (London: North West Thames Regional Health Authority).

King, R. and N. Nugent (1979) *Respectable Rebels: Middle-class Campaigns in Britain in the 1970s* (London: Hodder & Stoughton).

Kinsman, G. (1987) *The Regulation of Desire: Sexuality in Canada* (Montreal: Black Rose Books).

Kippax, S., R.W. Connell, G.W. Dowsett and J. Crawford (1993) *Sustaining Safe Sex: Gay Communities Respond to AIDS* (London: Falmer Press).

Kippax, S., J. Crawford, C. Waldby and P. Benton (1990) 'Women Negotiating Heterosex: Implications for AIDS Prevention', *Women's Studies International Forum*.

Kirk, M. and H. Madsen (1989) *After the Ball: How America will Conquer its Fear and Hatred of Gays in the '90s* (New York: Doubleday).

Kirp, D. and R. Bayer (1992) *AIDS in the Industrialized Democracies: Passions, Politics and Policies* (New Brunswick: Rutgers University Press).

Kiss and Tell [P. Blackbridge, L. Jones and S. Stewart] (1994) *Her Tongue on My Theory: Images, Essays, and Fantasies* (Vancouver: Press Gang Publishers).

Kitzinger, C. (1987) *The Social Construction of Lesbianism* (London: Sage).

Kitzinger, J. (in press) ' "I'm Sexually Attractive but I'm Powerful": Young Women Negotiating Sexual Reputation', *Women's Studies International Forum.*

Kitzinger, C. and S. Wilkinson (1993) 'Theorizing Heterosexuality: Editorial Introduction', in S. Wilkinson and C. Kitzinger (eds) *Heterosexuality: A Feminism and Psychology Reader* (London: Sage).

Kleven, K.V. (1993) 'Deadly Earnest or Postmodern Irony: New Gender Clashes?', *Young Nordic Journal of Youth Research*, Vol. 1, No. 4, November, pp. 40–59.

Kristeva, J. (1982) *Powers of Horror: An Essay on Abjection* (New York: Columbia University Press).

Komter, A.E. (1985) *De Macht van de Vanzelfsprekendheid: Relaties Tussen Vrouwen en Mennen* (Den Haag: Vuga).

Lacan, J. (1954–5) *The Seminars of Jacques Lacan. Book II: The Ego in Freud's Theory in the Technique of Psychoanalysis* (Cambridge: Cambridge University Press).

Lacan, J. (1982) 'Seminar of 21 January 1975', in J. Mitchell and J. Rose (eds), *Jacques Lacan and the Ecole Freudienne*, trans. J. Rose (London: Macmillan).

Lancet (1898) 'The Question of Indecent Literature', ii, pp. 1344–5.

Lancet (1910) 'Reviews and Notices of Books: *Studies in the Psychology of Sex*, Volume VI, *Sex in Relation to Society*', i, p. 1207.

Laqueur, T. (1990) *Making Sex: Body and Gender from the Greeks to Freud* (Cambridge, MA: Harvard University Press).

Larzelere, R.E. and T.L. Huston (1980) 'The Dyadic Trust Scale: Toward Understanding Interpersonal Trust in Close Relationships', *Journal of Marriage and the Family*, August, pp. 595–604.

Lasch, C. (1979) *The Culture of Narcissism* (London: Abacus).

Lasch, C. (1980) *The Minimal Self: Psychic Survival in Troubled Times* (London: Pan).

Laumann, E., J. Gagnon, R. Michael and S. Michaels (1994) *The Social Organization of Sexuality: Sexual Practices in the United States* (Chicago: University of Chicago Press).

Leidholdt, D. and J.G. Raymond (eds) (1990) *The Sexual Liberals and the Attack in Feminism* (London: Pergamon).

LeVay, S. (1991) 'A Difference in Hypothalamic Structure between Heterosexual and Homosexual Men', *Science*, Vol. 253.

LeVay, S. (1993) *The Sexual Brain* (Cambridge, MA: MIT Press).

Lewis, J. (1997) 'How Did Your Safe Sex Go Last Night, Daddy?', this volume, chapter 19.

Lloyd, E.B. (1917) Letter to Edward Carpenter, Sheffield City Archives Mss 368/28.

Lyotard, J.-F. (1984) *The Postmodern Condition: A Report on Knowledge* (Manchester: Manchester University Press).

Mac an Ghaill, M. (1995) *The Making of Men: Masculinities, Sexualities and Schooling* (Milton Keynes: Open University Press).

MacIntyre, A. (1985) *After Virtue: A Study in Moral Theory* (London: Duckworth).

MacKinnon, C. (1987) 'Not a Moral Issue', in *Feminism Unmodified: Discourses on Life and Law* (London: Harvard University Press).

MacKinnon, C. (1987) *Feminism Unmodified: Discourses on Life and Law* (London: Harvard University Press).

MacKinnon, C. (1990) 'Liberalism and the Death of Feminism', in D. Leidholdt and J.G. Raymond (eds), *The Sexual Liberals and the Attack on Feminism* (London: Pergamon).

MacKinnon, C. (1992) 'Pornography, Civil Rights and Speech', in C. Itzin (ed.), *Pornography, Women, Violence and Civil Liberties* (Oxford: Oxford University Press).

Macpherson, C.B. (1962) *The Political Theory of Possessive Individualism: Hobbes to Locke* (Oxford: Oxford University Press).

Macpherson, C.B. (1965) *The Real World of Democracy* (Toronto: CBC).

Macpherson, C.B. (1977) *The Life and Times of Liberal Democracy* (Oxford: Oxford University Press).

Mailer, N. (1971) *Prisoner of Sex* (London: Weidenfeld and Nicolson).

Mansfield, P. and J. Collard (1988) *The Beginning of the Rest of Your Life* (London: Macmillan).

Marcus, S. (1966) *The Other Victorians: A Study of Sexuality and Pornography in Mid-Nineteenth Century England* (London: Weidenfeld & Nicolson).

Marcuse, H. (1955) *Eros and Civilisation* (Boston, MA: Beacon Press).

Marcuse, H. (1964) *One Dimensional Man* (London: Routledge & Kegan Paul).

Marketing Direction (1988) *Youth Facts '88* (London: Marketing Direction).

Marx, K. (1973) *Manifesto of the Communist Party*, in D. Fernback (ed.), *Marx: the Revolutions of 1848* (Harmondsworth: Penguin Books).

Mason, M. (1994a) *The Making of Victorian Sexuality* (Oxford: Oxford University Press).

Mason, M. (1994b) *The Making of Victorian Sexual Attitudes* (Oxford: Oxford University Press).

Maticka-Tyndale, E. (1992) 'Social Construction of HIV Transmission and Prevention among Heterosexual Young Adults', *Social Problems*, Vol. 39, No. 3, pp. 238–52.

McIntosh, M. (1968) 'The Homosexual Role', *Social Problems*, Vol. 16, No. 2, pp. 182–92.

Mclean, J. et al. (1994) 'Regular Partners and Risky Behaviour: Why Do Gay Men Have Unprotected Intercourse?' *AIDS Care*, Vol. 6, pp. 333–44.

McRobbie, A. (1982) 'The Politics of Feminist Research: Between Talk, Text and Action', *Feminist Review*, No. 12, pp. 46–57.

Meakin Herford, E.B. (?1922) Letter to the Medical Women's Federation, in file 'Co-Education', Archives of the Medical Women's Federation in the Contemporary Medical Archives Centre, Wellcome Institute for the History of Medicine, SA/MWF/ [reference not yet assigned].

Melman, A. (1978) 'Development of Contemporary Surgical Management for Erectile Impotence', *Sexuality and Disability*, Vol. 1, pp. 272–81.

Meulenbelt, A. (1981) *For Ourselves: Our Bodies and Sexuality – From a Woman's Point of View* (London: Sheba Press).

Millett, K. (1972) *Sexual Politics* (London: Abacus).

Mintel (1988) *Youth Lifestyles*. Mintel Special Report (London: Mintel).

Mitchell, J. (1974) *Psychoanalysis and Feminism* (Harmondsworth: Penguin Books).

Modleski, T. (1995) *Loving with a Vengeance: Mass-produced Fantasies for Women* (Hampden, CT: Archon Books).

Moen, M.C. (1992) *The Transformation of the Christian Right* (Tuscaloosa: University of Alabama Press).

Morgan, P. (1995) *Farewell to the Family? Public Policy and Family Breakdown in Britain and the USA* (London: IEA Health and Welfare Unit).

Mort, F. (1987) *Dangerous Sexualities: Medico-moral Politics in England since 1830* (London and New York: Routledge & Kegan Paul).

Mort, F. (1994) 'Essentialism Revisited? Identity Politics and Late Twentieth-century Discourses of Homosexuality', in J. Weeks (ed.), *The Lesser Evil and the Greater Good* (London: Rivers Oram).

Mort, F. (1996) *Cultures of Consumption: Masculinities and Social Space in Late Twentieth-century Britain* (London: Routledge).

Murray, A.J. (1991) *No Money, No Honey: A Study of Street Traders and Prostitutes in Jakarta* (Singapore: Oxford University Press).

Murray, C. (1990) *The Emerging British Underclass* (London: IEA Health and Welfare Unit).

Murray, C. (1994) *Underclass: The Crisis Deepens* (London: IEA Health and Welfare Unit in association with the *Sunday Times*).

National Deviancy Conference (ed.) (1980) *Permissiveness and Control: The Fate of the Sixties Legislation* (London: Macmillan).

Nead, L. (1987) *Myths of Sexuality* (Oxford: Basil Blackwell).

Nestle, J. (1987) *A Restricted Country* (London: Sheba Press).

New York Times (1995) "Low-income Voters" Turnout Fell in 1994, Census Reports', 11 June.

Newburn, T. (1992) *Permission and Regulation: Law and Morals in Post-war Britain* (London: Routledge).

Newton, J. (1990) 'Historicism New and Old', *Feminist Studies*, Vol. 16, No. 3.

Nixon, S. (1992) 'Have You Got the Look? Masculinities and Shopping Spactacle', in R. Shields (ed.), *Lifestyle Shopping: The Subject of Consumption* (London: Routledge), pp. 157–73.

Oakley, A. et al. (1994) *Reviews of Effectiveness: HIV Prevention and Sexual Health Interventions* (London: Social Science Research Unit/Institute of Education).

Oetomo, D. (1990) 'Patterns of Bisexuality in Indonesia', unpublished paper (Faculty of Social and Political Sciences, Universitas Airlangga).

Paglia, C.(1992) *Sex, Art and American Culture* (London: Viking).

Paglia, C. (1995) *Vamps en Tramps* (Amsterdam: Prometheus).

Panos Institute (1994) *AIDS: Towards 2000*, Panos Briefing 1 (London: Panos Institute).

Parker, I. (1992) *Discourse Dynamics: Critical Analysis for Social and Individual Psychology* (London: Routledge).

Parker, R. (1985) 'Masculinity, Femininity and Homosexuality: On the Anthropological Interpretation of Sexual Meanings in Brazil', *Journal of Homosexuality*, Vol. 11, Nos 3–4, pp. 155–63.

Parker, R. (1995) *Torn in Two: The Experience of Maternal Ambivalence* (London: Virago).

Patton, C. (1990) *Inventing AIDS* (London and New York: Routledge).

Patton, C. (1991) 'Safe Sex and the Pornographic Vernacular', in Bad Object Choices (ed.) *How Do I Look?* (Seattle: Bay Press).

Patton, C. (1993) 'Tremble, Hetero Swine', in M. Warner (ed.), *Fear of a Queer Planet* (Minneapolis: Minnesota University Press).

Patton, C. (1994) *Last Served? Gendering the HIV Pandemic* (London: Taylor & Francis).

Pearsall, R. (1969) *The Worm in the Bud: The World of Victorian Sexuality* (London: Penguin Books).

Pearson, K. (1927) Letter to E. Cobb, 2 April (London: Pearson Collection, University College).

Perkins, R. (1983) *The 'Drag Queen' Scene: Transsexuals in King's Cross* (Sydney: Allen & Unwin).

Petchesky, R.P. (1984) *Abortion and Woman's Choice: The State, Sexuality and Reproductive Freedom* (New York: Longman).

Pethick-Lawrence, E. (?1918) Letter to Havelock Ellis, 26 November [undated, probably 1918], Autograph Letters Collection, Fawcett Library, London Guildhall University.

Phillips, A. (1993) *The Trouble with Boys* (London: Pandora).

Plummer, K. (1975) *Sexual Stigma: An Interactionist Account* (London: Routledge & Kegan Paul).

Plummer, K. (ed.) (1992) *Modern Homosexualities: Fragments of Lesbian and Gay Experience* (London: Routledge).

Plummer, K. (1995) *Telling Sexual Stories* (London: Routledge).

Pollack, R. (1980) 'The Twilight World of the Heterosexual', *Come Together*, No. 12, March 1972, reprinted in A. Walter (ed.), *Come Together: The Years of Gay Liberation, 1970–73* (London: Gay Men's Press).

Pomerantz, A. (1986) 'Extreme Case Formulations: A New Way of Legitimating Claims', in G. Button, P. Drew and J. Heritage (eds), *Human Studies*. Special Issue: *Interaction and Language Use*, Vol. 9, pp. 219–30.

Porter, R. and L.A. Hall (1995) *The Facts of Life: The Creation of Sexual Knowledge in Britain, 1650–1950* (London: Yale University Press).

Potter, J. and M. Wetherell, M. (1987) *Discourse and Social Psychology: Beyond Attitudes and Behaviour* (London: Sage).

Prendergast, S. (1995) 'Gender and Sex Education: Some Issues Explored', in D. Massey (ed.), *Sex Education Source Book* (London: FPA Press).

Prendergast, S. and S. Forrest (1996) ' "Shorties, Low-lifers, Hard Nuts and Kings": Boys and the Transformation of Emotions', in G. Bendelow and S. Williams, *Emotions in Social Life: Social Theories and Contemporary Issues* (London: Routledge).

Prendergast, S. and A. Prout (1980) ' "What Will I Do . . . ?": Teenage Girls and the Social Construction of Motherhood', *Sociological Review*, August.

Prout, A. and K. Deverell (1995) *MESMAC: Working with Diversity – Building Communities* (London: HEA/Longman).

Public Health Laboratory Service and collaborators (1995) 'Unlinked Anonymous HIV Prevalence Monitoring Programme England and Wales 1990–1993', published report, January.

Radford, T. (1996) 'New AIDS Risk Ahead', *The Guardian*, 1 March.

Radway, J. (1988) 'Reception Study: Ethnography and the Problem of Dispersed Audiences and Nomadic Subjects', *Cultural Studies*, Vol. 2, No. 3.

Ram, K. (1991) *Mukkuvar Women: Gender, Hegemony and Capitalist Transformation in a South Indian Fishing Community* (Sydney: Allen & Unwin).

Red Collective (1978) *The Politics of Sexuality in Capitalism* (London: Red Collective/ Publications Distribution Collective).

Reich, W. (1972) *Sex-Pol: Essays 1929–1934* (New York: Vintage Books).

Rempel, J.K., J.G. Holmes and M.P. Zanna (1985) 'Trust in Close Relationships', *Journal of Personality and Social Psychology*, Vol. 49, No. 1, pp. 95–112.

Rhondda, Lady (1933) *This was my World* (London: Macmillan).

Riley, D. (1988) 'Am I that Name?', *Feminism and the Category of Women in History* (Basingstoke: Macmillan).

Robinson, I., K. Ziss, B. Ganza, S. Katz and E. Robinson (1991) 'Twenty Years of the Sexual Revolution, 1965–1985: An Update', *Journal of Marriage and the Family*, Vol. 53, pp. 216–20.

Rogers, E.M. (1983) *Diffusion of Innovations* (New York: Free Press).

Rose, H. (1994) *Love, Power and Knowledge: Towards a Feminist Transformation of the Sciences* (Cambridge: Polity Press).

Roszak, T. (1993) *The Voice of the Earth: An Exploration of Ecopsychology* (London: Bantam).

Rotter, J.B. (1971) 'Generalized Expectancies for Interpersonal Trust', *American Psychologist*, Vol. 26, pp. 443–52.

Rotter, J.B. (1980) 'Interpersonal Trust, Trustworthiness and Gullibility', *American Psychologist*, Vol. 35, No. 1, pp. 1–7.

Rowbotham, S. (1977) *A New World for Women. Stella Browne, Socialist Feminist* (London: Pluto Press).

Rubin, G. (1984) 'Thinking Sex: Notes for a Radical Theory of the Politics of Sexuality', in C. Vance (ed.), *Pleasure and Danger: Exploring Female Sexuality* (London and Boston, MA: Routledge & Kegan Paul).

Rubin, G. (1991) 'The Catacombs: A Temple of the Butthole', in M. Thompson (ed.), *Leatherfolk: Radical Sex, People and Practice* (Boston, MA: Alyson Publications).

Rubin, L. (1983) *Intimate Strangers* (New York: Harper & Row).

Rubin, L. (1991) *Erotic Wars: What Happened to the Sexual Revolution?* (New York: HarperCollins).

Ruddick, S. (1989) *Maternal Thinking: Towards a Politics of Peace* (Boston, MA: Beacon Books).

Russell, D.E.H. (1982) *Rape in Marriage* (New York: Macmillan).

Russell, D.E.H. (1984) *Sexual Exploitation, Rape, Child Sexual Abuse and Workplace Harassment* (Beverly Hills, CA: Sage)

Ryle, J.A. (1943) 'Letters to the Editor: The Prevention of Venereal Disease', *Lancet*, i, p. 415.

Samuels, A. (1989) *The Plural Psyche: Personality, Morality and the Father* (London and New York: Routledge).

Samuels, A. (1993) *The Political Psyche* (London and New York: Routledge).

Samuels, A. (1995) 'The Good-enough Father of Whatever Sex', *Feminism and Psychology*, Vol. 5, No. 6, pp. 511–30.

Sartre, J.-P. (1976) *Critique of Dialectical Reason. Vol. 1: Theory of Practical Ensembles* (London: New Left Books).

Scott, J. (1988) *Gender and the Politics of History* (New York: Columbia University Press).

Schulman, S. (1984) *The Sophie Horowitz Story* (Tallahassee, FL: Naiad Press).

Schulman, S. (1986) *Girls, Vision and Everything* (Seattle: Seal Press).

Schulman, S. (1988) *After Delores* (New York: Dutton).

Schulman, S. (1991) *People in Trouble* (New York: Plume).

Schulman, S. (1992) *Empathy* (New York: Plume).

Schulman, S. (1994) *My American History: Lesbian and Gay Life During the Reagan/Bush Years* (New York: Routledge).

Schulman, S. (1995) *Rat Bohemia* (New York: Dutton).

Schwichtenberg, C. (1980) 'Near the Big Chakra: Vulvar Conspiracy and Protean Film/Text', *encritic*, Vol. IV, No. 2, Fall, 1980/Winter, 1991.

Sears, J.T. (ed.) (1992) *Sexuality and the Curriculum: The Politics and Practices of Sexuality Education* (New York: Teachers College Press).

Sedgwick, E. (1985) *Between Men: English Literature and Male Homosocial Desire* (New York: Columbia University Press).

Sedgwick, K.E. (1990) *The Epistemology of the Closet* (Berkeley: University of California Press).

Segal, L. (1987/1994) *Straight Sex: Rethinking the Politics of Pleasure* (London: Virago Press/Berkeley: University of California Press).

Segal, L. (1987) *Is the Future Female? Troubled Thoughts on Contemporary Feminism* (London: Virago).

Segal, L. (1990) *Slow Motion: Changing Masculinities, Changing Men* (London: Virago).

Segal, L. (1994) *Straight Sex: The Politics of Pleasure* (London: Virago).

Segal, L. and M. McIntosh (eds) (1992) *Sex Exposed: Sexuality and the Pornography Debate* (London: Virago).

Sharp, H.F. (1921) Letter to Edward Carpenter, Sheffield City Archives Mss 384/33.

Sharpe, M. (1885) Letter to K. Pearson, 15 November (London: Pearson Collection, University College).

Sharpe, M. (1889) Letter to K. Pearson, 30 May (London: Pearson Collection, University College).

Sharpe, M. (1890) Letter to K. Pearson, 1 April (London: Pearson Collection, University College).

Shields, R. (ed.) (1992) *Lifestyle Shopping: The Subject of Consumption* (London: Routledge).

Silkin, J.G. (1995) *Sex, Death and the Education of Children: Our Passion for Ignorance in the Age of AIDS* (New York: Columbia University Press).

Simpson, A. (1993) *Xuxa: The Mega-marketing of Gender, Race and Modernity* (Philadelphia: Temple University Press).

Sinfield, A. (1992) *Faultlines* (Oxford: Oxford University Press).

Sinfield, A. (1994) *The Wilde Century: Effeminacy, Oscar Wilde and the Queer Moment* (London: Cassell/New York: Columbia University Press).

Singaratnam, A.E. et al. (1991) 'Preventing the Spread of HIV Infection', *British Medical Journal*, Vol. 302, p. 469.

Singer, L. (1993) *Erotic Welfare: Sexual Theory and Politics in the Age of the Epidemic* (New York: Routledge).

Smart, C. (1995) *Law, Crime and Sexuality: Essays in Feminism* (London: Sage).

Smith, A.M. (1990) 'A Symptomology of an Authoritarian Discourse', *New Formations*, Vol. 10, Spring.

Smith, A.M. (1994) *New Right Discourse on Race and Sexuality* (Cambridge: Cambridge University Press).

Smith, P. (1988) *Discovering the Subject* (Minneapolis: University of Minnesota Press).

Smith-Rosenberg, C. (1975) 'The Female World of Love and Ritual: Relations between Woman in Nineteenth-century America', *Signs*, Vol. 1, No. 1.

Snitow, A et al. (eds) (1983) *The Powers of Desire* (New York: Monthly Review Press).

Squires, J. (ed.) (1993) *Principled Positions: Postmodernism and the Rediscovery of Value* (London: Lawrence & Wishart).

Stacey, J. (1994) 'Scents, Scholars and Stigma: The Revisionist Campaign for Family Values', *Social Text*, Fall.

Steedman, C. (1986) *Landscape for a Good Woman: A Story of Two Lives* (London: Virago).

Steedman, C. (1990) *Childhood, Culture and Class in Britain: Margaret McMillan 1860–1931* (London: Virago).

Stein, E. (ed.) (1990) *Forms of Desire: Sexual Orientation and the Social Constructionist Controversy* (New York: Garland).

Stoller, R. and I.S. Levine (1993) *Coming Attractions: The Making of an X-rated Movie* (New Haven, CT: Yale University Press).

Sullivan, A. (1995) *Virtually Normal: An Argument about Homosexuality* (New York: Knopf).

Tannen, D. (1991) *You Just Don't Understand: Women and Men in Conversation* (London: Virago).

Tapic, H. (1992) 'Masculinity, Femininity and Turkish Male Homosexuality', in K. Plummer (ed.), *Modern Homosexualities: Fragments of Lesbian and Gay Experience* (London: Routledge).

Taylor, C. (1992) *The Ethics of Authenticity* (Cambridge, MA and London: Harvard University Press).

Taylor, G.R. (1959) *Sex in History*, 2nd edn (London: Thames & Hudson).

Tebbit, N. (1986) *The Values of Freedom* (London: Conservative Political Centre).

Thatcher, M. (1993) *The Downing Street Years* (London: HarperCollins).

Theberge, N. (1991) 'Reflections on the Body in the Sociology of Sport', *Quest*, No. 43, pp. 123–34.

Thomson, R. (1994) 'Moral Rhetoric and Public Health Pragmatism: The Recent Politics of Sex Education', *Feminist Review*, Autumn.

Thomson, R. and S. Scott (1992) *Learning about Sex: Young Women and the Social Construction of Sexual Identity* (London: Tufnell Press).

Tiefer, L. (1986) 'In Pursuit of the Perfect Penis: The Medicalisation of Male Sexuality', *American Behavioral Scientist*, Vol. 29, No. 5, pp. 579–99.

Tiefer, L. (1995) *Sex Is Not a Natural Act and Other Essays* (Boulder/San Francisco/Oxford: Westview Press).

Tomlinson, A. (ed.) (1990) *Consumption, Identity and Style: Marketing, Meanings and the Packaging of Pleasure* (London: Routledge).

Trudell, B.N. (1993) *Doing Sex Education: Gender, Politics and Schooling* (New York: Routledge).

Turner, C.F. (1989) 'Research on Sexual Behaviors that Transmit HIV: Progress and Problems', *AIDS*, Vol. 3, Suppl. 1, S63–9.

ten Tusscher, T. (1986) 'Patriarchy, Capitalism and the New Right', in J. Evans et al. (eds) *Feminism and Political Theory* (London: Sage).

UNAIDS (1996) *The Current Global Situation of the HIV/AIDS Pandemic as of 15 December 1995* (UNAIDS Joint UN Programme on HIV/AIDS, Internet update).

US Supreme Court (1995) *Hurley v. Irish-American Gay Group*, 94–749, decision handed down 19 June.

Ussher, J.M. (forthcoming) *Fantasies of Feminity: Reframing the Boundaries of Sex* (London: Penguin Books).

Valverde, M. (1985) *Sex, Power and Pleasure* (Toronto: Women's Press).

Vance, C. (1984) 'Pleasure and Danger: Towards a Politics of Sexuality', in C. Vance (ed.), *Pleasure and Danger: Exploring Female Sexuality* (London and Boston: Routledge and Kegan Paul)

Vance, C. (1989) 'Social Constructionist Theory: Problems in the History of Sexuality', in A. van Kooten Nierkerk and T. van der Meer (eds), *Homosexuality? Which Homosexuality?* (London: GMP).

Vanwesenbeeck, I. (1994) *Prostitutes' Well-being and Risk* (Amsterdam: VU University Press).

Vanwesenbeeck, I., R. de Graaf, G. van Zessen, C.J. Straver and J.H. Visser (1995) 'Professional HIV Risk-taking, Levels of Victimization and Well-being in Female Prostitutes in the Netherlands', *Archives of Sexual Behavior*, Vol. 24, No. 5, pp. 503–15.

Vanwesenbeeck, I., G. van Zessen, R. de Graaf and C.J. Straver (1994) 'Contextual and Interactional Factors Influencing Condom Use in Heterosexual Prostitution Contacts', *Patient Education and Counseling*, Vol. 24, pp. 307–22.

Vicinus, M. (1985) *Independent Women* (London: Virago).

Waddy, J.L. (1975) Notice under Section 14(1) of the Indecent Articles and Classified Publications Act, 1975 (Sydney: Government Printer).

Waight, B.A. and E. Miller (1991) 'Incidence of HIV Infection among Homosexual Men', *British Medical Journal*, Vol. 303, p. 311.

Walkerdine, V. (1981) 'Sex, Power and Pedagogy', *Screen Education*, Vol. 38, pp. 14–21.

Walkowitz, J. (1992) *City of Dreadful Delight: Narratives of Sexual Danger in Late Victorian London* (London: Virago).

Walkowitz, J. (1980) *Prostitution and Victorian Society: Women, Class and the State* (Cambridge: Cambridge University Press).

Walter, A. (ed.) (1980) *Come Together: The Years of Gay Liberation, 1970–73* (London: Gay Men's Press).

Warner, M. (1993) Introduction to M. Warner (ed.), *Fear of a Queer Planet* (Minneapolis: University of Minnesota Press).

Watney, S. (1987) *Policing Desire* (London: Comedia).

Weeks, J. (1977) *Coming Out: Homosexual Politics in Britain from the Nineteenth Century to the Present* (London: Quartet).

Weeks, J. (1981/1989) *Sex, Politics and Society: The Regulation of Sexuality since 1800* (Harlow: Longman).

Weeks, J. (1985) *Sexuality and its Discontents* (London and Boston, MA: Routledge & Kegan Paul).

Weeks, J. (1986) *Sexuality* (London: Tavistock).

Weeks, J. (1993) 'Rediscovering Values', in J. Squires (ed.), *Principled Positions* (London: Lawrence & Wishart).

Weeks, J. (1994) *The Lesser Evil and the Greater Good: The Theory and Politics of Social Diversity* (London: Rivers Oram Press).

Weeks, J. (1995) *Invented Moralities: Sexual Values in an Age of Uncertainty* (Cambridge: Polity Press).

Wellings, K. (1994) 'AIDS Education: Targeting the General Population in Europe', *Soz Praventivmed* 37, Suppl. 1, 14–46 (Basle: Birkhauser Verlag).

Wellings, K. et al. (1994) *Sexual Behaviour in Britain: The National Survey of Sexual Attitudes and Lifestyles* (London: Penguin Books).

West, P., D. Wright and S. Macintyre (1993) 'Heterosexual Behaviour of 18-year-olds in the Glasgow Area', *Journal of Adolescence*, Vol. 16, Issue 4, December pp. 376–96.

White, S.K. (1991) *Political Theory and Postmodernism* (Cambridge: Cambridge University Press).

Wideman, J. (1995) 'Doing Time, Marking Race', *The Nation*, 30 October, pp. 504–6.

Williams, L. (1992a) *Hard Core: Power, Pleasure and Frenzy of the Visible* (London: Pandora).

Williams, L. (1992b) 'Pornographies on/Scene', in L. Segal and M. McIntosh, *Sex Exposed: Sexuality and the Pornography Debate* (London: Virago).

Williams, P. (1991) *The Alchemy of Race and Rights* (Cambridge, MA: Harvard University Press).

Williams, R. (1993) 'Accumulation and Evisceration: Urban Rebellion and the New Growth Dynamics', in R. Gooding-Williams (ed.), *Reading Rodney King, Reading Urban Uprising* (New York: Routledge).

Willig, C. (1994) 'Material Discourse and Condom Use', in P. Aggleton, P. Davies and G. Hart (eds), *AIDS: Foundations for the Future* (London: Taylor & Francis).

Willig, C. (1995) ' "I Wouldn't Have Married the Guy if I'd Have to Do That": Heterosexual Adults' Constructions of Condom Use and their Implications for Sexual Practice', *Journal of Community and Applied Social Psychology*, Vol. 5 pp. 75–87.

Willis, P. (1980) 'Notes on Method', in S. Hall, D. Hobson, A. Lowe and P. Willis (eds), *Culture, Media, Language* (London: Hutchinson), pp. 88–95.

Willis, P. (1990) *Moving Culture: An Enquiry into the Cultural Activities of Young People* (London: Gulbenkian Foundation).

Wilson, E. (1985) *Adorned in Dreams: Fashion and Modernity* (London: Virago).

Wilson, G. and D. Nias (1977) *Love's Mysteries* (London: Fontana).

Wittig, M. (1992) *The Straight Mind and Other Essays* (Hemel Hempstead: Harvester Wheatsheaf).

Wojnarowitz, D. (1992) *Close to the Knives* (London: Serpent's Tail).

Woolf, V. (1976) *Moments of Being: Unpublished Autobiographical Writings*, ed. J. Schulkind (London: Chatto and Windus).

World Health Organization (1994) *AIDS: Images of the Epidemic* (Geneva: WHO).

World Health Organization (1994) *Women and AIDS: Agenda for Action* (Geneva: WHO/UNDP/UN Division for the Advancement of Women).

World Health Organization (1995) *In Point of Fact*, WHO Briefing (Geneva: WHO, May).

Worth, D. (1989) *Sexual Decisionmaking and AIDS: Why Condom Promotion among Vulnerable Women is Likely to Fail*. Paper drawn from a seminar presentation at the Population Council, Montefiore Medical Center, New York.

Wright, W. (1982/1994) *The Social Logic of Health* (Hanover, NH: Wesleyan University Press).

Young, I.M. (1990) *Justice and the Politics of Difference* (Princerton, NJ: Princeton University Press).

Žižek, S. (1991) *Looking Awry: An Introduction to Lacan through Popular Culture* (Cambridge, MA: MIT Press).

Index